THE JENNINGS COMPANION

BY DAVID BATHURST

The corridor was a mass of waving arms and legs

First published in 1995 by Summersdale Publishers

Copyright © Summersdale Publishers 1995

Summersdale Publishers
46 West Street
Chichester
PO19 1RP
England

Published in association with Romansmead Publications
46 Mosse Gardens
Fishbourne
Chichester
PO19 3PQ

Printed in England by Selwood Printing Ltd., Burgess Hill.

ISBN 1 873475 49 7

A CIP catalogue record for this book is available from the British Library.

CONTENTS

FOREWORD

by Anthony Buckeridge

I am happy to write this Foreword as an introduction to the Jennings Companion by David Bathurst.

It is flattering to an author comfortably into his eighties to have such a diligent and appreciative assessment of his work - a book written in such a scholarly way by a young man of the stature of David Bathurst!

On reading these pages I find myself amazed at the detail revealed by his researches; he now knows the Jennings books far better than I know them myself. I feel that he should offer himself to Magnus Magnusson as a candidate for Mastermind, taking this subject as his speciality.

In this brief note of introduction, I should like to express my gratitude for the implication that my work is worthy of serious study - and I should like to commend David's book to what has now become several generations of Jennings readers.

Anthony Buckeridge

INTRODUCTION

By the time the Second World War ended, the traditional boys' public school story was in decline. This distinctive genre, which had begun with Tom Brown and Eric, been popularised by Talbot Baines Reed and Harold Avery, and had reached its climax with the work of Frank Richards and his Greyfriars tales, was not dead by 1945 but the essential elements which had produced these "ripping yarns" were already becoming the objects of ridicule and distaste. The didactic patriotic story, emphasizing the virtues of fighting for God, King and Country, now had a tasteless ring following the bloodshed of two world wars. Both wars had seen a narrowing of class distinctions and a greater suspicion of elitism, so that the "Well hit sir!" and "You're a bounder and a cad!" school of writing was no longer acceptable. The growth in popularity of radio communication and the austerity that was necessarily prevalent in Great Britain after the Second World War meant that fewer young people were buying books. They certainly preferred both radio and comic papers to the spongy, stodgy, stiff-backed volumes which had adorned the bookshelves for so many decades.

In the midst of this gloomy scene stepped one Anthony Malcolm Buckeridge, a preparatory school teacher whose teaching experience convinced him that there was a market for very funny yet believable stories set in an English boys' prep school. There was no need or room for patriotism, moral teaching, snobbery or elitism. Anthony Buckeridge decided on a hero, called him Jennings, gave him a friend called Darbishire, added a few form-mates, and school staff, and, using his own natural talents as a storyteller, began writing stories about their adventures at school. There were to be no dramatic sea rescues, no dicing with death in African jungles, no cliff edge heroics. There would instead be everyday incidents taken a stage further - real firemen hurrying in left-footed gumboots to a routine school fire practice, a piglet running amok on the school cricket field, or an unscheduled invasion of local ladies to a private jumble sale. The stories were written for radio and enjoyed huge success. As a result, the radio plays appeared in book form; these books have now appeared in thirteen languages and six million copies have been sold.

Recently a number of compilations of extracts from classic children's literature have appeared. It is no surprise to find the masters well represented - J.R. Tolkein, C.S. Lewis, Frances Hodgson Burnett to name but three - but quite baffling to find not a single extract from the Jennings books, which at least one critic, Joseph Connolly, regards as the funniest schoolboy books ever written. Peter Hunt's otherwise splendid 1995 publication, Children's Literature-An Illustrated History, makes only one cursory mention of the Jennings books. Yet when I mention to an acquaintance or friend that I have a passion for the Jennings books, I am more often than not met with a smile of recognition and the discovery that they, too, have at one stage had at least one of those six million copies somewhere about their home, even if it is now gathering dust in the cupboard under the stairs.

I was introduced to Jennings at the tender age of seven, and twenty-eight years later I am still laughing at his adventures, or more accurately the way in which they are recounted. It is my conviction that there are many others who share this enjoyment which has led me to produce this Companion volume. This book is first and foremost for the existing or erstwhile enthusiasts, in the hope that it will renew, strengthen or revive their love of the stories. Secondly it is intended to give valuable information to the existing or budding collector of the books, especially as the first editions of all but the last two books in the series are definite collectors' items and represent a very good investment. Thirdly I hope that it will provide an entertaining introduction for children's literature enthusiasts who have not had the pleasure of meeting Jennings and his friends at Linbury Court Preparatory School.

The book is divided into six sections. The first, THE STORY OF JENNINGS, provides the background to the author and to the stories. The second, WHERE TO FIND JENNINGS, lists the books and also the radio plays in chronological order. It also sets out the other radio and television programmes and books in which adaptations of the original stories have appeared. The third provides an in-depth investigation into the principal characters. The fourth is the real "meat" of the book, providing an A-Z guide to all the other characters and principal themes to be found in the books, together with a synopsis of each book and the original dustjacket illustration from each book. The fifth, COLLECTING JENNINGS, contains information for prospective and existing collectors on prices that the books will fetch, and information on how to obtain the books. The sixth and final section, JENNINGS FOR EVERYONE, is a nostalgic tribute to the books through the appreciative eyes of a number of contributors, including academics, experts on children's literature, and journalists. Scattered through the book are illustrations from the texts and some other interesting items of archive material.

The information contained within the book has been checked and double-checked for accuracy but mistakes can and do happen and I should be grateful to learn of any howlers of which I am unintentionally guilty.

This book could not have been compiled without the support of a large number of people. My primary thanks must be to the maestro himself, Anthony Buckeridge, whose humility, generosity and encouragement has helped to make the compilation of this Companion an immensely pleasurable and comparatively painless task, and who has allowed me to quote freely from the texts. I am grateful to Harper Collins for permission to quote from the dustjackets of the original titles and reproduce the illustrations. I would also like to thank those listed in the bibliography (to be found at the end of this book) for permitting me to quote from their work, and also Summersdale Publishers for their assistance in preparing this book for publication. Lastly I wish to thank my wife Lizzie, whose constant support and assistance has been invaluable throughout.

David Bathurst
Chichester, Summer 1995

1. THE STORY OF JENNINGS

Buckeridge in 1954

The man responsible for creating Jennings was Anthony Malcolm Buckeridge. Buckeridge was born in June 1912 in London. His father, a bank clerk, was killed in the First World War. The bank's "orphans" were swept up by a charity and sent to a boarding school on the Sussex coast where Buckeridge remained between the ages of 8 and 18 while his mother went to the bank to work. Thus it was that, like Jennings, Buckeridge received his schooling at a Sussex private boarding school; he is sure that had his father lived, he would have gone to a day school. He went on to study at London University; he also worked for a short spell in his father's bank which convinced him that he was not cut out for a career in finance. Having left university in the early 1930's he worked as a prep school master for many years, enjoying the work, although his teaching was interrupted by a five-year stint in the fire service during the Second World War. It was during this time that Buckeridge discovered he had both an enthusiasm and a knack for writing and story-telling. Of his own time as a pupil, Buckeridge recalls: **"During my first term at school, the boys of my form were told to write a story. Mine was tragic....Unfortunately, when the master read it aloud the whole form rocked with laughter, and I was so taken aback that I decided my next literary effort should be a comedy. Then if people still wanted to laugh, they might do so with perfect freedom."** The seeds of Buckeridge's humorous writing had been sown; and the combination of his teaching experience with his desire to write amusingly, fuelled by his love for the work of P.G. Wodehouse, made it natural that he should someday choose to write funny stories set in a boys' prep school. Interestingly, he did not set out to write school stories; his childhood ambition was to be an actor, and when he did develop an interest in writing his initial aim was merely to write humorous stories against a background with which he was familiar. Even more interestingly, he was to be the first boys' writer to use prep schools as a story setting.

Buckeridge's first "audience" for such stories were the boys at his Ramsgate prep school St Lawrence's, although during his years in the fire service he had improved the shining hour by writing radio plays intended for such programmes as the Wednesday and Saturday Matinee. He recalls that Jennings' character emerged gradually from the stories he told his pupils, usually as an inducement for them to do as they were told -**("finish up your prunes and custard in thirty seconds flat and I'll tell you a story")**. He recognised that there had to be a hero of these stories, and took the name Jennings from one of his contemporaries at school who was, in his words, **"a bit of an oddball...I just used his name because it seemed to fit."** A couple of the early fictional Jennings adventures- but no more - were based on adventures experienced by the real-life Jennings! It was from this that Jennings' character developed - a keen, eager, sometimes impetuous boy with strong qualities of leadership and a definite thirst for adventure. The characters were all drawn from a mixture of various people known to the author. Following his successful submissions of radio plays for the programmes mentioned above, Buckeridge submitted to the BBC Drama Department a script for a radio play about this Jennings character and tales of his life at Linbury Court Preparatory School, near Dunhambury, Sussex. The Drama Department passed the script to the producer of Children's Hour who liked it so much that he not only accepted it for broadcasting but immediately commissioned five more, and commissions came in regularly thereafter.

Buckeridge recalls: **"I cannot remember when the first Jennings story was told, for the character was never consciously created. He evolved gradually until he had become the hero of all the stories which I used to tell, evening after evening, in the dormitory. After that, his own personality took control, and all I had to do was to outline a situation and leave it to Jennings' peculiar methods of reasoning to work things out to their logical conclusion. The Jennings stories are humorous; and this is because there is so much humour to be found in studying the reactions of the juvenile mind to the corporate life of a school. Boys frequently do the most fantastic things, for reasons which the average adult is unable to appreciate. I could never have guided Jennings through his school career if I had not myself been a schoolmaster; for no author can write convincingly unless he is so familiar with his background that every undercurrent has an authentic ring."**

The first broadcast, Jennings Learns The Ropes, appeared on Children's Hour on 16th October 1948. The first words uttered were those of Mr

Carter: "Ration book, clothing book, identity card, sweet coupons, health certificate." Jennings'first words were "Me Sir, please Sir." The part of Jennings was taken by David Page, that of Darbishire by Loris Somerville. The first series ended on 5th February 1949, and a second series began on 1st October 1949, but even before the second series had commenced Jennings had the honour of appearing in a Children's Hour Request Week, for which a new script was written. All this time, Buckeridge, who certainly had not set out to create a series which would last him a life-time, was still teaching full-time and fitting his writing round his work, confessing not to be the speediest writer - a 35 minute play would take him 2 weeks to write. Most of the solid writing would be done during the school holidays.

In 1949 Buckeridge sent a batch of the radio scripts to William Collins, the publishers, with a suggestion that they might be incorporated into a book. William Collins readily agreed, and the resultant book, Jennings Goes to School, was published in 1950. Shortly afterwards Buckeridge gave up his job and became a full-time writer, although he would go back to St Lawrence's to teach drama once a week. Until 1961, he wrote the stories first as radio plays then converted them into novels, each one taking between three and four months to complete, and with one novel appearing roughly each year. Novels continued to appear annually even after the plays had ceased. The "joins" between each original play in each novel are extremely skilfully done, so that although one can perceive a pot-pourri of different adventures in one book, each book is a cohesive and satisfying unit in itself. Buckeridge would write in longhand and then the final draft would be typed up by a secretary. Altogether 62 plays - a total of 11 series plus some special editions - were written, the last being broadcast on 24th March 1962. There was often a considerable time lapse between a story appearing on the radio and being woven into a novel; Jennings and the Gift of Tongues, for example, was first broadcast on 10th January 1957 as a radio play, and was eventually incorporated into Especially Jennings, published in 1965. Jennings Abounding, published in 1967, was the very first book to contain no material at all that had previously been used on the air, and none of the succeeding books contained material previously used in that way. The first five books contained no illustrations in the text; According to Jennings, was the first to be illustrated, by S. van Abbe, who had produced dustjackets and frontispieces(some of which Buckeridge later described as embarrassingly dated!) for the first five books, and Douglas Mays was from 1955 to provide illustrations including dustjackets and frontispieces for the novels for the next fifteen years.

There were obvious difficulties about stretching the adventures of a single schoolboy over so many years. Elinor Brent-Dyer, the celebrated girls' school story writer, had allowed her Chalet School characters to move with the times and brought in new characters to replace them. Buckeridge, by contrast, effectively invited the reader to place Jennings outside the normal passage of time, wiping clean the slate of previous Christmas, Easter and summer terms he had spent in Form Three, and starting afresh with a new term, so that Jennings remained in Form Three right through the series. Broadly speaking, one term was covered by one book, although sometimes two books would cover a single term; a book about Christmas term adventures would follow with a book about Easter term adventures, and so on. There are occasional cross-references in the text to earlier adventures. Buckeridge did, however, take into account social change as the series progressed; one example is currency change, with references to shillings and pence in earlier books but decimal currency being used towards the end of the series. Like Elinor Brent-Dyer, Buckeridge was guilty of some inconsistencies although they tended to be fairly minor in nature; they are referred to in the A-Z section when discussing the character or subject giving rise to the inconsistency. The two most glaring instances of inconsistency are the location of Linbury Court's great sporting rivals Bracebridge School, and the age of the senior master Mr Carter. The other examples, however, are comparatively minor. The remarkable thing about the stories is that despite their great number, only very few characters play a regular part in the adventures, and even with those we get to hear very little about their personal backgrounds; similarly very few outside locations are used or even mentioned in the stories.

The individual characters and dominant themes and motifs are explored more fully in the A-Z of Jennings which follows later in this book. If one is asked, however, to summarise the world of Jennings and his Linbury Court School in a nutshell, one might describe it as a highly believable world, grounded in exact observation and consistent characterization; Buckeridge states: **"What I do really is start with a real-life situation - and take it just one step further. I didn't want to write anything fantastic but to keep my feet on the ground and bend the rules when I wanted."** The stories are emphatically not underpinned by stern moral, religious or authoritarian principles. They are populated by highly believable characters whose often farcical adventures are brought to life through narration of the highest quality - there are many shades of Wodehouse throughout - and the employment of a rich store of distinctive schoolboy terminology. One will never be able to think of Jennings without thinking of crystallised cheese-cakes, fossilised fish-hooks, petrified paint-pots and dehydrated eyewash. The distinctive slang arose from Buckeridge's realisation that everyday slang, especially schoolboy slang, changes from year to year, and his consequent decision to create his own phrases which would not go out of fashion. The realisation only really came to him after Jennings Goes To School, which has its own special brand of slang applicable to the year in which he was writing; years later, Buckeridge still found this book embarrassing to read for that very reason. Incidentally, the word "clodpoll," which is frequently to be found in the stories, was very much in vogue in Shakespearian times! Readers will note a subtle change in the style of the books as the series progresses; the earlier books contain far more of what Buckeridge calls word-quibbling and verbal nonsense; he regards the later books as **"not so rumbustiously funny. The style does change, and I think it's probably because I was learning the job as I did it. The early ones possibly went over the top, rather, became slightly too farcical at times, which means you can lose in other directions. I think the style has improved, as some of the farcical elements have been toned down a bit."** The absence of moral or establishment overtones in the stories may well be explained in part by the fact that ever since he lost his father in the First World War, and went to a boarding school which offered no real opportunity to develop a creative side, Buckeridge has been sceptical of officialdom and he even donated one of his original Jennings scripts to raise funds for the Labour party.

Whatever it was that prompted it, the formula of the Jennings books - escapist to a degree, but containing much with which the juvenile reader could easily identify - was hugely successful. Throughout the 1950's and 1960's the children's sections of bookshops throughout the country but also overseas contained copious supplies of Buckeridge's work, which with the books of Enid Blyton, Richmal Crompton and Captain W.E. Johns enjoyed popularity which exceeds that of any modern writer, the popularity extending to girls as well as boys, and even adults too; as Buckeridge says, **"These aren't for girls or boys, they're for any age."** A nostalgic tribute to the world of Linbury Court is to be found at the end of this book. Other spinoffs were to appear as the popularity of the books increased. The Jennings stories continued to appear regularly in Children's Hour Request Week right up until Children's Hour ended in 1964. Short stories were inserted into the BBC Children's Hour Annual, BBC Fourth Dimension and Collins' Boys' Annuals, and even the Boys' Brigade's Omnibus where incidentally an accompanying illustration was prepared by Thomas Henry, the artist for the William books. Buckeridge does insist that all the short stories, like the radio plays, were incorporated into or taken from one or more of the novels. Jennings made further appearances on BBC Television and Radio, and in 1991 a double cassette of his adventures was issued as part of the BBC Radio Collection. Jennings' appearances in sound and vision are more closely examined in a subsequent section of this book. In 1978 a Jennings musical, entitled Jennings Abounding, was written, with lyrics by Buckeridge and music by Hector Cortes and William Gomez; the acting edition, published by Samuel French, is still in print at the time of writing. The Jennings books were successfully translated into twelve foreign languages and marketed abroad; to date the books have appeared in French, German, Norwegian, Spanish, Dutch, Welsh, Swedish, Finnish, Indonesian and even Modern Hebrew; Jennings has been renamed Bennett in France(because apparently Jennings is unpronounceable in French), Fredy in Germany and Stompa in Norway. Indeed the Jennings books are most popular of all in Norway, where there have even been three full-length Jennings films, and Jennings' doings are still dramatised annually on Norwegian state radio.

"Cover illustrations for Norwegian and French translations of the Jennings books"

By the end of the 1960's, however, things were changing. Television was becoming increasingly dominant and it became less and less economical to produce hardbound books for children. Suddenly the school novel became transformed. No longer was there a demand for books about private schools; as Stephen Pile puts it, **"the heirs of Tom Brown went to Grange Hill."** The relationship between Buckeridge and his publishers had always on the face of it been harmonious; he would submit the script to their offices and they would reproduce exactly what he had written. However, after Douglas Mays' association with the series ended, Buckeridge was in need of an illustrator for the cover of his next book in 1971. Quentin Blake, who went on to illustrate the Roald Dahl books so successfully, produced some pictures which were used in the 1970 adaptation of some Jennings stories for the BBC Jackanory programme. Buckeridge thought they would be just right; his publishers would not agree and Blake's artwork was never seen on the dustjacket of a Jennings title. After a Jennings book had appeared virtually annually right through the 1960's and into the 1970's, no new Jennings book appeared in 1972, but merely a reprint of the compilation volume, A Bookful of Jennings, under a new title, The Best of Jennings. Then in 1973, after Speaking of Jennings(the 22nd title, including the compilation volume which had appeared seven years previously) William Collins decided to stop the series, and instead produce paperback reissues of the existing books under the Armada imprint.(In fact, Puffin Books, the children's imprint of Penguin Books, had issued two titles in paperback, but the paperback rights were bought back by Collins) Buckeridge, who would have been quite happy for the series to continue, did write one paperback original for Armada, Jennings at Large, which appeared in 1977, before a drought of 14 years. People would ask Buckeridge why he was not writing any more books; he had to reply that it was because nobody wanted to publish them, and at one stage he believed he would not write another Jennings book. The drought was broken only in 1991 when Macmillan Children's Books requested Buckeridge to write a new Jennings book in order to boost sales of their own paperback reprints(see section 5 below). The result was the publication of Jennings Again; the publishers were sufficiently satisfied with the response to this new title that it was followed three years later by the twenty-fifth and latest book, That's Jennings. Although Buckeridge was 82 when this book was published, he prided himself upon his continuing awareness of the juvenile world; he was no doubt helped by the fact that his wife Eileen was a teacher!

**"Examples of illustrations on the edited paperback editions
published by Macmillan and Armada"**

By the end of the 1970's, all the Jennings books had gone out of print.
However, in the early 1980's, John Goodchild publishers began to issue
new editions of the books with updated language, terminology and
ambience; for instance, a prohibition on parking in a certain place on
odd dates became a dull old yellow line in the new edition, and, to
reflect the growing public distaste for smoking, references to smoking
were also deleted. Short trousers, however, were allowed to stay in,
after consultation with a scholastic agency! Subsequently Pan Macmillan
published these revised editions in paperback; by 1995 sixteen of these
paperback editions were available. Despite the claim by Buckeridge,
who himself undertook the updating at the publishers' request, that the
amendments were minor, the original texts were undoubtedly distorted.
Although Buckeridge would have been happier not to update the texts,
the publishers felt that old jargon, terminology and currency would be
off-putting to new readers.

What is perhaps more significant and more gratifying is the fact that in
recent years there has been a revival of interest in Buckeridge's work, by
collectors and others who fondly remember the Jennings books from
their youth. This may be a reflection of growing disillusionment with

the comprehensive school system and a greater enthusiasm for private education; Robert Leeson, author of many of the Grange Hill comprehensive school stories, says **"In my opinion, Jennings has come back because the books themselves as pieces of work were too good to be totally neglected."** The original texts are now fetching considerable sums on the second-hand book market. One wonders, indeed, whether most of the purchasers of Jennings Again and That's Jennings were nostalgic adults rather than the children for whom the books were notionally intended! By 1995, it is estimated that six million copies of the Jennings books had been sold worldwide, and there is still a constant demand by book collectors, book dealers and Jennings fans for copies of the early editions of all the William Collins titles.

Sales of the Collins hardback editions in English total just over 1.6 million copies; France and Norway have each sold around 1.75 million copies, and indeed a number of new translations in Norwegian have just been produced. The Jennings play has been performed as recently as 1994, by the King's School, Worcester.

Buckeridge undertook one other major series, again a series of school stories, about Rex Milligan, a London grammar school boy. He also edited three compilation volumes of boys' stories, and a "one-off" adventure story. None of these have achieved the success of the Jennings books.

Buckeridge in 1994

Anthony Buckeridge now lives with his wife Eileen in the tranquil village of Barcombe Mills, near Lewes in East Sussex, and close to Glyndebourne where he has taken small walk-on parts in the world-famous theatre. He has been there since 1964, after living in Sandwich, Kent, and then for a time in London. He has two children, Sally and Tim, by his marriage to Sylvia which ended in 1962, and a son, Corin, by his marriage to Eileen. Even in his eighties, he continues to send off radio play scripts, although with no real expectation of getting them produced. He has said that he would like to write another Jennings book if given the opportunity to have a further one published. When asked which is his favourite Jennings book, he replies that his favourite is always the one being worked on at the time, although he has expressed a strong preference for Jennings in Particular and prefers his later books to the earlier ones. He displays no bitterness about Jennings' wilderness years, comforting himself with the fact that the books remain bestsellers abroad, in countries that do not even have boarding schools. What is perhaps most surprising is his attitude to boarding schools per se; he is totally opposed to sending children to boarding school in order to have rough corners knocked off them, and says **"I am not terribly in favour of them at all. The only reason for sending children to them is if they can get something there that they can't get at home."** Two of his three children went to day schools, and the third boarded only because it offered greater musical opportunities. Surprisingly for a man who has done so well out of writing about fee-paying school life, Buckeridge remains a Labour voter, as well as a strong advocate of nuclear disarmament.

Buckeridge still has a full postbag, mostly from people in their 50's(who would have been Jennings' age when the stories began) and although the stories are inexplicably accused by some librarians of being elitist and sexist, he says he has never had a "hate" letter about Jennings. Although the Jennings books do not feature amongst his bed-time reading, he says he has always enjoyed writing them. He can relax in the knowledge that no other fictional schoolboy since the war has inspired such affection and had his tales chronicled in such delightful English.

2. WHERE TO FIND JENNINGS

Jennings In Print

For the contemporary Jennings enthusiast, access to Jennings as originally written must necessarily be by the printed page rather than the spoken word. The most obvious reference point is the series of Jennings books, of which there are twenty-four, excluding the compilation. Buckeridge has asserted that all the Jennings stories ever written are included somewhere within the books. Those books are listed below together with the publisher, the year of publication, and the abbreviation used in respect of each as and when they are cited during the remainder of the book.

Jennings Goes to School - JG - Collins, 1950
Jennings Follows a Clue - JF - Collins, 1951
Jennings' Little Hut - JL - Collins, 1951
Jennings and Darbishire - JA - Collins, 1952
Jennings' Diary - JD - Collins, 1953
According to Jennings - AT - Collins, 1954
Our Friend Jennings - OF - Collins, 1955
Thanks to Jennings - TT - Collins, 1957
Take Jennings, For Instance - FI - Collins, 1958
Jennings as Usual - AU - Collins, 1959
The Trouble with Jennings - TW - Collins, 1960
Just Like Jennings - LJ - Collins, 1961
Leave it to Jennings - LI - Collins, 1963
Jennings of Course! - JO - Collins, 1964
Especially Jennings! - EJ - Collins, 1965
Jennings Abounding - JB - Collins, 1967
Jennings in Particular - JI - Collins, 1968
Trust Jennings! - TJ - Collins, 1969
The Jennings Report - JR - Collins, 1970
Typically Jennings! - TY - Collins, 1971
Speaking of Jennings! - SO - Collins, 1973
Jennings at Large - JE - Armada, 1977
Jennings Again! - AG - Macmillan, 1991
That's Jennings! - TH - Macmillan, 1994

The compilation, A Bookful of Jennings, appeared in 1966, published by William Collins; it was reissued in 1972 as The Best of Jennings but with the original text unaltered.

Jennings stories(all of which were included in the texts listed above) have been featured in the following books:

BBC Children's Hour Annual
Collins Boys' Annual
Boy's Brigade Omnibus(including illustrations by Thomas Henry)
BBC Children's Annual
BBC Fourth Dimension Annual

There is also available the Samuel French Acting edition of the script of
the play Jennings Abounding published in 1980.

Jennings In Sound and Vision

Jennings was originally broadcast on Children's Hour, and the complete
list of the broadcasts, in chronological order, is set out below. Each
broadcast title is followed by the date of the
broadcast, the series number and then the
number in that series, so, for instance, the
notation S1,1 after Jennings Learns the Ropes
indicates that this was the first broadcast in
the first series.

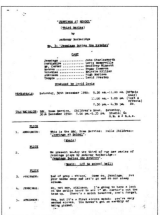

**"An extract from the original script of one of the early
radio plays"**

1. Jennings Learns the Ropes - 16.10.48 (S1, 1)
2. Jennings and the Poisonous Spider - 6.11.48 (S1, 2)
3. Jennings and the Friend of the Family - 27.11.48 (S1, 3)
4. Jennings Sees the Light
 - 18.12.48(S1, 4)
5. Jennings and the Very Important Parent - 15.1.49(S1, 5)
6. Jennings and the Unwelcome Gift - (a) 5.2.49(S1, 6) (b) 2.4.51(2nd
day Request Week)
7. Jennings Sounds the Alarm - (a) 5.4.49(Request week edition)
(b) 30.4.57(3rd day Request week)
8. Jennings and the Tinkling Glass - (a) 1.10.49(S2, 1) (b) 24.11.55(S8, 1)
9. Jennings Breaks the Record - 29.10.49(S2, 2)
10.Jennings and the Kettle of Fish -(a) 10.12.49(S2, 3) (b) 2.5.50(Request
week edition) (c) 28.9.54

11.Jennings Presents the Prize - 14.1.50(S2, 4)
12.Jennings and the Present for Matron - 11.2.50(S2, 5)
13.Jennings Takes the Cake - (a) 11.3.50(S2, 6) (b) 27.2.52(S4, 5a)
14.Jennings Follows A Clue - 7.11.49(Request week edition)
15.Jennings Joins the Search Party - (a) 28.10.50(S3, 1) (b) 5.4.57(S9, 4)
16.Jennings Gets Into Hot Water - 25.11.50(S3, 2)
17.Jennings Buries the Hatchet - 30.12.50(S3, 3)
18.Jennings Runs Cross Country - (a) 27.1.51(S3, 4) (b) 13.6.57
19.Jennings and the Paying Guest - (a) 24.2.51(S3, 5) (b) 15.3.56(S8, 6)
20.Jennings Packs His Trunk - 24.3.51(S3, 6)
21.Jennings Watches the Match - 10.10.51(S4, 1)
22.Jennings and the Penny Black - 7.11.51(S4, 2)
23.Jennings to the Rescue - 5.12.51(S4, 3)
24.Jennings' Diary - 2.1.52(S4, 4)
25.Jennings and the Secret Pet - 30.1.52(S4, 5)
26.Jennings takes the Stage - (a) 5.4.52(S4, 6) (b) 12.12.57
27.Jennings and the Roman Remains - (a) 25.10.52(S5, 1) (b) 14.2.57(S9, 2)
28.Jennings' Happy Thought - 22.11.52(S5, 2)
29.Jennings' Half Term - 20.12.52(S5, 3)
30.Jennings and the Farewell Gift - (a) 17.1.53(S5, 4) (b) 26.10.54 (c) 14.11.57
31.Jennings Entertains the General - (a) 14.2.53(S5, 5) (b) 28.11.57
32.Jennings and the Assistant Masterpiece - 14.3.53(S5, 6)
33.Jennings takes the Wrong Turning - 22.10.53(S6, 1)
34.Darbishire takes the Plunge - (a) 19.11.53(S6, 2) (b) 19.1.56(S8, 4)
35.Jennings and the Fateful Date - (a) 17.12.53(S6, 3) (b) 24.10.57
36.Jennings and the Scientific Frogman - (a) 14.1.54(S6, 4) (b) 1.4.54(5th day Request Week) (c) 19.10.54
37.Jennings and the March of Progress - 11.2.54(S6, 5)
38.Jennings and the Tricky Predicament - 11.3.54(S6, 6)
39.Jennings and the Train of Events - 28.10.54(S7, 1)
40.Jennings and the Abominable Snowcat - (a) 25.11.54(S7, 2) (b) 29.1.59(S10, 5)
41.Jennings and the Furtive Feasters - 30.12.54(S7, 3)
42.Jennings and the Organised Outing - (a) 27.1.55(S7, 4) (b) 21.4.55(Request week edition) (c) 10.10.57
43.Thanks to Jennings - 24.2.55(S7, 5)
44.Jennings and the Next Best Thing -24.3.55(S7, 6)
45.Jennings Takes Charge - 27.10.55(S8, 1)
46.Jennings and the Christmas Spirit - 22.12.55(S8, 3)
47.Jennings and the Best Laid Plans - 16.2.56(S8, 5)
48.Jennings and the Gift of Tongues - 10.1.57(S9, 1)
49.Jennings and the Planned Operation - 14.3.57(S9, 3)
50.Jennings and the Unique Antique - 16.5.57(S9, 5)
51.Jennings and the Key to the Mystery - 28.12.57(S9, 6)

52.Jennings and the Mixed Assortment - 1.1.59(S10, 1)
53.Jennings and the Handy Gadget - 8.1.59(S10, 2)
54.Jennings and the Surprise Item - 15.1.59(S10, 3)
55.Jennings and the Watchful Eye - 22.1.59(S10, 4)
56.Jennings and the Old Folks at Home - 5.2.59(S10, 6)
57.Jennings and the Tide of Fortune - 13.1.62(S11, 1)
58.Jennings Weathers the Storm - 27.1.62(S11, 2)
59.Jennings and the Unconsidered Trifles - 10.2.62(S11, 3)
60.Jennings and the Lure of the Jumble - 24.2.62(S11, 4)
61.Jennings and the Camouflaged Textbook - 10.3.62(S11, 5)
62.Jennings and the Mysterious Raindrops - 24.3.62(S11, 6)

The success of the Children's Hour broadcasts and the Jennings books led to a number of adaptations of the stories. Jennings made a return to radio in 1968 when Buckeridge himself read from JI in "Storytime," and again in 1972 in a Saturday afternoon Radio 4 series for children entitled Fourth Dimension. 1990 saw readings of Jennings stories on Radio 5 by Stephen Fry.

There were two BBC television series of Jennings, rewritten from the radio scripts, one in 1956(ten episodes) and one in 1966(six episodes). In June 1970 Ronnie Corbett read some Jennings stories in the children's programme "Jackanory;" these were repeated in August 1971. In addition, there have been some cassette recordings of the Jennings stories; one cassette, which is no longer available, contains readings by Buckeridge himself from JG, whilst 1991 saw the issue of a Jennings double cassette in the BBC Radio Collection, with readings from JG and AG by Stephen Fry from his Radio 5 readings.

The only colour illustrations within the books were contained in the frontispieces. This example is taken from TAKE JENNINGS FOR INSTANCE.

T.J.F.I.
" Ah! How do you do, Dr. Hipkin."
(See page 040)

3. THE PRINCIPAL CHARACTERS

John Christopher Timothy Jennings

Many well-known writers of school stories have chosen not to single out one particular character or even one particular school in their narratives. Even some of those who have done - for instance, Charles Hamilton(as Frank Richards) writing about Billy Bunter - have spent considerable portions of their narratives dwelling on other characters. The Linbury Court School books of Anthony Buckeridge, however, are centred very definitely around Jennings. Every single book in the series contains some reference to Jennings in the title.

Jennings and the old bicycle parted company at the bottom of the hill.

The name Jennings came from a boy the author knew, described by the author as **"a bit of an oddball."** Some of the Jennings stories were based on incidents from the life of this real boy called Jennings. The charisma of the fictional character is such that it is rare for dealers and collectors to talk of "Anthony Buckeridge books" or "Linbury Court books." They will rather refer to the "Jennings books" which will instantly conjure up pictures of the irrepressible, impetuous schoolboy and his adventures, and the collection of twenty-five books which chronicle them.

Perhaps before beginning a detailed analysis of Jennings' character, Buckeridge's own words should be considered: **"Jennings(is)not a rebel, he gets into trouble because he falls over backwards, as a rule, to put things right that have gone wrong. It's his fault they went wrong in the first place."**

It is difficult to describe Jennings in a few words. There is a huge range of adjectives which can be used to identify the many varied traits of his character. Virtually all of them, however, depict a positive, enthusiastic, active, assertive individual, who is determined to make the very most of every second - one who, in the words of Kipling, can fill the unforgiving minute with sixty seconds worth of journey's run. If he were to have carried these traits through into adult life, he would almost certainly be running a school of management, instilling these positive qualities into poorly motivated employees of select client companies.

Even before the Jennings chronicles begin, in the Introduction to the opening book in the series we get some idea of the character of this charismatic schoolboy. We are told the inscription in his Shorter Latin Primer, (carefully altered to read A Shorter Way of Eating Prime Beef):

If this book should dare to roam,
Box its ears and send it home, to
J.C.T. Jennings,
Linbury Court School,
Dunhambury,
Sussex,
England,
Europe,
Eastern Hemisphere,
Earth,
Near Moon,
Solar System,
Space,
near More Space.
(JG)

That is Jennings in a nutshell; irresponsible, imaginative, innovative and always entertaining: yet Chapter One of the first story is yet to commence!

John Christopher Timothy Jennings is introduced to us as a boy of **"ten years, two months and three days last Tuesday(JG)"** but later he becomes eleven and fortunately for us remains of that tender age until his young readers have reached

Jennings rushed to rescue his property.

middle age and possibly beyond. He is a friendly-looking boy with an untidy fringe of dark brown hair and an average sort of face for boys of his generation. Half a head taller and a few months older than his best friend Darbishire, he lives in Haywards Heath, his father is an engineer, and he is the owner of a rabbit named Bobtail. He is good at sport, starting as a First Eleven footballer and then finding a niche in the Second Eleven. His keenness to get out for his first practice match is such that he is reduced to tears when detained from it by Mr Wilkins, and when he does get out there he has omitted to remove his day clothes that remain under his football gear(JG). Later we hear that he is junior cricket captain for his house Drake, scoring 51 runs against Raleigh house(JB); he also becomes a 2nd XI cricketer and succeeds in bowling out Mr Wilkins at the nets(JL); and he runs in the 440 yards in the school sports(JF). His prowess at sport is not matched by his piano-playing skills, which are described as only fair(AU). Academically he is even less gifted, his first term at Linbury seeing him about halfway down the class(JG). It takes 7 postcards for him to write something even remotely comprehensible to his parents on his first night at Linbury Court(JG); he is admonished by both Mr Wilkins and the Headmaster for defacing, or failing to take care of, school text books(JG, JF); he uses lesson-time to write letters to his aunt(JA) and update his diary(JD); and his lack of knowledge of history means he is unable to remember the numbers of his combination lock using the mnemonic Mr Carter has provided(FI). On two occasions at least he does come out on top; Mr Wilkins' imposition on him of having to learn 6 pages of history means he is able to impress Mr Macready(TT) and, although his drawing of a farmyard earns him a miserable two out of twenty, he does manage to come top of the class in French(EJ).

Jennings does have a number of very positive characteristics. Fortified by his father's entreaty to him to stand up for himself (JG) he is a born leader, asserting his authority on many occasions. The formation of a club, such as the Natural History Club(FI), Jennings Membership Club(EJ) or the secret society devoted to tracing Tim MacTaggart's time capsule(TH) will usually see Jennings in charge of it, with others having to accept a more submissive role.

When Jennings leads, he does so from the front, and his pioneering approach to problems and challenges highlights his thirst for adventure. Who but an adventurous soul would try and escape from school on his second day and even have the cheek to ask for the bus fare first(JG); would spearhead an investigation into the late-night illuminations in the sanatorium(JF); would cook a parcel of raw fish instead of disposing of it as ordered to do so(JA); would organise a rooftop fishing expedition to retrieve a parcel stuck in a master's chimney(JA); would try a downland short cut from Pottlewhistle to Linbury rather than the safer road route(JA); would hitch a lift to a cricket match when left behind by the rest of the party(AT) and in a later story, hitch a lift to enable successful completion of the Sponsored Trot(JE); would assist in the apprehension of a thief of a county cricket team's valuables(AT); would interfere with a neighbouring school's plumbing to try and obtain hot shower water(TJ); or, having obtained a cheap camping stove by accident, would instead of throwing it away, take it up on to the Downs with a view to camp cookery?

Jennings' spirit of adventure also manifests itself in a strong distrust of routine. He cannot be bothered to exchange small-talk with his parents about "ordinary" aspects of school life(JG), and he sees "outside-school" projects or appointments as a perfect opportunity to indulge in other adventures, such as his using his dental appointment as a pretext for dealing with Swing-Wing(JB). Such is his wish to break from mundane routine that his imagination often runs away with him. Sometimes this simply manifests itself in harmless fantasy, such as imagining tuckboxes to be police cars for the purpose of a game(JF) or visualising a special

The figure was wedged tight in a gap in the hedge.

school where the boys are in charge and it is the masters who have to come to heel(LI). On occasions, however, he invests everyday mundane occurrences with an importance they do not merit. When his diary goes missing, complete with coded messages, he has visions of the diary falling into enemy hands and embarrassing the government, prompting him to report the loss to the local police officer(JD), and when he meets Dr Tiddyman, the birdwatcher, he believes the Doctor's recording equipment to have much more sinister possibilities, and feels it is his duty to notify the authorities(LJ). When Miss Tubbs, the assistant at the

Linbury General Stores, assumes the title Madame Olivera at the village fete to raise money by some harmless amateur fortune telling, Jennings, having had his fortune told, not only hopes but expects to see the prophecies fulfilled(LI). The discovery of a wheel - which in actual fact is the remains of the Dunhambury Borough Council's sand and gravel cart - is assumed to be a Roman chariot wheel simply by virtue of the letters BC inscribed on the rim(JD). A snippet of an overheard conversation between Matron and Mr Wilkins regarding the latter's weekend arrangements leads Jennings to assume that Mr Wilkins is leaving Linbury for good(AU). The removal of Mr Wilkins' defective car from a car-park by a bona fide mechanic leads Jennings to the belief that Mr Wilkins' car has been stolen; and Mr Wilkins, climbing through a classroom window after dark, is taken for a burglar, and the matter is reported accordingly(AU). Sometimes, Jennings' wish to escape routine places him in conflict with authority; this is discussed more fully below.

Hand in hand with his thirst for adventure and dislike of routine go a very necessary spirit of creativity, curiosity and ingenuity. Whether it is photography(TT), setting up a detective agency(JF), assembling a collection of objects for a Natural History Museum(JD), pioneering a space craze(AT), learning ventriloquism for a school concert(JO), creating his own time capsule(TH) or thinking up novel ways of raising money for famine relief(TJ), Jennings loves to think of new and interesting things to do, and involve himself fully with what is going on around him. Only a boy with his curiosity and interest in his surroundings would enquire of a fireman why all firefighters have two left feet(JG), would place his head in a glass case to see if it would fit(AT), and would try out a crystal set **"just to improve our education you might say(EJ)."** His ingenuity manifests itself in many ways. It may be his use of a protractor and compasses to cut a cake(JG); his use of a piece of glass from a photo frame to replace a cucumber frame he has broken(JL); his use of a snorkel to clean out a fish tank(TW); his substituting a food parcel with Temple's house shoes to ensure a successful midnight feast(LJ); his jumble sale to return goods from the overflowing lost property cupboard to their rightful owners(JO); his creation of a "home-made" box of chocolates for Matron after Aunt Angela's box was gobbled up by his colleagues and himself(EJ); his pretext of helping to push a trailer in order to implement his piano-selling plan(TJ); his trail of red herrings which enables him to recover Old Sleepy(JI); his suggestion that air be let out of the school minibus to allow it to proceed into the garage from its jammed position(TY); his plan for advertising school property for sale as a useful source of revenue(SO); his use of a pocket radio in class to communicate vital

Test Match information(TY); his plan to make tea for the masters with fizzy drink because no water is available(TY); and his knowledge of home-made cake competition standards which enables him to enter a cake he hopes will win the third prize(LJ). Virtually all of his bouts of creativity have a positive aim in mind, and on many occasions Jennings exhibits an admirable spirit of compassion and warmth for his fellow-beings. We see this in his **"let's-be-decent-to-Wilkie"** campaign following the downland search for him in which Mr Wilkins was a none-too-willing participant(JA); his term's catalogue of Good Resolutions culminating in an "At Home" party for the masters(TW); his willingness to break off his imaginary mountaineering to come to the rescue of a cat in distress(LJ); his suggestion that the firework night be used as a means of obtaining money for famine relief(TJ); his determination to raise a round ten-pound figure for the cause of famine relief(TJ); his compassion for the vulnerable hedgehog which results in his adoption of Old Sleepy(JR); and his campaign to save Emma Sparrow's animals and at the same time help Mrs Hockin's Animal Rescue(JE).

Problems do inevitably arise from Jennings' activity, creativity and enthusiasm. Without the wherewithal and the maturity which an adult would bring to the situations in which he finds himself, Jennings is often guilty of thoughtlessness; quite simply, he fails to appreciate the consequences of what he does. He will hurtle round the corners of corridors without thinking that the headmaster may be proceeding towards him on a collision course(JG); he does not think about the consequences of calling the fire brigade out to a non-existent fire(JG); he gives stamps freely from an approval sheet without reading the small print and realising they have to be paid for(OF); he places his head through park railings to photograph a squirrel without thinking that he might get his head stuck(TT); he applies rubber bicycle pedals to his written work to erase an ink blot without thinking that the pedals themselves might leave a far worse mark(FI); he uses exercise books full of school notes for paper chains without thinking that the notes in the exercise books might be needed again(AU); he places a snorkel in his bath water without thinking what might happen to the bath water as a result(TW); he displays a poster indicating that his jumble sale is open to all without thinking that some people, for instance Mrs Hackett, might think that meant outsiders were welcome(JO); he fails to read the small print indicating that payments as well as tokens are required for a consignment of lethal space guns(EJ); he writes the word Ditto instead of his name on one of his shoes without thinking that this device will give no clue as to the owner of the shoe(JB); he throws some young poplars on the school bonfire without thinking to ask if they ought not to have been planted instead(TJ); he assumes, without advance enquiry, that he will automatically receive a cash payment from the music shop in Dunhambury for Miss Thorpe's honky-tonk piano(TJ); he presents a card to Mr Wilkins without looking inside and seeing that it wishes the recipient a **"Happy 80th birthday, Grandad**(TH);" he assumes that a retailer of new sports equipment may have second-hand tennis rackets to spare for only a few pennies(TY); he places letters addressed to himself in the post tray, with a view to obtaining First Day Cover postmarks, without thinking that the caretaker will hand them straight back to him(JI); and when invited to tie a guy-rope to anything he can find, he chooses the bumper of the school mini-bus without thinking that the vehicle may need to be driven(JE). Occasionally, Jennings' assumption that things will go the way he wants them to, without thinking of the feelings of others affected by his behaviour, displays itself in a rather mercenary attitude. Having indirectly caused the music room ceiling to collapse on Mr Wilkins and himself, through flooding the bathroom, he proceeds to ask Mr Wilkins if he can have a bath because all he has done so far is run the water(TW)! On three occasions at least he prevails upon his Aunt Angela's generosity in the most unsubtle fashion, assuming that she will come up with the goods and his plans can continue. He writes to remind her to send a postal order so he can replace the glass in the shattered cucumber frame(JL); he writes asking her for a new bike so he can join the Natural History Club outing(FI); and he hints strongly that she should come and take him out(EJ).

The second major problem is Jennings' inability to perceive adults' point of view in any situation. He is perhaps understandably baffled when a piece of his behaviour is met with disapproval - e.g. the locking of General Merridew in the library - but condoned when exactly the same behaviour is perpetrated by an adult(AT). He cannot understand why a grass snake at breakfast time(LI), a rhubarb plant in a peanut butter jar(TH) or a jet-propelled greetings card(AU) should fail to prompt a grateful response from the recipient staff member. He erroneously sees Mr Wilkins' anger over a broken vase not as the salutary warning to boys to maintain a respect for others' property but as the anguish of one who has lost a treasured possession(LJ). Often he fails to see either the need for, or the purpose of, certain school rules. He is quite prepared to break school rules if need be in order to further his aims, but we may be prepared to forgive him after we have heard his justification for so doing. Finishing a cross country run by bus seems the only way of satisfying Mr Wilkins' wish that he and Darbishire return to school in reasonable time(OF); an illegal Saturday afternoon trip to Dunhambury is the only way of cleaning clothes soiled by Jennings' falling into a ditch when he should have been walking(JO); Old Sleepy's welfare is ample justification for foxing out to fetch the hedgehog from the wild(JR); the welfare of Swing-Wing(JB) and Miss Thorpe's fish(AG) presents in each case a pretext for breaking bounds with a view to safeguarding their vulnerable lives; it is at Uncle Arthur's insistence that the boys go into the cinema, where they should not be going(OF); and it seems the most natural thing in the world that having been encouraged by his teachers to take an interest in nature and

The creature had no external limbs.

countryside, he should fox away from school one afternoon on a boat trip(FI)! Jennings is no rebel, and would never deliberately disobey authority for disobedience's sake; there will usually be a good reason for it with which the reader can sympathise. It is again as a result of thoughtlessness, and failure to see the purpose of a school rule, that Jennings will not think to ask permission to do something proscribed by school rules. That having been said, Jennings does have a mischievous streak, retribution for which is necessary and well-deserved; he devises an underwater breathing competition with a view to making apple-pie beds for the participants(EJ), and there are a number of instances of after-dark escapades in which Jennings is ring leader, such as telephoning other dormitories(AU), dormitory-cleaning(LI) and of course feasting(LJ). Even then, however, moral justification for such behaviour may be found - for instance, the master's own alleged propensity to furtive feasting(TT). Jennings is not above a spot of cheeky repartee; when asked by an irate Mr Wilkins what he is doing in a particular place, the response may well be that he is **"just coming out Sir."** Occasionally, when Jennings knows he has gone too far, he tries to redress the balance by being especially well-behaved, such as staying indoors one sunny day to re-copy his history notes into a new exercise book(FI). The imposition of punishment or the administration of harsh words by officialdom does have a salutary effect on the boy; his potential deprivation of football in his very first term ends in tears(JG) and the uncomfortable time he spends in the Head's study following his sleepwalking episode prompts him to try and improve relations with authority by way of a party for them(TW).

When Buckeridge was asked what he thought Jennings might have done in later life, he guardedly suggested Jennings might have become a vet; yet in some ways this seems a rather undistinguished and unsatisfactory destiny for a very special schoolboy. Jennings, often known as "Jen" by his friends, may test the patience of Job; his irrepressibility may be a constant headache to all those, particularly Mr Wilkins, who fail to properly understand the workings of the juvenile mind; his unpredictability makes it impracticable to legislate for the harm he may cause next; but he is impossible to dislike. In an age where so many have learnt to go along with the crowd, Jennings' creativity and ingenuity provide a welcome and very necessary antidote.

Charles Edwin Jeremy Darbishire

Darbishire, normally known as Darbi, is Jennings' best friend, and in most of the adventures in which Jennings is involved, Darbishire will also be in the forefront of the action. His creator admits to being more of a Darbishire at school than a Jennings. Buckeridge, whose favourite character is Darbishire, describes him as **"really rather endearingly stupid, I think. He doesn't have very much macho and I rather like him for that."**

Darbishire is the only character besides Jennings to be awarded the accolade of a mention in one of the book titles(JA), and the only character with whom Jennings' name is bracketed when the latter's foibles are being commented adversely upon in official circles. The relationship between the two, which begins when they are placed next to each other at the tea-table as new boys on the first afternoon of their first term(JG) has a comfortable, carefree feeling, where argument is unusual and any hostility is the **"shortlived exasperation of two eleven-year-olds sharing the day-to-day frustration of rules and routines(TY)."** In the main, they will remain loyal to each other and rally to each other's support in times of crisis, or as much as it is practicable to do so having regard to their differing personalities. Although Darbishire has a weak, some might say ineffectual personality, Jennings himself would be the first to admit that many of his exploits and achievements could not have been attained without the support of his friend.

As has been intimated, Darbishire is 11 years of age with fair curly hair, a pink and white complexion, and mild blue eyes in front of which are his ink-splashed spectacles. His home is in Hertfordshire; his father, to whom he makes frequent references in the series, is a clergyman with similar physical characteristics to his son. A few months younger and half a head shorter than Jennings, he has an earnest disposition, is solemn in appearance, has a distinctive voice which often gives the impression he is speaking in capital letters, and is cautious and law-abiding by nature. He does have a hearty appetite, and three helpings of shepherds pie after a stint as linesman is certainly not beyond him(JA).

Workwise his performance is adequate rather than brilliant. He is a few places higher than Jennings in class and usually manages to hold his own; during one term he comes fifth in French(JA) but lets himself down with just four out of ten in a Maths test(JL), and shows a lack of intelligence by writing to his parents a postcard which simply says **"I hope you are quite**(JG)**."** He is not a great artist(JF) or hairdresser(TJ) but enjoys playing the recorder(TW). He can, we are told, do a better imitation of a train going through a tunnel than anyone else in the school(JL), and his head is full of statistical information(JL) and poetry(JF). We are told he contributes an article on Steam v Electrification for the school

magazine(LJ), he helps to launch "The Miser's Secret(OF)" and also writes the first story about the fictional detective, Flixton Slick(JG). Of one thing there is no doubt. From the moment he emerges on to the football pitch with his boot laces tied together(JG) we realise that he is no good at sport, and he is soon demoted to the rabbity "D" game at football. He is also a hopeless athlete as demonstrated in his performance at the school sports, failing to finish his race until after another has started(JF). His missed catch and subsequent overthrow almost help his House to lose the junior House match in

Caught off-balance Darbishire was sent reeling . . .

which, through sickness of others, he has secured a place(JL). As an Australian batsman in an impromptu evening game he is mocked by Jennings for running away from the first ball he receives on English soil, and when he gets round to bowling a good ball it is contemptuously hit for six(JL). His sighting of Swing-Wing causes him to miss the easiest catch in the history of cricket(JB), and indeed his performance at cricket is likened to that of a **"flat-footed starling**(JB)." He only finds he can swim after slipping accidentally into the swimming pool(AT). His incompetence at cross country running means that the boys have to catch the bus in order to reach the school in reasonable time(OF), and his cycling career is in doubt after his inability even to mount the saddle of the machine hired from Mr Lumley, let alone ride it(JD). He tries to make up for his sporting ineptitude by writing sporting articles(JG, JA), taking photos of the game(JA), concentrating on the theory of cricket(JB) and cricket statistics(AT), and acting as linesman(JA).

Darbishire is often portrayed not so much as a person with initiatives and attributes of his own, but as the frequently unwilling accomplice of Jennings as he tries to carry out his plans. Indeed his outstanding characteristic is his loyal submissiveness to Jennings' irrepressible authority, even if such submissiveness only comes after a struggle. The combination of Darbishire's loyalty, and Jennings' assertiveness, means that Jennings will always get his way. On three occasions - the Natural History Club(FI), the Jennings Membership Club(EJ) and the society devoted to finding the time capsule(TH) - Darbishire finds himself honorary secretary while Jennings takes on an executive role. It is only loyalty to Jennings rather than a desire to make his mark, which sees him collaborating with his best friend on such tricky manoeuvres as recovering the fish parcel(JA), the expedition for the purpose of dry-cleaning Jennings' mud-stained clothes(JO), and the boat-hiring expedition(FI). Loyalty to Jennings means that he is prepared to defend him against the taunts of others, as he does when Jennings is being punished for trying to arrange a midnight feast(TW) and it takes a major misunderstanding over what exactly is being swapped for what in providing a birthday present for Darbishire, to produce a quarrel between them.

Darbishire's personality has several other important differences from that of Jennings. He is less easy-going; his early days at Linbury Court are marked with a tearful homesickness(JG), he sees his downland walk from Pottlewhistle as an ordeal rather than the adventure Jennings sees it as(JA), and on such matters as Christmas cards, he is a definite

He launched the missile on its maiden flight.

traditionalist(AU). While Jennings treads boldly and confidently, Darbishire is gauche in his movements; he performs poorly as a look-out as Jennings marches in to recover the sports cup he believes Mr Higgins has purloined(JF); he is unable to be "natural" in the presence of a master prior to a midnight dormitory feast(LI); he sets up a hidden camera to catch an alleged rainfall-statistic-spoiler but without inserting a film in the camera first(LI); he goes on stage with a toothbrush instead of his recorder(TW); he deposits an aerial out of a window thereby ruining the planned construction of a radio listening post(EJ); and he makes a mess of his fishing-tackle purchase mission(SO). He also lacks Jennings' emotional resourcefulness, coming close to tears when confronted with an angry bus conductor during their early escape attempt(JG); being seized with numbness when bidden to speak by the inspector Mr Macready(TT); and panicking when they are almost detected during the secret dry-cleaning mission(JO). When one of Jennings' plans goes wrong, as it frequently does, Darbishire is prone to bemoan:**"Why do these frantic hoo-hahs always pick on us to happen to?"**

What Darbishire lacks in assertiveness, resourcefulness and intelligence, however, he more than makes up for in his imagination, helped by his liking for science fiction or adventure stories such as those about the Fearlerss Four(JF) or the Mystery of the Secret Galleon(LI). Darbishire's outstanding characteristic is his propensity to imagine himself being, or doing, something quite outside the normal run of school life, or alternatively according, in his imagination, exaggerated consequence and moment to ordinary goings-on in school. During the series he visualises himself as Dr Livingstone, as he crosses the inhospitable land owned by Major Rudkin(JE); Professor Darbishire, the expert in Stone Age cooking pots(AG); as he diagnoses a case of housemaid's elbow, a medical specialist(AT);a space-ship designer(AT); a primitive cave-painter(TY); a professor of zoology, specialising in hedgehogs(JR); Space

Pilot C.E.J. Darbishire, also known as Daring Darbi, as he flies Venables' kite(LJ); a Special Foreign Correspondent, as he works on the Form Three Times(JA); a visitor from Planet X, arriving on Earth to explain the mysteries of particle physics while shaking off the alien agent Mr Wilkins from Planet Z(AG);a helper of tribesmen to protect their homelands from encroaching desert(AG); a business tycoon planning to corner the market in industrial plastics(EJ);and, as he scribbles on the board adjoining his cricket scoring box, a cafe owner exhibiting his price list(JB). He has the habit of investing his doubtful achievements with titles out of all proportion to their real magnitude, such as naming himself Official Investigator(when assisting Jennings in his report on television watching(JR)) or Official Calendar Compiler(JG) and claiming to have patented the Darbishire Method For Removing Heads From Railings(TT) and the Darbishire Method For Improving The Vocabulary(LI). He will ascribe to everyday or mundane situations an imaginary gravity which bears no relation to their actual importance, such as asking Mr

" Duck your head!   He's just in front!" croaked Darbishire
63

Wilkins for a rocket-launch-style countdown by the end of which the boys should have changed out of their cricket gear(LI), and going to great lengths to prepare a speech for what he believes to be Mr Wilkins' last lesson with them(AT). He will also become pre-occupied with the imaginary consequences of certain factual or fictional situations that are presented to him. He will speculate on the practical consequences of Mr Wilkins' assertion that in ancient times a squirrel could jump from tree to tree right from Sherwood Forest to Land's End without ever setting foot on the ground(AG); he will spend a football match speculating on the consequences of a visitor from another planet arriving on the football field(TJ);he is intrigued by the vision engendered by Bromwich's abbreviated notes on the Theorem of Pythagoras which begin **"The squaw on the hippo**(JI);" and he fantasises on the rarity value of a supposedly poisonous spider he and Jennings have discovered, and the consequent interest to the British Museum(JG). A delicious piece of dialogue which sums up Darbishire's apparent wish to identify with, and imagine himself to be part of, the goings-on of the outside world, but lacking the practical common sense and intelligence that he would need when he got there, comes when application forms for the Jennings Membership Club are being drawn up:

"They'll have to be proposed and seconded, of course, and then we'll need another little space FOR OFFICE USE ONLY."
"What's that for?"
"So they can leave it blank. You always have it on forms when you apply for dog licences and things."(EJ)

In many ways it might be said Darbishire is a rather sad character; a boy doomed to spend his school life and possibly his adult life in a supporting role, with only his imagination to sustain him through times of frustration and under-achievement. Indeed, Buckeridge suggests that Darbishire might have gone on to become a librarian! Again, however, the vital importance of the role he plays as a helper and supporter of our principal hero cannot not be exaggerated. Life needs the Darbishires as well as the Jenningses.

Venables, Temple and Atkinson

These three boys, rather like the Famous Five who have the dubious pleasure of sharing a class with Billy Bunter, are Jennings' and Darbishire's most featured companions in Form Three. They feature in every book in the series, and play a prominent part in almost all of the incidents described in the stories.

All three are keen participants in Linbury Court life and what it has to offer. They enjoy hut-dwelling(JL), pretending to be cat-burglars(JF), 2nd XI cricket, impromptu cricket with composition balls(JI), collecting frogs(FI), fortune-telling with spinning knives(LI), participating in the space craze(AT), using Latin words to imitate gunfire(JF), and midnight feasting(TT). They enjoy their food, discussing whether they had kippers or sausages for breakfast the previous Friday week(JA), moaning about having only one helping of shepherds pie instead of three(JA), and seeking to get on friendly terms with anyone in possession of a tuck parcel(TW, LJ). They participate enthusiastically in mopping dormitories Jennings has flooded(TW), preparing projects on bathwater consumption(JR) and engage in hobbies as diverse as creating an African landscape with corrugated iron, a patchwork wigwam and a patent invention for putting a jumper on before taking a pyjama jacket off(JA). In short, they are ordinary schoolboys, no different in many ways from Martin-Jones, Nuttall, Pettigrew, Marshall, Bromwich and the many others who grace the pages of the Jennings series.

The chief function of the trio is to act as foils for Jennings and Darbishire. Anthony Buckeridge had a keen understanding of the youthful mind, and cleverly identified the fickle nature of friendships between a boy and his peers, sometimes amicable and co-operative, sometimes hostile and resentful.

There are numerous instances of the three boys colluding with Jennings and Darbishire, or providing them with loyal co-operation in times of need. They willingly writhe on the floor of their dormitory to simulate the consequences of the imaginary fire which the Headmaster has asked

Hostile hands grabbed his legs.

Jennings to deal with(JG); they applaud the efforts of Jennings' detective agency(JF); they try to bail Jennings out after he has fallen into the pond after an illegal Sunday excursion(JL); they offer encouraging and sympathetic words for the two boys when a caning is in the offing(JL); they assist in assembling objects for Jennings' Natural History museum, even if they do only consist of sticks and a distemper brush(JD); they contribute to a collection for Mr Wilkins' presumed departure from Linbury(AT); they agree to take part in Jennings' play(OF); they willingly join Jennings' mountaineering expedition on the back stairs(LJ); they provide support for the "At Home" party in pursuance of Jennings' Good Resolution(TW); they give support to the fund-raising bonfire party and Plan of the Secret Piano(TJ); they willingly participate in Darbishire's Prehistoric Joke(TY); they support the Sponsored Trot(JE); they assist in finding Tim MacTaggart's time capsule(TH); and they take part in the conspiracy to recover Jennings' unflattering cartoon of Mr Wilkins which he believes to have found its way into the master's custody(AU).

However, their relationship with Jennings and Darbishire is not always happy. On their very first evening at the school, Jennings and Darbishire are made to feel distinctly uncomfortable about their Linbury futures after the trio, all with Linbury experienced, have promised them unspeakable punishments for stepping an inch out of line, and bashings-up before tea(JG); the trio, having laughed at Jennings' unintentioned winding-up of Mr Wilkins, turn angrily on the former when as a result of the winding-up they are given detention on the afternoon of a Bracebridge football match(JG); they blame Jennings and Darbishire for the hut ban despite the fact that their huts would have been equally susceptible to damage from the Headmaster(JL); having contributed to a leaving present for Mr Wilkins, they demand some recompense when they learn that Mr Wilkins is not leaving after all(AU); having agreed to take part in the Miser's Secret, their enthusiasm wanes with the passing of time and Jennings is forced to make alternative plans(OF); they mock Jennings when they believe his aunt has provided him with a ramshackle second-hand bicycle instead of the new one Jennings hoped for(FI); they react angrily and derisively when Jennings claims he is ill and cannot attend a detention class(JD); they will not concede possession of the table-tennis table so that Jennings and Darbishire can have a game(JO); they pour scorn on Jennings' proposed fishing trip, dismissing it as **"another of Jennings' disastrous fiascos**(SO);" they do not hesitate to tell Jennings that a detention was **"your fault as usual**(TW);" they round furiously on Jennings when the latter's plan to relay the latest cricket score via pocket radio is discovered and the boys are deprived of being able to watch the highlights on TV(TY); and they conceal from Jennings the fact that it is a waste of time to set up a crystal set because of a broken cat's whisker, leaving Jennings to languish in the cold February air after he has gone in search of the misplaced aerial(EJ). Truly, when the going gets tough, Jennings and Darbishire cannot count on the support of their peers if giving that support is going to inconvenience them!

None of the three boys has the individuality of Frank Richards' Famous Five of Greyfriars. We receive no insight at all into their backgrounds or home lives; we do not know where they live, what their parents do for a living, and we never get to find the Christian name of one of them! It is true that there are some subtle differences in their physical characteristics, and in some stories one of the three may rise to greater prominence. However, given the similarity between the three of them, and the fact that they play stereotyped roles in the action, it matters little which one it is. Jennings and Darbishire, whose characters are so fascinating in themselves, are the two star performers; Venables, Temple and Atkinson are stock characters, merely providing vehicles to help or hinder Jennings and Darbishire in their adventures.

Of the three, Graham J. Venables appears in the thick of the action the most. A thin, lanky, gangling boy, size in collars 13 and sufficiently tall for his age to arouse a bus conductor's suspicions(TT), he is described as being both eleven and twelve years of age. He is an untidy boy, with a clumsiness which makes him spill bat oil along the corridor(AT), perpetually trailing shoe laces, an untucked shirt, toes poking through his bedroom slippers, and according to Mr Carter is an ideal choice for the role of Yeti where to play that role demands dangling long hair and the uttering of uncouth noises(LJ). He believes in steering clear of trouble, as for instance when Jennings takes his Latin book to be sold on the very day the Headmaster holds a book inspection(JA); he has a sharp nose for ferreting such secrets as Jennings' ventriloquism(JO) and the time capsule(TH); he is drawn by the sight of food, but is not a good cake-maker(JL). He sticks up for Cambridge, Arsenal and Lancashire, and has a penchant for carrying chessmen on his head(JF). Having just lost his health certificate, it is he who is commanded to show Jennings the ropes(JG). He is a 2nd XI footballer and cricketer, appointed Chief Birdwatcher in the Natural History Society(FI),a keen philatelist who is horrified at Jennings' treatment of a supposed Penny Black(OF), a good artist(EJ), gerbil owner(SO), and holder of the Dormitory Four underwater breathing record(EJ). Incidents in which he plays a significant role include his putting Jennings' clothes on under his own in order to rescue Jennings from the ill-effects of his fall into the pond(JL); removing the fish parcel from Mr Wilkins' chimney but only telling Jennings after he has been up on the roof trying to hook the parcel out himself(JA); composing a poem that is, sadly for Jennings, good enough to win a sponge cake that has not arrived(JA); treating Jennings and Darbishire to tea without the wherewithal to finance it(JA); taking Jennings' bicycle without consent, and then allegedly having it stolen from him(FI); undermining Jennings' position as dormitory captain by borrowing Jennings' after-dark reading equipment at just the wrong time(AU); appropriating Darbishire's recorder in exchange for a telescope, and being threatened with having to play in the school concert, which hastily precipitates another swap(TW); indirectly introducing Jennings to the birdwatcher Dr Tiddyman when his kite is let loose into Miller's Wood(LJ); taking

Jennings' socks by mistake, and getting Jennings into hot water in more ways than one(LI); asking Jennings to accompany him to Lumley's for tea and then expecting Jennings to pay his share(LI); speculating as to the consequences of going through a hedge backwards(LI); challenging Jennings' ventriloquial skills(JO); prompting a campaign to be decent to Matron, with the consequent breakfast-serving assistance and the Krunchie-Whispie space gun saga(EJ); unknowingly lodging a drawing-pin in the sole of his shoe and then suggesting the missing pin may be in Matron's new bath salts(JI); devising a Plan(The Venables Plan) to enable Mr Laxton to see Old Sleepy in secret(JR); chaining Jennings to a roller and consequently making him late for class(AG);and assisting in the recovery of what Jennings believes to be a Penny Black(OF).

Robin Atkinson is a fair-haired, excitable boy, described variously as being ten and eleven years of age, and who has joined Linbury Court two terms before Jennings. His birthday is in October. He is introduced to us as the unfortunate boy whose father has conveyed him to school at the start of term and then sets off again for the city with his trunk key(JG). He is not the most intelligent boy; his poem about a zoo visit fails to impress the competition organisers of the Form Three Times(JA), he laments that Mr Wilkins, whom he dislikes, moans at him about his maths(TY) and believes a box of drawing pins is in fact a rattlesnake(FI). However he has an admirable range of interests, including collecting stamps(especially Canadian and Australian ones), model aircraft, Second Eleven cricket and football, the violin, specialising in duets with Rumbelow at the piano(JO) and the Natural History Club, where he is placed in charge of **"Moles and Voles(if any)(FI)."** It is he who introduces Jennings to the joys of Linbury Court slang by use of the word "ozard(JG);" at the risk of severe retribution, he submits to the urge to try on Merridew's Homburg hat when the General is paying a visit(JL); he tries to capture the headlines of the Form Three Times with the account of the caterpillar in his cabbage(JA); the discovery of an old knife handle that he has buried, which Jennings firmly believes to be a petrified fang, encourages the Natural History museum to take root(JD); being the only one apart from Jennings who knows that Darbishire cannot swim, he keeps watch when Darbishire is given a secret swimming lesson by Jennings(AT); his illness brings a visit from his grandmother and the gift, not of the hoped-for food, but of the notorious guinea pig F.J. Saunders(TT); his handkerchief is used to help clean Mr Wilkins' car even though the cleaning mission ends in disaster with Jennings' handkerchief shoved in the exhaust(FI); he is the one who incites Jennings to draw the unflattering cartoon of Mr Wilkins(AU); he misinterprets Jennings' instructions by buying for the "At Home" party not a sponge cake but a foam rubber washing sponge(TW); it is his idea to use food packets to hide the cleaning materials in the Great Dormitory Four clean-up(LI); it is he who is with Jennings when Swing-Wing's temporary home in the attic is discovered, and he is let in on the elaborate conspiracy to feed him(JB); it is his paraffin, serving as an ant's cattle-grid, which spills, sending him out to Dunhambury with the little insects crawling all over both him and his mother(JR); and he is the lucky recipient of two tennis rackets, gratis, after Jennings has just paid 25p for an old cooking stove and dreadful painting(TY).

We never get to know what C.A. Temple's initials stand for. We do know, however, that he is a sturdy, burly, broad-shouldered, square-rigged boy, whose birthday is in August.

We are first introduced to him as a boy who has been on an air trip to Guernsey and who produces an identity card with a hole punched through it(JG). To begin with - although not for long - he is also known as Bod. The journey from C.A. Temple to Bod is a masterpiece of logic; his initials CAT lead naturally to Dog, lengthened to Dogsbody and shortened to Bod. We are told he has the best handwriting in Form Three; he is also a Second Eleven footballer and cricketer, a keen philatelist(OF), the Curator of Caterpillars in the Natural History Society(FI), and possesses a fair amount of bravado, having foxed out on his own to Valenti's to buy some rock(JG). It is this daredevil feat which, on Jennings'

With a cry of desperation, Mr. Wilkins seized the snorkel.

first night, together with his threat of a bashing-up for Jennings on the second day of term, shows him as quite a formidable character. However, very soon afterwards he loses this dominance and slides back happily into his stock role. Unlike Venables and Atkinson, though, Temple has a significant craving for food. He is well known for his hearty appetite, offering to buy sweets and cakes from boys receiving food parcels from home(TW), regarding the fare provided at tea-time of more importance than tracing the missing Jennings and Darbishire(LJ), and suggesting a "slap-up blow-out" as a means of dealing with the funds from the Jennings Membership Club(EJ). He does not like to see good food going to waste, shovelling scrambled egg into his mouth in one forkful in case Jennings should regain his appetite and demand it back(SO) and hurriedly swallowing the remains of his first plateful of food in the hope of obtaining a second(AG). He is a keen critic of school tea, on one occasion saying it is **"so weak it can hardly crawl out of the urn**(JO)**;"** he has a propensity to talk at the top of his voice with his mouth full despite Mr Wilkins' warnings; and his major consideration in his participation in the Sponsored Trot is the provision of suitable refreshment on the way(JE). After the first night of Jennings' Linbury career, when Temple is outraged that Jennings should borrow the washbasin he considers his private property(JG), there are a number of other incidents in which Temple is the star player. He is the one who discovers Jennings' glove during the evening search party(JA); he is the delighted assistant to Mr Wilkins as he endeavours to get Jennings rescued from the park railings(TT); he leads Mr Macready towards the gasmeters, believing the school inspector is really the gasman(TT); he accompanies Jennings to a Dunhambury junk shop to buy a music stand, knowing where the shop is and having a good laugh at Jennings' expense when the latter believes the shopkeeper is French(TW); it is the borrowing by Jennings of Temple's moonman's helmet which leads to a commotion that sees Jennings despatched away from the main party and on to their very own special train(LJ); and his illness(through overeating perhaps) leads on one occasion to an intensive search for a substitute 2nd XI cricketer(with one being discovered under one of Mrs Lumley's tea tables(LI)), and on another occasion to the locum Doctor Wooderson attending Linbury Court and being mistaken for a hedgehog expert(JR).

Bit part players maybe; but all three boys provide important foils for Jennings and Darbishire, as well as plenty of entertainment value of their own.

The Headmaster

Martin Winthrop Barlow Pemberton-Oakes, M.A. Oxon is the headmaster of Linbury Court School, and rejoices in the nickname "the Archbeako." Our first meeting with him sees him showing Darbishire's father round the school premises. Mr Pemberton-Oakes is a tall man in his mid 50's with thinning grey hair, and 35 years' experience of teaching. He is a softly spoken and rather reserved man, but amiable and kind-hearted too, and well versed in the **"difficult art of pouring oil on troubled waters(TT)."** He is a liberal-minded man who prides himself on holding enlightened ideas about education, and progressive views on the upbringing of the younger generation. For all that, it should not be thought that he is a soft touch. His dignified presence, exemplified by Miss Thorpe inviting him to the church bazaar as a "distinguished guest(LJ)" ensures that the Linbury staff and pupils are kept under control, and when he

Mr. Pemberton-Oakes leaped for cover behind his roll-top desk.

107

does feel the need to assert himself he will not hesitate to do so - even when it is a new boy whose kick on the Headmaster's shins in a corridor is entirely accidental(JG). The first indication of such assertiveness may consist of a **"cold unwavering stare"** such as he gives when he finds the boys engaged in an unorthodox street collection(TJ); we also hear that the more deeply he will feel about something, the less he shows it, hence the expressionless face which we hear will precede a thirty-five minute lecture(in which he specialises) and caning(JL). Miscreants may, besides a lengthy homily, receive the benefit of his often rather sarcastic, pompous language. He regards Darbishire's return to a supposedly burning building as showing a **"masterly grasp of the correct procedure to be followed(JG);"** he believes that the influence of the strip cartoon **"cannot but cause consternation in the minds of those whose duty it is to supervise the literary tastes of the rising generation(AT);"** and Jennings' india rubber fire is regarded by him as a **"particularly obnoxious conflagration(AU)."** However, we are left in no doubt that he is not being vengeful but merely protective towards the boys in his care - shown, for example, in his concern over the bona fides of camera salesman Mr Russell(JF). He is happy to tolerate and sometimes encourage creativity - for example, hut building(JL), the Natural History Club(FI), the Form Three Times(JA), pre-breakfast exercise(EJ), Old Sleepy's awakening from hibernation(JR), environmental friendliness(AG) and leisurely Sunday recreation(JB), and will only intervene when things get out of hand - as for instance they do when he finds himself stuck in the small back room of Jennings' hut(JL), or the victim of Rumbelow's space-gun(EJ) or rampaging pig(JI). He is certainly no tyrant, and seems happy to leave the smooth running of the school in the capable hands of his staff, only occasionally testing it for himself(JD). He does not, however, distance himself totally from day-to-day activity; there is evidence that he teaches(JF) and also bowls at the nets(JI). Nor is he a superman, and indeed is as susceptible to human frailties as any of his staff; he is regarded by pupils as more or less human when he is in the mood! He confesses to finding General Merridew difficult; he refrains from coming on school picnics because on a previous picnic he was plagued by ants; although a classics scholar he admits he is not a maths genius(JG)nor indeed typist(JL); and in a moment of aberration he fails to see that Darbishire will be letting his House cricket colleagues down by helping in the school kitchens(JB). He is somewhat mercenary; his proposed punishment for Jennings and Darbishire for going to the pond with Roger Merridew is cancelled when he learns that purely as a result of the incident Roger's mother decides to enrol him as a Linbury pupil(JL); he stops Mr Wilkins punishing Jennings for fraternising with Henri Dufour when it turns out Henri is to become a pupil(EJ); and he decides against punishing Jennings for breaking bounds in the attic and defacing it when the consequent investigation of the attic reveals woodworm infestation, prompt attention to which will save the school a lot of money(JB). He does not possess Mr Carter's canniness. Mr Carter correctly predicts that Diana and Roger Merridew will not like the superhuman display of neatness that he insists on providing(JL); he does not question the real motive for calling the fire brigade which Mr Carter is all too well aware of(JG); and he accepts at face value the reason for Jennings' involvement with the Dunhambury & District Gazette(JB) and the reason for his late-night study of Latin(JA) and Shakespeare(TW). He is perceived as somewhat inconsistent in his application of sanctions for misconduct, such as Mr Wilkins' cucumber-frame-smashing Boundary six(JL) and General Merridew's library prank(AT).But perhaps the most endearing flash of humanity is provided when on one busy morning he confides in Mr Carter that he has hardly a moment to call his own, hastily concealing the TIMES crossword puzzle which has kept him busy for most of the morning(OF)!

Mr Carter

Michael Carter is the Head's senior assistant master, and, like the Head, a graduate of Oxford. Although given the name Benedick in the first book(JG) - derived from the Latin word in the school grace "Benedicata"

- this does not stick. A friendly, calm, unhurried man with a keen ear for music, he is variously described as being in his early 30's, early middle-aged, 35 years of age, in his mid-30's, and at university fifteen years before when he excelled at rugger. Although prone to the occasional error of judgment(TT) he presents throughout as the model schoolmaster, without the inconsistency and pomposity of the headmaster, and without the hot-aired bluster of his junior colleague Mr Wilkins. Indeed on more than one occasion - e.g., Mr Wilkins' "cancelling" the Bracebridge match(JG) and confiscating food for the "At Home" party(TW) - he acts almost as a Jeeves to Mr Wilkins' Bertie Wooster of Wodehouse fame, advising him against certain actions, the advice being ignored, but Mr Carter inevitably being proved right in the end. His calmness manifests itself in a number of ways. He regards the Bathroom 3 flood as merely "awkward" while Mr Wilkins runs round in circles with worry(TW); it is his calm approach, rather than the flustered approach of Mr Wilkins, which persuades the bargain-hunting ladies to leave Jennings' jumble sale(JO); and he reacts with amusement rather than apoplexy to Mr Wilkins" problems with Atkinson's guinea pig - as he says, **"If I meet you tip-toeing along the corridor trailing a cabbage leaf on a piece of string, I shall know the chase has begun in earnest(TT)."** His friendliness is part of a broadly philanthropical make-up which is evident in his anti-litter campaign(TW), his commitment to an organisation devoted to the welfare of deprived children, which inspires him in two books to encourage the boys to raise money for famine relief(EJ, TJ), and his interest in badgers, which has led him to spend all night in other parts of the country watching the activities of a badger community(TH). Carter versus Conscience is, we are told, a keen contest, and it is pure luck which prevents him from telling the Head the real reason for Jennings calling the fire brigade(JG)!

His fifteen years' teaching, we are told, have provided him with a profound understanding of the workings of the juvenile mind, and with his receptive selfless nature the boys find him the obvious person to whom to turn in times of difficulty and crisis. Indeed the boys regard it as unthinkable to try to take advantage of him. It is he who is approached when the alarm clock gift to Mr Wilkins goes so badly wrong(AT); when Jennings is unjustly punished when Venables appropriates his socks(LI); when Jennings is worried about what to do with Swing-Wing(JB); or when money is required to help Mrs Hockin's Animal Rescue(JE). In short, he can **"always be trusted to set right the grievances and injustices that (are) so much a part of boarding school life(TY)."** He has a perceptive awareness of juvenile psychology, and is amused by Mr Wilkins' lack of such awareness. He recognises it will be premature to nip the boys' escape plan in the bud too early(JG); he reminds Mr Wilkins that **"if you stop them playing one sort of game they'll only think up another one**(JF)**;"** he will put off as long as possible any decision about a match cancellation so as not to disappoint the boys needlessly(FI); he refuses to conceal from Jennings the fate of his midnight feast despite Mr Wilkins' view that he should, in order to avoid further impetuous behaviour on Jennings' part(TW); he deduces that in schoolboy language, a piece of work that is "not quite finished" is in reality not quite started either(EJ); he recognises that Roger Merridew will not like the posh display the Head insists on providing for him(JL); he correctly predicts that a bird craze, which so worries Mr Wilkins, will be over by the following term(JB); and he suggests that retribution is better carried out when the offending boy is in a position to receive it and learn from it, than in the immediate heat of the moment as Mr Wilkins might like - as for instance when Jennings imprisons himself in a sleeping bag(JI). He reflects that the boys' intentions are excellent; they are not usually intentionally impertinent and their hearts are in the right place; their difficulty is that they just do not know when to stop - especially Jennings(EJ)!

Mr Carter's tolerant, positive view of the boys' activity often leads him to intercede on their behalf when others might be minded to take a stand against them. He treats Jennings and Darbishire to baked beans on toast rather than punishing them for their escape(JG); he impresses on a doubtful headmaster the values of hut-building(JL); he types the Form 3 Times for the boys despite its questionable literary merit(JA); he is instrumental in seeing Jennings gets another chance to show he can be a responsible individual following his disastrous attempts at dormitory captaincy(AU); he takes the boys' side against the bullying Major Rudkin(JE); he speaks up for the boys after they(although not Mr Wilkins) feel that they have done the right thing in reporting the classroom 2 burglary, Mr Wilkins, unbeknown to them, being the burglar(AU); he is not prepared to condemn the boys for smartening up the dormitory in a secret after-lights-out operation(LI); when Mr Wilkins "pounces," against his advice, to confiscate food for the "At Home" party, he not only accepts the party invitation but suggests purchasing extra party food(TW); he refuses, unlike Mr Wilkins, to see anything sinister in Jennings' ventriloquism(JO); he does not sympathise with Mr Wilkins over the unintentioned donation of his sports jacket for the guy(TJ); and he refuses to condemn the boys for bringing Old Sleepy back to school despite it being against Mr Wilkins' orders(JR). He goes out of his way to help the boys too; he encourages the boys in the Natural History Club(FI) and the

Camera Club(TT) to the extent whereby an outing is organised for them; he and Robinson combine to dig up the time capsule which is beyond the boys' power to shift(TH); he is happy to allow the boys to bend the normal dormitory rules so they can sing the school song on the last night of term(JE); he helps the boys organise their sponsored trot(JE); and he provides the last 10p needed for Jennings to raise a total of ten pounds towards famine relief(TJ).

The problem with Mr Carter is, as the boys find, that nothing can be kept secret from him. However much they try and conceal from him what they are doing, he will always find out in the end. There are numerous instances of conduct which the boys believe they can keep secret from him, but the boys are wrong. They include Jennings' first falling into the pond and then smashing a cucumber frame(JL); the discovery of the food list for the "At Home" party(TW); the fish parcel Jennings and Darbishire obtain from the French fishermen(JA); Jennings' lost diary and his consequent altercation with PC Honeyball(JD); Jennings' and Darbishire's chestnut roasting and, in the same book, their trip to the cinema(OF); and the Jennings Relief Fund, set up when Jennings has been made to pay for a new maths book(LI). He is perceived as having eyes like the Greenwich Observatory(SO) and he himself says **"all schoolmasters have eyes like photo-electric burglar alarms."** Although he agrees with Mr Wilkins that he would rather not know in advance what mischief Jennings was going to get up to next, there never seems any doubt that he will not be equal to it when the time comes!

Mr Wilkins

Lancelot Phineas Wilkins, M.A. Cantab, otherwise known as "Old Wilkie," is the most famous or perhaps infamous master at Linbury Court School, and junior to Mr Carter. A tall, broadshouldered man, with a voice like a loud-hailer, a short temper and a vigorous disposition, Mr Wilkins is no weakling, being 13 stone 6 lbs in weight, and 38 round the middle. It is no surprise that he has a hearty appetite, tucking into cake with **"the single-mindedness of ten year old third-formers(LJ)"** and mellowing when roast chicken is on the staff supper menu(JO). He is a strong man, only too pleased to help Matron with Jennings' trunk - although not so pleased when asked to repeat the process(JD)! He smokes tobacco, reads the Guardian, and although he enjoys crosswords and cricket - his boundary 6 from the cricket nets smashes a cucumber frame and is described as a **"remarkable stroke(JL)"** - his musical abilities extend merely to teaching the choir how to sing sea-shanties. As a

" What in the name of thunder is going on up there?"
Mr. Wilkins spluttered.

Cantabridgian, he was in the crew that won the Boat Race three years running. Although he is apparently ten years younger than Mr Carter, we also hear that he is in his 30's - as Mr Carter also is! He has to teach form 3 for 14 periods a week, and has the somewhat disconcerting tendency to start some lessons whilst still five yards from the classroom door.

There are a vast number of adjectives that can be used to describe Mr Wilkins. Many of these can be described under the general heading "mercurial." He has a fiery temperament, being known to go **"into the attack like an armoured column**(JA)**;"** we are told he **"hurtled and exploded his way through life like a radio controlled projectile**(JG)**;"** his entry to a room is described thus - **"as though attacked from without by a battering ram, the door hurtled open and Mr Wilkins was among those present**(JG)**;"** later that term he slams the staff room door behind him with a crash(JG); and he reacts angrily to comments about his car(FI). His excitable temperament is exemplified in his catchphrases, about more of which below. He is careless; he causes a fire in the staff room(LI), he leaves a car door unlocked with the ignition key inside(TJ) and he loses Jennings' watch(TJ). He is inconsistent, cancelling a well-deserved punishment for Jennings and Darbishire because their bungling has inadvertently produced a new cook(JO), insisting that the fruits of the Natural History Club be displayed, rather than destroyed, because of Dr Hipkin's visit(FI) and he expects the Head to sacrifice his poplars for the school Guy Fawkes bonfire after being criticised for his churlishness about parting with his sports jacket for the same purpose(TJ). He is prone to bursts of exaggeration; an overflowing bath becomes **"torrents of water cascading down the stairs like the Niagara Falls**(TW)**"** and his concerns about the bird-fancying craze prompts him to have visions of **"cormorants on the cricket pitch, swans in the swimming bath, buzzards in the bicycle shed, a vast flapping maelstrom of feathered**

songsters(JB)**."** Whilst he is often critical of the boys for their impetuous, thoughtless and unpredictable behaviour, with a tendency to jump to over-hasty conclusions, there are numerous examples in the series of Mr Wilkins' exhibiting exactly the same traits, often with disastrous results. His impersonation of Snodgrass hinders, rather than helps Mr Carter and Sergeant Hutchinson to solve the mystery of the intruder in the san(JF); his belief that Jennings has described him as the "missing link" rather than having a cuff link missing leads to a punishment which Jennings might feel is unjust(JD); his rough handling of the rattling relic, when gentler treatment is called for, causes damage to the school banisters(JD); Jennings' perfectly innocent inquiry as to whether there are any "old fossils" in the staff room to add to his archaeological collection is greeted with more than a little anger(JD); his sticking a knife into the music room ceiling brings the whole ceiling down(TW); his attempt to get the supposedly sleepwalking Jennings back to bed by means of the electric bell brings the whole school cascading downstairs for an unwanted choir practice(TW); his hastiness in confiscating the "At Home" provisions nearly deprive the staff of being entertained by the boys(TW); he wrongly believes the boys have been sabotaging the rainfall records during a dry spell(LI); he believes the boys' attempts to clean their dormitory are part of a midnight feast(LI); his hastiness to impound the entire contents of the lost property cupboard for the village jumble sale leads directly to the school receiving far more jumble back then they had before(JO); he is over-hasty in condemning Jennings' entertainment of Henri Dufour(EJ); he agrees to take on the part of Henry V and then pulls out, most inconveniently, at the last moment having realised he does not know the part(OF); he automatically thinks a shoal of missing tadpoles have turned into frogs, thus prompting him to ask the boys to find frogs for him and being suitably rewarded(FI); he mistakes for impertinence the friendliness the boys show him when they think he is leaving Linbury(AT); he believes the school inspector Mr Macready to be a police inspector regarding a minor traffic violation he has committed(TT); and his command to Jennings to tie a guy rope to anything he can find prompts the boy to tie the rope to the bumper of the school bus(JE). It seems almost inevitable that Fate, as if looking with disapproval on his antics, will hand to him more than his fair share of bad luck. It is he who believes he will have to stay up all night and add up 10,000 marks(JD). It is he who has to change Jack Carr's wheel(TT) and take responsibility for the Dunhambury Borough Council wheel left by Jennings in the Roman gallery(JD). And it is he whose journey home from Dunhambury is interrupted by PC Honeyball investigating the theft of his car which Jennings has reported(EJ).

Mr Wilkins' mercurial unpredictability is perhaps matched only by his lack of canniness and worldly wisdom. However much he might like to think he should have more authority(JG) he often displays a naivete and lack of sophistication which suggests that he is not, during this series at any rate, ready to step into Mr Carter's shoes. He dislikes fancy vases(LJ) and it is his dislike of fizzy drinks which prompts Jennings to try to brew picnic tea for him with his new paraffin stove(TY). He has no time for modern motors, preferring his old black Austin saloon which inevitably is the butt of much ridicule(FI). He is less than comfortable in the company of the fairer sex, and when turned upon is mere putty in their hands. His sister Margaret completely disarms him when he is ready to deliver earth-shattering punishments to Jennings for missing his detention class(JA) and Matron successfully intercedes on Jennings' behalf both when he thinks the boy is malingering(JD) and when he is minded to punish the boy for mislaying his mark book(JD). He tends not to notice things - he

blithely and unknowingly drives the cat Pyewacket to Linbury in order to report the loss of same(LJ), and he fails to see through the trail of red herrings which Jennings successfully lays in order to recover Old Sleepy(JR). He is not terribly practical - he offers a compressed liquorice allsort to the guinea pig for whose care he is responsible(TT), and his camping skills in the fields of tent erection, water drawing and camp cooking leaves much to be desired(JE). Rather more worrying is his failure to understand the eleven year old mind; he can never quite fathom why boys of eleven will neither reason nor behave in the intelligent manner of their elders. Perhaps it is this lack of understanding which

"*. . . you look like a thornbush in a blizzard.*"

makes it harder for him to establish control in his classes; we hear that Form Three's silence is the **"shallow silence of necessity not the deep silence of respect(JG)."** He is perplexed and anxious, rather than amused, by Jennings' "gred and gutter practice(JO);" he looks on most new crazes, particularly the space craze, as time-wasting, and believes that the boys' evening activity should be planned to the last detail; he has little time for Western films(OF); he demands immediate explanation for Jennings' imprisonment in a sleeping bag rather than waiting until the following morning when he will be in a better position to give such explanation(JR); he looks with alarm on the prospect of the "silly little boys" out in the world trying to earn their living, forgetting that he was once a silly little boy himself(JI); and he claims dogmatically **"I'm the one who has the worries - boys like Jennings don't even know the meaning of the word**(JR)**."** When he sees the boys playing football with an old school globe, his immediate thought is that since he cannot see any reason for doing such a fantastic thing, why should the boys do so?

It should not, however, be thought that Mr Wilkins is all bad. He has a sense of humour; whenever he sees the funny side of anything, we are told, it cannot be kept secret(JD). He has an explosive laugh, he is always in a jovial mood on the last night of term, and his self-mocking melodrama of a long-suffering teacher always goes down well with the boys(JE). He is genuinely fond of the boys in his care, and is touched at the idea of the boys buying a present for him believing that he was leaving Linbury; he reflects that they cannot be as bad as he supposed(AT)! Underneath the bluster, the impetuosity, the naivete and the lack of understanding is a kind heart which just occasionally asserts itself, seemingly against the owner's wishes. He is a fair-minded man, determined to make it up to Matron when he realises he has falsely accused her of being hoodwinked by a malingering Jennings(JD); he makes amends for his "At Home" food confiscation by making a special journey to Linbury to buy extra food(TW); he immediately compensates Jennings the cost of his new maths book when he finds the lost one was in his possession all the time(LI); he saves Jennings from becoming the laughing-stock at the end-of-term concert during the boys' conjuring act(JO); he resolves the deadlock over Mr Findlater's presentation bat(AT); he intercedes for Darbishire who faces punishment for watching the same rubbishy Western film three times(OF); he agrees to play the part of Henry V for the boys' Shakespeare excerpt(OF); he is willing to do all he can to put the matter right if a boy is treated badly by one of his fellows(FI); he spares the utterly dejected Jennings a further telling-off and punishment after the boy, following his disastrous attempt at dormitory captain, further lets himself down by appearing in class in a roller skate(AU); he is concerned that his demeanour may have caused the boys to abandon their sparkle derived from Old Sleepy's antics(JR); he helps with the sponsored trot in aid of Mrs Hockin's Retreat(JE); he recognises that punishment must stop somewhere(AG); and he is relieved, rather than angry, when Jennings turns up after his underground adventure(AG).

Mr Wilkins is unique in having his very own stock of personal catchphrases and expressions which carve a unique place for him in Linbury folklore. Here is a selection:

"But if I have any more nonsense from either of these two boys, I'll - I'll - well, there'd better not <u>be</u> any more nonsense!"(OF)

"Be quiet, Venables...I never heard such a lot of trumpery moonshine in my life..."(JD)

"Doh! I-I-Corwumph!" Mr Wilkins broke in. "What did you want to poke your head through for, you silly little boy!"(TT)

"I-I-Corwumph!" he spluttered. "What-what-what! Who on earth...! Goodness gracious! I've never, in all my life...What in the name of thunder is going on up there?"(TT)

"Doh! Picnics in the library!" he spluttered. "I never heard such a...Who in the name of thunder told Mrs Hackett she could invite all her friends here!"(JO)

"I shall count ten," he informed them. "And anyone who's still in here by that time will be - will be - we'll, he'd better look out."(LI)

"Tut! I'd like to know where on earth the silly little boy has got to."(LI)

"Silence! Silence!" Mr Wilkins roared in a voice as powerful as a loud-hailer. "I have never in all my life heard such a disgraceful exhibition of unruly hooliganism!"(TW)

"Jennings!.....Darbishire!...What on earth is the meaning of this foolhardy tomfoolery!"(AT)

"I'm warning you boys; I've had just about enough of this trumpery tomfoolery," he threatened. "And if there's any more trouble as a result of these ridiculous games, I'll...I'll...Well, there'd better not <u>be</u> any more trouble!"(AT)

4. THE A-Z OF THE JENNINGS BOOKS

This section features synopses of all the Jennings books, quotations from them, and entries for all the characters, apart from the principal characters, who appear in them, as well as pupils and staff who do not appear but are referred to by name. Where an "outside" character does not physically appear, that character will be allotted an entry of their own if they play a significant role in the surrounding action. A number of animals are referred to in the stories; they are only allotted an entry of their own if, again, they play a significant role in the surrounding action.

This section also contains features about the fictional locations used in the series, and highlights recurring themes in the series.

All the information provided below is based on the wording of the virgin texts, as originally written. A number of the books were re-issued in the Collins paperback imprint, Armada, with minor(often imperceptible) changes and updates, in the early 1970's. These have little or no value for collectors, and can be bought cheaply. Macmillan have, at the time of writing, re-issued sixteen titles in paperback, but the texts have been interfered with and, as stated elsewhere, they are worthless to both collectors and traditional Jennings enthusiasts.

Note:
Where the commentary refers to a book being illustrated, this means that there are illustrations in the text in addition to any frontispiece and dustjacket illustration, for which the illustrator would also have been responsible. Where the commentary refers to a book NOT being illustrated, information will be given as to the illustrator of the dustjacket and any frontispiece.

According to Jennings(AT) Sixth book in the series, first published by William Collins in 1954, 255 pp. Dedicated to **"David Davis, Head of BBC Children's Hour, whose keen understanding of the youthful mind brings the characters of Linbury Court School to life so vividly on the air."** The first Jennings book to be illustrated - for this one book only, by S van Abbe, who had already drawn the dustjackets and frontispieces for the first five books. Douglas Mays was to take over in the next book. With nineteenth century memories of General Merridew, and a devotion of a number of chapters to the craze for space exploration which at the time of writing was in its infancy, this is one of only very few Jennings stories which have dated.

Synopsis

Chapter 1 - The March of Progress - The space craze hits Linbury, the masters being tormented by groups ranging from the Form Three Space Pilots' League to the Form 1 and Early Bedders' Guided Missiles Club.

Chapter 2 - Attention All Space Shipping - The glass cover for a stuffed woodpecker makes not only unsuitable but very painful headgear for one budding spaceman.

Chapter 3 - Prisoner in the Library - The antics of the would-be space explorers include a prank which results in the most distinguished Old Linburian, General Merridew, being locked in the library during a flying visit.

Chapter 4 - An Old Boy Remembers - The General forgives his captors, regales the boys with some fond memories of his own, and goes about reconstructing one of his more successful pranks.

Chapter 5 - Mr Wilkins Rings The Bell - Mr Carter and Mr Wilkins are victims of the prank, being imprisoned in the library and ringing the old school bell every time they try to pull the door. The General is so delighted he asks for the school to be granted a day off.

Chapter 6 - Indoor Cricket - The day off is to see the school's top cricketers, plus scorers, attend a county match. Jennings' and Darbishire's wild celebrations result in the invitations to them being withdrawn by Mr Wilkins.

Chapter 7 - Distinguished Company - Jennings and Darbishire, anxious to show their detention work to Mr Wilkins at the match, hitch a lift with the international cricketer R.J. Findlater.

Chapter 8 - Autograph For Darbishire - Darbishire's realisation that RJF still has his autograph book in the changing room for signing results in an encounter with a burglar about to make off with the players' possessions.

Chapter 9 - Token Of Thanks - The burglar is apprehended with the assistance of Jennings and Darbishire, who are rewarded with a specially autographed bat.

Chapter 10 - Jennings Jumps To Conclusions - From an overheard snatch of conversation, Jennings erroneously believes Mr Wilkins is about to leave Linbury for good, and sets up a Farewell Gift fund.

Chapter 11 - Darbishire's Secret - Darbishire is forced to reveal to Jennings, who has pencilled him in to the Drake team for the Junior Swimming relay, that he cannot swim.

Chapter 12 - Troubled Waters - A hastily-arranged swimming lesson is cut short by the arrival of officialdom.

Chapter 13 - Decorations in the Dark - The resultant refuge taken by the boys in a cubicle ruins the fresh paintwork therein. Darbishire's efforts at repairing the damage are not an unqualified success. Luckily Robinson puts things right.

Chapter 14 - Ring Out, Wild Bells - It is decided to give Mr Wilkins an alarm clock as his present. Unfortunately it goes off in the middle of what the boys think is his last lesson, and he mistakes the whole exercise for a practical joke at his expense.

Chapter 15 - Darbishire Takes The Plunge - Darbishire is replaced by Bromwich for the relay, only to get so carried away in the race itself that he nosedives into the water - and finds he CAN swim!

Chapter 16 - Farewell to the Gift - The problem of how to dispose of the clock and pacify the angry contributors is solved by Matron's birthday occurring just at the right time. Darbishire's speech is mercifully drowned by yet another rude jangle from the alarm clock.

"And if I find any more disgraceful exhibitions of - of extremely courteous conduct, I'll - I'll - well, they'd better look out!"

**"You see, there's no air on the moon. That's why the chaps in this comic had to go about with their heads in things like goldfish bowls."
"Golly! They took the fish out first, I suppose?"**

Ackroyd Red-haired, tooth-braced member of Form One, who together with Clayton, stuffing grass down the neck of Cameron, is one of a party of walkers whose presence on the River Dun disrupts Jennings' and Darbishire's ill-fated fishing expedition. Ackroyd incurs Mr Wilkins' displeasure by splashing his form-mates through throwing a clod of earth into the water(SO).

Alsop With Perry, Binns minor and Plackett, a potential recipient of Darbishire's undersized cake(JG).

Animals and Birds There are several visitors from the animal kingdom into the pages of the Jennings stories, some invited, some not. They include the spider who crawls out of the Jamaican banana crate and who frightens the life out of Mr Wilkins(JG); the cows that provide the first real test of Darbishire's nerve as assistant detective(JF); Elmer the goldfish whose adventures include exercising in the swimming bath and being stored in a kettle in the woodshed(JL); the parcel of dead fish which Jennings secretes firstly on top of his head and then up Mr Wilkins' chimney(JA); the cow which Jennings and Darbishire try to return to its friends during a cross country run(OF); F.J. Saunders the guinea-pig whom Jennings and Darbishire and also Mr Wilkins take it in turns to adopt(TT); Matron's cat George The Third; the tadpoles, caterpillars and other insects which are so keenly sought after by the Form Three Natural History Club culminating in a speech day exhibition especially for the benefit of the day's guest(FI); the goldfish which provide Jennings and his companions with further uses for a snorkel(TW); Pyewacket, Margaret Wilkins' cat, which Jennings believes to be a stray and hands into the police while the owner's brother is searching high and low for it(LJ); the grass snake which Jennings presents to Mr Wilkins to accompany his breakfast(LI); Swing-Wing, the racing pigeon, whose arrival at Linbury leads to adventures that involve phantom woodworm and a ride on a fire engine(JB); the runt which Jennings wins in a sideshow at the Linbury fete and which causes devastation both in the pen of the rather more prestigious Susannah The Eighth and on the school playing field(JI); the hedgehog Old Sleepy whose rescue and awakening from hibernation provide a better report for Mr Wilkins than data regarding TV-watching habits of the local populace(JR); Jason, Miss Thorpe's bounding boxer, whose apparent indifference to obedience classes manifests itself in the mayhem he causes in Miss Thorpe's house, on Farmer Arrowsmith's land, and on the school premises(JR, AG, TH); Mrs Maverick, the Southdown sheep whose antics firstly amuse Jennings and Darbishire, and later, in a cave, terrify school picnickers(TY); Venables' gerbils Gerald and William whose temporary escape causes consternation to both the owner and those whose allegedly poisonous toadstools they have allegedly eaten(SO); and the birds for whom the boys leave scraps of unwanted school food(SO, TH). It is the discovery of Mrs Hockin's Animal Retreat which gives Jennings a great idea of how to assist Emma Sparrow in the disposal of her illegal menagerie in her London high-rise flat, and which leads to a big fund-raising campaign to keep the Retreat open. On the way, we meet, among others, a rabbit suffering in a petshop, Epaminondas the donkey, Ben the playful black-and-white mongrel, and the cows who block the route of the support vehicle for the Sponsored Trot(JE). Lastly, Jennings and Darbishire pretend that the secret society they have set up to find MacTaggart's buried time capsule is really a bird-watching society(TH).

Archer Pupil at Bracebridge School who coincidentally bowls Temple out and is then bowled by Temple, each player scoring 4 runs, in a 2nd XI cricket match(FI).

Arrowsmith, Mr & Mrs Jim Owners of Kettlebridge Farm and large tracts of land immediately adjoining Linbury. Although they do not have to put up with as much as Farmer Jenks, the Arrowsmiths' equivalent in the William stories, their relationship with the Linbury boys and staff is not always smooth. Their first confrontation with Jennings and Darbishire arises when Mrs A erroneously believes that the two boys have let one of their cows out of a meadow during a cross country run. When it is revealed that they were in fact trying to do the reverse, Mrs A offers the boys compensation in the form, inter alia, of chestnuts - the attempted consumption of which gets them into more trouble(OF). Mrs Arrowsmith inadvertently causes problems for the boys by presenting them with ALL the unsold jumble from the Linbury jumble sale(JO). When not crossed, the farmer can be of great assistance to Linbury Court, as he is when Mr Wilkins maths project takes Form 3 members on to his land for research purposes(JR). The ugliest altercation between the farmer and the boys comes when Jennings and Darbishire try to place their carelessly-won pig, an unbelievably ugly specimen, into the pen occupied by the potential show-winner Kettlebridge Susannah the Eighth(JI). Things are patched up reasonably soon afterwards, when the Arrowsmiths are invited to the school's charity firework night(TJ), only to be threatened again when Miss Thorpe's bounding boxer, Jason, temporarily in Darbishire's charge, runs amok on Arrowsmith's land(JR). However, reconciliation again takes place, when the boys, out on a picnic on the Downs, discover one of Mr Arrowsmith's sheep stuck at the end of a downland cave, and Mr Arrowsmith is able to rescue his Mrs Maverick(TY). Towards the end of the series Miss Thorpe is encouraging Mr Arrowsmith towards organic farming!(AG)

Uncle Arthur Like Aunt Angela, one of Jennings' more kindly relatives, but without as much time to devote to his nephew as Angela clearly has. We first hear of him through his sending five shillings to Jennings which is used to finance a trip to Dunhambury ostensibly to buy Matron a present, although things do not work out quite like that(JD). He appears in person for the first and only time one half-term, when an urgent appointment elsewhere causes him to put Jennings and Darbishire through a highly illegal afternoon in the Empire Cinema in Dunhambury.

Before that, however, he generously treats the boys to a meal in the Red

Lion which includes baked beans between courses(OF). In a later book he lends Jennings a collection of old coins, the half-sovereign from which falls into the untrustworthy hands of Mr Pink(SO).

****
"It's got - er - well, you know, four legs and a tail, of course."
"Most cats have. I've noticed that myself."(LJ)
****

Atkinson, Mrs Two Mrs Atkinsons appear in the narrative, both related to Robin Atkinson, one of Jennings' Form Three associates. The first to appear is his grandmother; her only appearance in the series is as a result of her grandson's ill-health, for which she prescribes barley water, grapes and a guinea-pig which she is forced to take back after it wreaks havoc on the school routine(TT). Later in the series, in the Bell Hotel in Dunhambury, we meet the boy's mother, despairing over the ant infestation for which her son has been responsible at the start of the exeat weekend(JR).

Attic Antics The junk-filled attic at Linbury Court, out of the way as it is from colleagues and officialdom, is the setting for a number of adventures involving Jennings. These include the attempted concealment of FJ Saunders(TT), the search for glass to replace a shattered cucumber frame(JL), the nurturing of Swing-Wing(JB) and the boys' incarceration there after trying to retrieve cricket balls from the roof, culminating in Jennings going to bed imprisoned in a sleeping bag(JI). We hear that the a tuck-box key can open the attic(JB) but in the next book it seems that cannot come to the aid of two boys who are trapped inside, and a store-room key is needed instead(JI).

Aunt Angela See Birkinshaw, Miss A.

Barlow, Thomas Cantankerous second-hand bookseller in Dunhambury whose business canniness causes him to rapidly deflate the value of books when he realises he is being asked to buy rather than sell them(JA).

Barney A gloomy individual, who together with Rocker, a sturdy, bare-headed youth in jeans and gumboots, and Mr Fouracres, a large man in donkey jacket and woollen cap, comprise a trio of farm workers who in between puffs of home rolled cigarettes load the honky-tonk piano on to Miss Thorpe's trailer for conveyance into Dunhambury where it is hoped the boys will get £5 for it(TJ). Barney appears in the next book in the series, as one who is somewhat indifferent to the plight of a vulnerable hedgehog and indirectly prompts Jennings to take care of the animal himself(JR).

Bathos **"Gosh, no; that's no earthly use. Who wants to see your face plastered all over the wall? What we want is something like the winning goal in the Cup Final, or jet fighters zooming into a power dive." "Or the semi-final of the Form Four chess championship."**(JA)

"It's frightfully invaluable, sir. It's got all sorts of people in it - sporting characters, television stars, famous authors, and our window-cleaner's brother who won a football pool, sir."(AT)

Ben The black-and-white mongrel whose escape causes problems for Emma Sparrow and Jennings in their conveyance of Emma's menagerie to Mrs Hockin's Retreat(JE).

Binns Major The elder brother of one of the two youngest boys in the school is mentioned only in passing; as a competitor in the half-mile with Darbishire(JF) and as a member of the 2nd XI football team that has to form a search party for Jennings and Darbishire(JA).

Binns N.(Binns Minor) and Blotwell, R.G. The two youngest boys in the school, eight-year-old members of Form One, and the only boys junior to Jennings and Darbishire to make regular appearances in the series. That having been said, Blotwell(who is younger than Binns) does not appear until the fifth book(JD) when Mr Wilkins is unable to find a bed for him, as a new boy, in Dormitory 3(this being hardly surprising, as Jennings is enjoying unscheduled occupation of it) and this hardly eases the discomfiture the new recruit feels. Both have loud, penetrating, squeaky voices; their announcements are trumpeted with ear-splitting shrieks; and much of their dialogue is "shrilled" or "squawked." At refreshment times they can be seen squabbling happily over mid-morning snacks or perhaps looking ahead to the next meeting of the Form One Percussion Band of which Blotwell is the conductor. On organised walks - which they as juniors must take part in more frequently than their elders - they can be found tripping along with chirruping prattle at the side of the long-suffering duty master, speculating as to whether school tea tastes more like diesel oil or cabbage water. Both boys spend much of their time trying to identify with and take a part in the lives of their Form Three colleagues. Binns manages to achieve a place on Darbishire's Cake List(JG); he secures a position as Chief Salvage Officer and Deputy

Armourer at the school sports to rank alongside Venables' directorship of Campanology(JF); he builds a hut forbidding hawkers(JL); he is so anxious to achieve inclusion in the Form Three Times that he wildly exaggerates the importance of the temporary loss of his left football boot, and composes improbable doggerel about a melancholy pirate(JA). He and Blotwell invite themselves into the quest for fossilised objects, proud of their collection of **"smooth round stones - probably fossilised but probably not"** and are included in the party to visit Dunhambury Museum where they speculate on the Romans' ability to build glass cases to house their treasures(JD); they offer, in vain, to assist in the production of The Miser's Secret(OF); they establish their Early Bedders Club as their part of the space craze and then when interest turns to swimming they form the Shallow Enders Frogmens Union(AT); they set up their own Form 1 Telephone Exchange and create a spinning machine with cardboard discs and loops of cotton in answer to Form Three's craze for ingenious inventions and methods of communication(AU); they mirror Jennings' enthusiasm for festive fun by creating fairylights(Blotwell as Chief Electrician) and experimenting with jam jars full of cold water and chalk dust to create a snow effect(AU); they mirror Jennings' criminological pursuits by taking up fingerprinting(LJ); they cultivate civilised crafts such as the creation of toadstool patterns(SO); they happily conspire to put Mr Wilkins off the scent when Jennings organises an illegal fishing trip(SO); they are eager patrons of Jennings'jumble sale, obtaining a perished hot water bottle and 5 year old calendar as trophies of the occasion(JO); they are keen observers of Old Sleepy's awakening from hibernation, breathing down the ears of Jennings and Darbishire so much that some of their breaths are taken for Old Sleepy's(JR); and they insist on joining the Jennings Membership Club, and participate enthusiastically in the quest for convincing replacement chocolates for Matron by providing colourful wrappers(EJ). Not surprisingly, there is little love lost between them and Jennings and his friends. They regard Form Three boys as the **"lowest form of animal life known to science,"** this opinion being reinforced by the fact that Jennings' newly-won pig has just run amok and ruined their almost-complete jigsaw puzzle, prompting them to assert that **"Darbishire is a rota and Jennings is a bigger one(JB)."** They relish the thought of Jennings' misdeeds earning him punishment, preferably harsh physical punishment; they are liable, when not imitating jet-propelled aircraft, to imitate the sound of the Headmaster's cane crashing down on the hapless victim. They are quick to spell out the dreadful consequences of Jennings' supposed turning off the water-heater for Miss Thorpe's aquarium(AG). Despite their hankering after equality with their elders, their attitude is refreshingly juvenile. They speculate that Mr Hind's pipe may be the reason for an after-lights-out fire drill(TW); they believe that carrots are good for eyesight because donkeys are not seen wearing glasses(TY); they wish to throw Miss Thorpe's umbrella out of the window to see if it falls like a parachute or a pancake(prompting the headmaster into wondering the same thing!)(TJ); they contemplate with relish the smell given off by burning tyres on the bonfire(TJ); they believe they can combat the greenhouse effect by standing beside a tree and breathing deeply(AG); they speculate on the possibility of an albatross landing on Darbishire's nose in the middle of a Test match he was playing in(JB); they play golf with pingpong balls(TY), use houseshoes to hammer biscuit tins(JL), trampoline on beds(TT), execute wardances on the 1st XI cricket pitch(FI), experiment with a plastic space gun on a train(LJ), engage in a tug-o'war for possession of a cricket ball(LJ) and storm castle ramparts with a water pistol(TT). The last book of the series still sees them on fine form - making music with blades of grass, and producing Robin Hood and His Merry Men with a cast of two. Not only do they try to secure a frying pan for Friar Tuck; they believe his "habit" might be biting his nails. Notable in the production is Blotwell going back on stage without his beard; it is presented to him by means of a cricket stump(TH). Truly they are as delightfully juvenile as they ever were!

Birchingdean Village close to East Brinkington where Mrs Goodman optimistically believes Jennings can pick up an early bus to Dunhambury after his unsuccessful expedition with Swing Wing(JB).

****

"Don't be ridiculous, boy! Why, I could play the part on my head, if I wanted to."
"We wouldn't want to surprise the audience all that much, sir," Darbishire assured him solemnly. **"If you'd just play it the right way up, that'd be good enough for us."** (OF)
****

Birkinshaw, Miss A. Known throughout the series as Jennings' Aunt Angela, she is Jennings' favourite aunt. An attractive, amiable woman in her early thirties - Jennings describes her as **"decent unless you happen to rub her up the wrong way and then she can be a bit awkward(EJ)"** - she is a supporter of disarmament(EJ), her handwriting consists of a nasty illegible scrawl(FI)and her two outstanding characteristics are generosity and absent-mindedness. Her generosity, which sometimes needs a little unsubtle prompting from Jennings, is considerably more than one might be entitled to expect from an aunt, extending as it does to a new bicycle(FI), termly postal orders(JL), home-made cakes(she is an excellent cook and her cake, when entered for the church bazaar, wins a prize)(LJ), a diary(with a promise of ten shillings if it is written in every day)(JD), a fountain pen(to help her nephew come top in French)(EJ), assistance with the counting of TV aerials(JR), tuckbox topups(JR), theatre trips(EJ), monthly letters(JL), a printing outfit which helps to start the Form Three Times(JA), a replacement arithmetic book which even has answers printed in it(LI), boxes of chocolates(LI, EJ) and entertaining both Jennings and Darbishire to lunches and teas out in Dunhambury(EJ, JR). Her absent-mindedness may lead her to send Jennings a seed catalogue while her nurseryman gets Jennings' postal order(JL); to write to her nephew to expect parcels that never come(TW); and to forget that she is double-booked and can't come and see her nephew as planned(although the lollipops and cake are ample compensation)(TW); and to leave umbrellas on buses(JL). Aunt Angela makes a mere handful of appearances in the series; indeed we hear that her visits to Linbury are rare. Her first appearance comes when Matron has just handed round a box of chocolates hastily cobbled together by the boys after the first box, that she sent, was consumed by them but intended for Matron(EJ); later that day, as she entertains the boys for lunch, she faithfully reports the theft of Mr Wilkins' car even though the thief is none other than a garage mechanic doing as instructed by the owner(EJ). Her second visit is largely unexpected - Jennings thinks she is not coming because of her car problems - but she arrives nonetheless and because Jennings has gone off on an illegal mission, it is left to Darbishire to smuggle her out of the building in his own gauche fashion(JR). Far from the comfortable genteel lady-of-leisure that we take her for, it is to our surprise that we learn late in the series that she is a social worker living in a tall block of flats in south-east London and finds herself heavily involved in her nephew's efforts to save Emma Sparrow's animal menagerie(JE). Apparently Jennings comes and sees her at 64 Gaitskell Court every so often, and is allowed to tinker with the motor-mower - one wonders why she needs it(EJ).

Birthdays The fact that Jennings, and his Linbury colleagues, remain in the same class for over forty years does not stop them having birthdays. The first birthday which the reader is privileged to witness involves Jennings being given a camera and a printing outfit, with which two pieces of equipment he indirectly proceeds to disrupt school life for the best part of the rest of term, and, better still perhaps, being let off a punishment by Mr Wilkins(JA). The happy coincidence of Matron's birthday and a present that was intended for, but did not reach Mr Wilkins as it was supposed to, helps Jennings to solve a knotty problem(AT). By contrast, a coffee party Matron conceives for Mr Hind's birthday is nearly a washout when the party cakes are appropriated by midnight dormitory feasters(TT). Darbishire's birthday is a partial failure when he finds he has no use for the music stand Jennings has given him(he having swapped his recorder for a telescope for Jennings to go in a leather case which Jennings has also disposed of)(TW). Mr Wilkins' birthday coincides with Bromwich's need to place the master in a favourable mood in order that his confiscated set might be returned to him, and throughout the day, Mr Wilkins is inundated with birthday greetings from Bromwich of a most unsubtle nature, culminating in his receipt, from Bromwich, of a particularly repulsive oil painting(TY). There is considerable debate as to when the best time of year for a birthday is; Temple thinks August is best so he can enjoy it during a month of freedom, Atkinson regards his October birthday as a red letter day sandwiched between the days of school routine, and Bromwich has the best of both worlds with his birthday at the end of March, and if it happens to be breaking-up day, he can have his cake and eat it!(TW)

Boddington, Messrs S & S Stamp merchants whose enticing magazine advertisement tempts Jennings and Darbishire into sending for lists and approval sheets fondly believing the contents of the sheets to be free. Having had their misleading ads exposed, the dealers further antagonise Jennings and Darbishire by making them believe they have created an imitation Penny Black(OF).

Boland's Wood See entry for Three Acre Marsh.

A Bookful of Jennings Sixteenth book in the series, first published by William Collins in 1966, 320 pp, and reprinted as **The Best of Jennings** in 1972. No dedication or illustrations; dustjacket by Douglas Mays. This is a compilation volume, with no new stories, and the only compilation volume to have been produced. It consists of a mixture of long and short extracts from all fifteen books which had been published up until then (the most recent being EJ). Although the long extracts are given headings which are mostly the same as chapter headings in the originals, the content may have been extracted from other chapters in the same book or even other chapters in other books, in order to create continuous narratives. The long extracts, which where necessary are preceded by an introductory resume in italics, are as follows:

Anthony Buckeridge

A BOOKFUL OF JENNINGS

1. Hazardous Journey(JG) - the boys' attempt to run away from school.

2. The Rattling Relic(JD) - the boys' adventures with the wheel and chain.

3. An Old Boy Remembers(AT) - General Merridew and the locked library.

4. The Snake in the Grass(LI) - The unappetising breakfast present for Mr Wilkins.

5. Cross Country(OF) - The boys' ill-fated cross country run.

6. The Planned Operation(TW) - The attempted midnight feast.

7. Tangled Web(JO) - Jennings' dry-cleaning operation.

8. First Rehearsal(OF) - The launching of "The Miser's Secret."

9. Curtain Up(OF) - The performing of the Henry V extract.

10. High Altitude(LJ) - Mr Wilkins' vain efforts to teach Form 3 about the rigours of Everest.

11. The Scientific Frogman(FI) - Dr Hipkin's visit to Linbury.

12. The Handy Gadget(TW) - Jennings' snorkelling exploits.

13. The Furtive Feasters(TT) - The boys' discovery of the supposed secret eating by the masters.

14. The Farewell Gift(AT) - The boys' doomed attempt to give Mr Wilkins a happy send-off from Linbury.

15. The Organised Outing(TT) - Jennings getting entangled in the park railings.

16. The Mobile Man Trap(AU) - Jennings rollerskates into trouble in a geography lesson.

17. In Contact(EJ) - Jennings believes he has infected his demob-happy colleagues - but with what?

18. An Inspector Calls(TT) - Mr Macready's eventful visit to Linbury.

19. The Great Rainfall Mystery(LI) - Whilst drought conditions persist, why does the rain gauge disagree?

20. The Old Folks At Home(TW) - The boys' attempts to lay on a party for the staff.

21. Venables Stands Treat(JA) - Venables forgets to bring money to pay Jennings' and Darbishire's tea.

22.Ici on Parle Francais(EJ) - Jennings' efforts to master the French language - with a little help from Henri Dufour.

23.The Scarlet Runner(JD) - The boys attempt to master Chas. Lumley's hired bikes.

24.False Whiskers For Two(AU) - Jennings and Mr Wilkins each become Father Christmas.

25.The Incomplete Anglers(JA) - The boys' attempt to rescue a fish parcel from Mr Wilkins' chimney.

26.The Lure of the Jumble(JO) - Linbury Court is invaded by bargain hunters.

27.The Key to the Mystery(EJ) - The boys are locked out whilst trying to recover a radio aerial.

28.The Unique Antique(JL) - Jennings' successful bid to win a vase for Mr Wilkins.

Three chapters consist of much shorter extracts from one or more book on a common theme, but without a continuous narrative thread:

1. Hardly Cricket(LJ, AT, JL) - all on a cricketing theme.

2. All Right on the Night(JO) - all related to preparations for the end-of-term entertainment.

3. Trouble After Dark(AU, LI) - both relating to goings-on after "lights-out."

There are three other chapters of a more general nature:

1. A Word About Jennings - an introduction to the world of Jennings and Linbury Court.

2. In Brief - a sequence of fairly short unconnected extracts(LI, LJ, EJ)

3. And Similarly... - an assortment of similes from the series.

In addition, there are scattered through the book, in smaller type, choice "mini-extracts" of a dozen lines or even fewer.

Criteria for selection for the compilation is unclear; many first-rate stories from the first fifteen books are omitted, and some books are hardly touched at all. Nonetheless, it is a splendid appetiser for those wishing to be introduced to the world of Linbury Court. Like many of the more recent Jennings books, copies are scarce and even without dust-jackets they are valuable collectors' items.

Borrowmore, Irving(a.k.a. Alfred Hubert Mudd) Shakespeare actor whose appearance at Linbury on the same day as the end-of-term revue, owing to an oversight by Mr Wilkins, gets Jennings and his fellow thespians out of a tight spot when he agrees to play Henry V after Mr Wilkins has less than graciously bowed out(OF).

****

Atkinson didn't think much of the picture. He wrinkled his nose and said: "Somebody's spilt gravy-browning all over it."
"That's just because it's old. You can easily clean it up a bit with an india-rubber."(TY)
****

Bracebridge School The great sporting rivals of Linbury Court, providers of substantial post-match teas. Presided over by Mr Parkinson, Bracebridge is one of only two other schools mentioned in the whole series, although extremely little of the action takes place there. The location is uncertain; in one book it is a train journey away from Dunhambury(JA) whereas in two others it is within walking distance of the town centre and indeed the grounds are well situated for a furtive shopping spree(JO, SO); and just to confuse the issue, a fourth book has it as ten minutes' drive from the centre of Dunhambury(TJ)! It has a modern block containing a sports hall, a well-lit changing room and spacious showers and knee baths. Our first visit to Bracebridge sees Darbishire being imprisoned in a detention class by mistake; the prisoner has time to notice the same smell of ink and chalkdust, the same overfull desks with lids that will not quite shut, the lost rubbers under the radiator and the badly-aimed balls of old blotting paper(JA). Subsequently Jennings and Darbishire are conveyed there by Mrs Hipkin to avoid - or so they think - Linbury officialdom after an illegal boat trip(FI); and on a more lawful visit, Jennings' attempts to heat up the cold shower after the match lead him to believe he has emptied the school swimming pool(TJ). It is against Bracebridge that Jennings makes his First Eleven soccer debut, scoring the winning goal(JG).

"Supersonic tea, they gave us, wasn't it? That shepherds pie was the wizardest garbage I've tasted for months. I had three refills."(JA)

Bretherton House School The opposing side in the first football match in which Jennings is selected to represent his school. Tragically illness prevents him from doing so(JG). Thereafter the school is never mentioned again, and Bracebridge School is the usual rival for Linbury Court.

Bromwich, I.K. Until the very last book, his first two initials seem to be without doubt; in at least two books(TY, FI) he has the initial I. Somewhat to our surprise, however, we are then informed that his name is in fact David Jonathan Bromwich(TH)! It is beyond dispute, however, that he is Bromwich Major, with a brother in the first form(although his brother is reported to win the Form TWO pingpong championship!). With his thick black curly hair Bromwich is, after Venables, Temple and Atkinson, the most frequently mentioned third-former in the series, but is set slightly apart from the latter three friends and contemporaries of Jennings and Darbishire. He is Head Newt Keeper in the Natural History Society(FI), holds the Dormitory 6 underwater breathing record with a count of 38(JA), and he is also a 2nd XI footballer(JA), table tennis fan(TT), model aircraft constructor(OF), footprint plastercast creator(JD), swimmer for Drake House(AT), keen stamp collector and swapper(TW, OF), and cricket enthusiast despite an ignorance of the whereabouts of a backward short leg(TH). In some books he shares a dormitory with the five aforementioned characters(he is actually a rather bossy dormitory captain in one such book(AU)) but in others he clearly sleeps elsewhere. He is an intelligent boy; he is able to decipher Aunt Angela's handrwriting(FI), he is wise to Jennings' chalk-dust tricks(LJ), he leads an agricultural fact-finding group for Mr Wilkins' maths project(JR), he suggests that imitating a sleepwalker might be an effective way of gathering material for a dormitory feast, he comes top of form 3 and receives an honourable mention in five subjects(FI) and is regarded as more level-headed and dependable than the others, hence his appointment as junior house match umpire(JB), minder of the boys whilst Mr Wilkins goes in search of Jack Carr(TT) and dormitory captain(AU). However he can also be as irresponsible and juvenile as his friends when the mood takes him. His rhymed couplets about rabbit hutch construction cut little ice in the poetry competition(JA); he tries to solve a mathematical problem using a snail rather than the intended homo sapiens(JA); he suggests a naval battle on the river Dun during a nature trip(LI);his geology essay degenerates into a crass study of the domestic properties of chalk(LI); he is in two books said to be anxious to avoid a weekly French test((EJ, JI); and he busies himself with building a rabbit hutch without a rabbit to put inside it(JA). Bromwich is referred to as a lone wolf and a law unto himself, and a number of incidents highlight his individuality. He is less keen on the structural wizardry of his contemporaries' huts than on his pet goldfish Elmer, his companion in his hut(JL); he continues his rubbish scavenging on his own whilst the others are working in groups(AG); his lack of interest in Jennings' unflattering cartoon of Mr Wilkins causes him to collect for marking a book in which Jennings believes the offending artwork is contained(AU); and he has to be coaxed into looking at the Form Three Times(JA). Despite a keen appetite - he once eats a picnic lunch before leaving the premises(AT)- he is a stern critic of the table manners of another hearty eater, Temple, claims not to like school food, and is not always in the best of health. His illness on various occasions causes Jennings to take responsibility for his goldfish and lose it(JL), turns Jennings into an unwilling dormitory captain(AU), forces Jennings to give Darbishire emergency swimming coaching(AT) and enables Jennings, to his great dismay, to appropriate and then have confiscated his pocket radio(leading to a painfully long "chatting-up" process to have the set returned from Mr Wilkins(TY)). On a number of occasions he plays important bit-parts in Jennings' exploits and misadventures. He is dropped to allow Jennings to become a First Eleven footballer(JG); he spills the beans to the Headmaster about Jennings' dash to the forbidden hut area with Roger Merridew(JL); his loan of a tin trumpet ensures himself a place in the Henry V excerpt(OF);he is the owner of the glass Jennings uses which creates a conflagration during a book inspection(AU); he admits a horde of women to Jennings' supposedly private jumble sale(JO); his confinement to the sickroom with an ankle bruise prompts Jennings to believe he may have put himself in quarantine(EJ); his father's ownership of a metal detector, which may help locate Tim MacTaggart's time capsule, leads to a bout of friendliness towards him which comes to an abrupt end when Darbishire lets him down badly in a House match(TH); he escorts hedgehog expert Mr Laxton into the school, believing him to be a doctor(JR); his errant boxing glove upsets the chess pieces which leads to Jennings seeking other forms of leisure activity, including turning detective(JF); he places the jacket of a work of pulp fiction round Jennings' textbook rather than the brown wrapper intended, thus creating yet more problems for Jennings(LI); and his painting of a worthless red stamp makes Jennings believe he has discovered a Penny Black(OF).

Brown Major Centre half in Jennings' first practice match, fellow team member in Jennings' first First Eleven game(JG), muddy-shoed hut dweller with serious misconceptions about military attaches and little time for Darbishire's crumbs of statistical information(JL), with a brother who has a penchant for filling inkwells with stale cake crumbs(JG). See also Paterson below.

Brown Minor See entry for Brown Major.

Bullying   Linbury Court appears to be blissfully free of aggressive types, and none of the stories contain episodes of bullying. The closest we get is on Jennings' very first night at the school, when Temple threatens him with a bashing-up, but even this is qualified when his threat is described by the author as **"a mild rebuke to Jennings, so that he might know his lowly station in life and not get above himself(JG)."**

****

This report proves that people living in two houses, plus twenty-three hundredths of all people living in another house watch more television in the country than in the town.(JR)
****

Mrs Caffey   Housekeeper at Linbury Court, otherwise known as Mother Snackbar, responsible for admitting Mr Higgins into the school to collect the House sports cup for engraving, arousing suspicions from the Linbury Court Detective Agency(JF). After this book she is not heard of again.

Cameron   First former and stage manager of Binns' and Blotwell's "Robin Hood and His Merry Men" slot in the school Drama Evening. When Blotwell goes back on stage without his false beard - it has been tossed behind a radiator - Cameron shows a commendable degree of ingenuity by presenting it to the hapless actor on the end of a cricket stump(TH). Also see entry for Ackroyd.

Carr, Jack   Elderly and somewhat senile owner of the car jack with which Darbishire extricates Jennings from the park railings. By way of compensation Mr Wilkins kindly changes his wheel for him, after taking some time to persuade the hapless owner that the property really is his. **"Yes, of course! I see what you mean. You didn't mean `This is your car, Jack old man' - you meant `This is your jack, Carr old chap!' Eh? H'm!"**(TT)

Mr Catchpole   The anxious sales manager of the Grossman Cine Camera Company who mistakenly believes Jennings is a wealthy aristocrat, and sends Mr Russell down to Linbury Court in order to effect the sale of a movie camera(JF).

Charlie   Two characters in the series have this name. The first is the driver of fire appliance in an abortive mission to rescue Jennings from park railings(TT). The second is the sale room porter at the Dunhambury

Auction Mart who lumbers Jennings with goods he has unwittingly put in a bid for(TY).

Cherry, Mrs School cook-housekeeper, who departs to take up a new post in London; after she leaves, the standard of food at the school, which was excellent when she was at the helm, suffers considerably at the hands of the washing-up supremo, Mrs Hackett(JO).

Chester, Andy The man in charge of the Dunhambury Youth Club. A genial, bearded young man who when we meet him is dressed in a vast sweater and faded fawn trousers, he not only relieves the boys of their honky-tonk piano but, to test it out, organises an impromptu concert party in the otherwise uninspiring Denton Street, and thereby helps to bump up Jennings' famine relief fund(TJ).

Christmas Because the boys are at home for Christmas, this exciting time of the year does not achieve the prominence it receives in, for instance, Richmal Crompton's William books. The most exhaustive coverage given to the festive season during one book includes Jennings folding a Christmas card into a paper dart and throwing it into the staff room, his using old exercise books full of valued notes as paper chains, and dressing up as Father Christmas to return a missing pen to Mr Wilkins(AU). It is the coincidence of the accumulation of unwanted jumble and the end of the Christmas term which prompts Jennings and Darbishire to hold a disastrous jumble sale in the gym, although it provides an unexpected Christmas present for the school in the form of a new cook(JO). We are informed of Blotwell having had to spend Christmas in bed at school through contacting someone with a contagious disease right at the end of the Christmas term(EJ). A surge of environmentally friendly behaviour by the boys prompts them to suggest that they should ask for trees as Christmas presents(AG).

Clarke With MacTaggart, one of Darbishire's competitors in the half-mile race(JF).

Clayton See entry for Ackroyd.

Clive The man who locals believe will turn up and exceed Jennings' score of 47 in the "Bowling For A Pig" at the village fete. It is his non-attendance which results in Jennings winning the competition and finding himself with a most unwelcome prize(JI).

Clough, Mrs Bertha Mrs Hackett's neighbour in Linbury village, who together with Mrs Clutterbuck, Ethel Pinmill, Doris, Gladys and many others creates havoc by attending a jumble sale Jennings has organised in the school gymnasium to get rid of the jumble left inadvertently by Mrs Arrowsmith. It is at Mrs Hackett's suggestion that she attends with other womenfolk of the district, drawn to the school by the offer of Fabulous Free Gifts For All and free admission too. We are told that although she is gifted with obvious powers of leadership, Mrs Clough is somewhat disorganised in her plans for rallying her supporters in a frontal assault on the gymnasium. When they finally arrive in the Promised Land, it is hardly surprising that Mrs C should resent being told by Mr Wilkins that she and her comrades are trespassing, and has no qualm about not only loudly complaining about the quality of the goods in the millinery department,but also waving an umbrella in Mr Wilkins' face(JO).

Clutterbuck, Mrs One of Bertha Clough's partners in crime, who after the arduous half-mile walk from the village to the school jumble sale, rests her weary limbs with a picnic in the library(JO).

Cooper, Alfred Of the firm of A.Cooper & Son, Builders & Decorators, it is his inspection of the school which prompts the Headmaster to renovate the music room ceiling; how fortunate that Jennings should assist by being instrumental in bringing it crashing down(TW).

Correspondence Jennings, being at boarding-school, often feels the need to communicate with the outside world - after all, we hear that his mother writes to him each week(SO) and he corresponds with his mother each Sunday(JE)- and with no telephone available, he often puts pen to paper. His letter-writing is one of the most delightful aspects of the series. Letters are wont to begin with polite enquiry:

Dear Emma,
I hope you are well and having weather.(JE)

Letters even to officialdom produce solicitous inquiry as to the addressee's health, and provision of sports news:

Dear Mr S and S Boddington,
I hope you are quite well. We are having decent weather. Are you?
I shall be obliged if you will send me some of those stamps which you

are giving away without obligation. And if you could let us have them soon, so much the better, as we are in rather a hurry to get started. Last week the Second XI played Bracebridge School at football. We won 3-2. (OF)

Letters may be mercenary in nature, such as a letter to Aunt Angela in which he tries gently to remind her that she promised him a bicycle as a present:
It is a long time since Christmas. I hope you enjoyed the card with the robin on that I sent you. Almost everybody has a bike except me, it is good exercise. You can send them by train and the van brings them. It comes quite often. I expect they will all enjoy the picnic, except me.

As Jennings then reflects, **"I've only dropped a veiled hint here and there among the rest of the news."**(FI)

Jennings is anxious to explain the reason for delays to his correspondence:
I did not write because I was in bed with a sore throat so I did not write but I am not in bed now as I am well, so I will write.(EJ)

It is not surprising that Mr Carter should refuse to pass some of Jennings' unpunctuated paragraphs for public consumption - such as this:
We tried to send him back before, but he flew home(i.e. viz back to school) and we did not know your address until Mr Carter found out which we should never have done by ourselves if I had not put my name on the beam in drawing pins so it really was a Blessing in Disguise. (JB)

Some equally incoherent letters do, however, slip through the net:

Thank you for writing asking why I hadn't answered your letter, it is because I had to sell a person your old unused stamp to buy another unused new one, but as you have sent me a used new one I will get my money back from another person and buy an old unused one for your letter, so that will be all right.(JI)

Correspondence from Jennings is liable to be "singed" rather than "signed:"

To the Chief of Police, Linbury...Dear Sir, I hope you are well and having weather. I expect you do not know, but there is a suspicious character in Miller's Wood who may be a secret agent. You can tell

him because he has a beard and quite a lot of cable coming out of the back of the car. Also dark glasses and some more things but I could not get his prints on the bottle owing to gloves. I have no motive and hope this does not matter. Yours sincerely(singed) JCT Jennings. (LJ)

And Jennings has the perfect pretext for ending a letter promptly...
Must stop now as have no blotch so can't turn over. (LI)

....although there may be a solicitous enquiry instead, even if the potential recipient lives only just down the road:

I hope you are having good weather.(TJ)
The weather here is clement as I hope it is also in your locality(AG)

Jennings' finest letters are those written to his parents when he first arrives at Linbury, the Grossman Cine Camera Company, and Mr Laxton concerning his hibernating hedgehog. Each is worth reproducing in full:

Dear Mother, I gave mine in to Mr. cater Darbsher has spend 4 and a half of his my healthser ticket was in my pocket he said I had got bubnick plag it was a jok he is called Benny Dick toe I think it is. We had ozard of wiz for tea Atkion said wiz is good and oz is garstly so do I. Love John. P.S. Temple is a brain, he is short for dogs boody.(JG)
Dear Sir, I would like to buy one so how much are they and please send me one at once but not if they are more than eleven and eight if so just a catalog. We beat Bracebridge School in the end. There was sports practics last Wedednesday only there was not any owing to the wet it was scratched. Hopping you are quit all rit.(JF)

I hope it is all right writing to you, but it is because you are a professional expert on a certain subject i.e. viz-hibernation. We have got a hedgehog who is doing this and would like your advice. We are looking after him secretly for certain reasons which are known to us, but it is all right telling you about this provided you do not spread it. Please will you write back in the enclosed stamped-addressed envelope which I shall put in giving us confidential advice and correct answers to these questions, i.e. - viz - 1. We think he is nearly awake sometimes only not properly because of the weather and will not eat and is getting thinner, so what should we do? 2. If we put him out to eat and he goes off somewhere, will he get eaten by a fox if he goes to sleep again because it is not warm enough to stay awake? 3. If you are hibernating is it all right to wake up for a bit and then go off again, or do you do it

all in one go because you are only sleeping and are not properly hibernating any more? 4. If you did this, i.e. viz see Question 3 would you eat in the times when you were awake? I hope you are quite well and having decent weather.(JR)

Darbishire's communications can be frank and to the point:
I enjoyed it very much also the jelly and ice-cream even though it was pink. The car was not stolen he had gone to the garage for a new thing... And he signs off, unusually, **Yours trolley.**(EJ)

Cowpatch Wood   The wood adjoining Pottlewhistle Halt station where Jennings and Darbishire are seen beginning their walk on to the Downs in their attempt to get back to school after losing the rest of their party(JA).

Crazes   Although Jennings and Form Three remain constant throughout the series, times change and Linbury Court will find itself as susceptible as any other school to passing juvenile crazes and ephemeral pre-occupations, or **"those wild enthusiasms which sweep through a school like a prairie fire**(AU).**"** It may be hut-building(JL); it may be coin-collecting or toadstool patterns(SO); it may be stamp-collecting(OF); it may be natural history, particularly the accumulation of insects and amphibians(FI, JB); the interest in space travel, which became intense during the 1950's and 1960's, crops up in many titles and summed up aptly by Mr Wilkins as involving **"silly little boys with smudges of green chalk all over their faces, pretending they're Martians or Mercurians, or some such nonsense**(AT);**"** it may be telecommunications, assisted by tobacco tins linked with twine(AU); it may be snorkels, and the various things one can do with same, be they cleaning out goldfish bowls or flooding bathrooms(TW); it may be amateur criminology, as Jennings tries to solve the mystery of the bearded man in Miller's Wood(LJ); it may be the swopping of matchbox labels or even exploits with crystal sets, both activities being carried out under the auspices of the Jennings Membership Club whilst waiting for space guns to arrive - which they do not(EJ); it may be ornithology, arising from the advent and subsequent departure of Swing Wing(JB); it may be stamp-collecting, with the attendant excitement of a new issue of stamps(JI); or it may be a desire to stave off the greenhouse effect(AG). One thing is certain; next term will bring something different! As Mr Carter says,   **"In seven weeks' time they'll be back again, bursting at the seams with some new interest which has just taken their fancy**(JB).**"**

Crime Because Buckeridge strove to make his stories believable, there is little of the daredevilry or heroism which are such a feature of the (Billy Bunter) Greyfriars books. Linbury is hardly a hotbed of crime and violence. Even suspected offenders turn out to be perfectly harmless, such as Doctor Tiddyman, the mysterious stranger(LJ); or boys may report the theft of bicycles, only to find that it was merely a colleague who had borrowed the machine in question(FI, JI). When evildoers need to be thwarted, it is more by luck than judgment that they are brought to justice. Leslie Perks is unlucky because Jennings and Darbishire happen, by a fluke, to be in the laundry van and discover the missing trophies(JF); the thief of R.J. Findlater's possessions and those of his team-mates rather unwisely takes cover in a shed which Jennings can secure, rather than mingling with the departing crowds(AT). Mr Wilkins, no less, is responsible for one minor traffic violation and when he hears there is an inspector in the school shortly after the incident he immediately jumps to the wrong conclusion(TT). A tapping at the window in Dormitory Four, which is supposed to signal the start of some earnest interplanetary communication, sets off a train of events which lead to the school staff searching for a burglar which turns out to be a key-less Mr Wilkins(AU). Mr Wilkins suffers even greater inconvenience a few terms later, as firstly Jennings' nocturnal search for a coil of wire makes him suspect that there is an intruder in the grounds(EJ); then his car is reported stolen by Jennings(it has in fact been driven off by a garage mechanic) and he is later stopped whilst driving it back to Linbury(EJ). The one named criminal to whom Jennings and Darbishire fall victim is Linbury's petty thief Wally Pink, as he first sells them a stolen fishing rod and then accepts(and sells on) Jennings' valuable half-sovereign in exchange(SO). Lastly, Jennings witnesses the theft of Dr O'Connor's wallet on the London Underground but soon after the stolen property is recovered, the criminal manages to escape(AG).

Cronk, Archie Driver of a delivery van bringing a bicycle for Jennings as a present from his aunt. Jennings believes Mr Cronk's dilapidated bicycle is the present in question, not realising that Mr Cronk has a more impressive offering awaiting him(FI).

Culture and Creativity Despite the inevitable obstacles, teachers at Linbury Court endeavour to instil some cultural appreciation into their charges as well as teaching them how to make the most constructive use of leisure time. Linbury Court has a well-stocked hobbies room and a hobbies' hour is a popular feature of the day's timetable, with such pursuits as chess, aero-modelling, and LP records. Linbury Court has a scout movement, and we hear that Venables is a keen tenderfoot in the Peewit patrol(JI). There are numerous contrasting examples of the boys letting off steam; our first hint of this is Mr Wilkins taking a choir practice shortly before a fire practice is held, drowning his keyboard incompetence with his stentorian baritone(JG), although even that is probably preferable to Jennings' attempts to learn the piano(AU) or Venables' pathetic efforts on the recorder - the same recorder which Darbishire will eventually use to impress Mr Hind's musical evening audience with "The Bluebells of Scotland (TW)". Mr Carter is happy to type out the Form Three Times for Jennings and Darbishire(JA), and indeed we are informed that a school magazine is also published(JO). An end-of-term revue leads the boys to write a play the second draft of which contains an earthquake and head-on train collision, later to be replaced by an excerpt from Henry V(OF). A revue in a subsequent term prompts the boys to seek after excellence in the areas of ventriloquism and conjuring, whilst more conventional tastes are satisfied by choral and instrumental groups(JO). At the end of the very last book in the series, there is a Drama Evening including such delights as Robin Hood & His Merry Men starring two people only, and Jennings' and Darbishire's depiction of the discovery of the time capsule left by MacTaggart and Merridew. This replaces a previous play idea involving a **"mad scientist who's invented something, such as - er, well, some invention, and these crooks steal the plans and there's a fight and the good guys win(TH)."** Reference is made in one book to a school production of Julius Caesar(LI) but neither of the boys appear in a fully costumed production during the series. We are told that in the hot days of the summer term, the Sunday walk is relaxed and pupils allowed to indulge in more sedentary outdoor activity, which is fine providing no pigs are in the vicinity(JI). Sometimes a particular interest will become an obsession for a term; see Crazes above. It should not be thought that the boys' creative activity is entirely hedonistic; the Form 3 Fireworks Fund, at Mr Carter's suggestion, becomes a vehicle for helping famine victims, and the £10 total is achieved through collection of a copyright fee Jennings claims for an essay he has written for Mr Carter(TJ).

Cuppling, Archie Leading Fireman at Dunhambury Fire Station and, along with his subordinates Long and Short, aghast when the school requires his services on the very day that he decides to give his appliance a much-needed spring clean. His problems are compounded with the discovery of a temperamental carburettor and a distinct shortage of right-handed gum boots. Well might he utter **"Well, darn my socks(JG)!"** Incidentally, the Dunhambury fire service is also required to deal with Jennings' imprisonment between two park railings - or would have been, had he not freed himself before they arrived(TT).

****

"Nobody's likely to pick Darbishire to play for England in a <u>hundred</u> years - let alone ten."
"Ah, no, sir, because he'd be over the age limit in a hundred years."
(JB)
****

Cyril See entry for Perce.

Darbishire, The Reverend Percival and Mrs Parents of Jennings' most loyal ally. Darbishire's father is the first "outside" character to be mentioned in the whole series, as he admires the air-conditioning in the school dining-hall, and later, with his wife, supplies his offspring with winter-weight underwear(JG). He does not often appear at Linbury in person, and indeed on at least one occasion his son has to go with Jennings and his uncle because his parents have let him down(OF). His knowledge of Latin and family history knows no bounds; he is however most notable for the unending stream of wise words and adages which his son, though nobody else, finds invaluable in a crisis.
"My father was asked to say a few words to the infants' school in his parish last term," said Darbishire, looking around with an important air. "He had to present the plasticine modelling prize to the under-fives, and he told them that education was derived from the Latin word <u>educare</u> meaning to lead out and..."
"That's just the sort of thing your father would say," Atkinson broke in.(JF)

"Oh, golly, I wish we'd never done it!" lamented Darbishire. "We must just keep very calm and think out what to do. My father knows a quotation from <u>Horace</u> about keeping a balanced mind in adversity."
Jennings snorted. "It'd be more to the point if <u>Horace</u> had told him one about how to get things out of chimneys. I can't think why you have to clutter the place up with your father's famous wise sayings."(JA)

"Oh, fish-hooks! I hadn't thought of that. Why do these frantic hoo-hahs always have to pick on us to happen to? My father says that..."
"Never mind what your father says! And stop jigging about like a cow on an escalator - your giving me the fidgets. We'll manage all right."(JA)

"My father says there's an art in packing a trunk. You have to keep cool and calm, and use lots of patience. He says an ounce of patience is worth a ton of..."
"It's a pity your father isn't here! He'd be quite welcome to try his hand at this one," said Mr Wilkins grimly. (JD)

His cricket is not to be sneezed at either:
"Oh, yes, he made 236 all in boundaries once."
"Phew! Not bad!" Atkinson was impressed. "Who was he playing against?"
"Well, that time he was playing on the beach and my mother was bowling with a tennis ball."(JL)

Donaldson, Mr Water-bailiff employed by the River Authority Catchment Board to superintend the stretch of the River Dun upon which Jennings and Darbishire choose to do their fishing with the rod bought, in good faith, from Wally Pink, but actually belonging to Mr Donaldson's companion Richard Rogers. After he has apprehended the boys and allowed Mr Rogers to give them a pompous lecture about the evils of fishing without a licence, he assists them in their ultimately successful attempts to recover the half-sovereign they have paid to the said Mr Pink(SO).

Doris See entry for Clough, Mrs Bertha.

Dormitories There is evidence that Jennings occupies both Dormitory Four and Dormitory Six(JD, AT) during his Linbury career; one can put that down either to administrative convenience, or a slip of Buckeridge's pen. Several stories within the books are set in one or other of these dormitories, equipped as they are with washbasins, beds and clothes cupboards. One book devotes several chapters to dormitory goings-on, in the form of elaborate devices for reading under bedclothes, Jennings' disastrous experiences as dormitory captain, and the chain of events following attempts by two dormitories to communicate with each other by home-made telephones(AU). Other memorable dormitory events include Jennings' miserable first-night experiences closely followed by an account of his amateurish attempts at coping with the outbreak of a fictitious fire within the confines of his sleeping quarters(JG), the sight of the light in the sanatorium(JF), Darbishire's going to bed in frogs' feet after an illicit swimming lesson(AT), Jennings' going to bed with Darbishire's school cap perched on his head(OF) or an unyielding sleeping bag covering all but his head(JI), and Jennings' imprisonment in the boiler room and attempts at escape causing strange things to happen to the dormitory lights(OF). There are a number of attempts at midnight-feasting involving the preparation of sausages and potatoes in a biscuit tin in the boiler room(TT); an impersonation of Lady Macbeth and Plans A to F(TW); and, at last, a successful midnight feast as Jennings smuggles Aunt Angela's cakes under the bedclothes, even if Temple's house-shoes have to be thrown out of the window in the process(LJ). If cleanliness is next to godliness, then the boys are positive saints when they smarten their dormitories in the hope of winning Matron's cup for the tidiest and best-behaved dormitory, even if Dormitory 4(the eventual winners) do almost ruin their chances by carrying out cleaning operations after "lights-out" under the guise of a dormitory feast(LI)! One totally unproductive after-dark episode involves the attempted use of a crystal set, frustrated by the cat's whisker being broken and Darbishire dropping the aerial out of the window(EJ). Nearby, the bathrooms offer further scope for misadventure, such as the double flooding caused respectively by faulty towel rail and mischievous snorkel(TW) and the underwater breath-holding competition which also ends in flooding(EJ). The last night of term will see the dormitory ring to renditions of celebratory song as well as space games(JE).

Dufour, Monsieur and Henri The only foreign flavour to be found in the whole series. Somewhat fortuitously Monsieur Dufour's car breaks down close to Linbury Court, and as a result Jennings gets to meet his son Henri and swap matchbox labels with him, although Mr Wilkins is convinced Jennings needs Henri for something altogether more crafty. Eventually Henri is booked into Linbury for the following term, so there is no need for Jennings to worry about his supremacy over the rest of Form Three in French during the spring term(EJ). The following term we hear that Henri is now a pupil at Linbury Court, having great difficulty in understanding cricket, but his finest hour comes when Jennings, admittedly in a pit of despair, loses his wicket one afternoon to one of Henri's deliveries. By the end of the book, he has fallen for one of Linbury's frequent crazes, namely that of bird-watching - in this case, counting the number of starlings on the telephone wire.(JB)

So far as he could understand the pitch meant wicket and the wicket meant the stumps. Surely, then, the pitch and the stumps must be the same thing! (JB)

"The birds were there tomorrow, so I think they will be here yesterday, also. No?" (JB)

Dun River flowing five miles to the west of Linbury village but through Dunhambury. The river sees several adventures involving Jennings and Darbishire, including their illegal boat trip(FI), their field trip and the discovery of the local rainfall records(LI), and the fishing trip which almost leads to the boys' summons for fishing illegally(SO).

Dunhambury The Sussex market town that lies five miles to the west of Linbury, separated from Linbury by a hilly road with steep gradients which apparently reduces the average speeds of buses to twelve miles per hour(AT). Throughout the series it provides the only regular taste of urban life for Jennings and his friends whilst at school, and an obvious place for parents and relatives to entertain the boys and top up their tuck supplies during half-terms and exeats, as well as a convenient place to visit the dentist(TY) and if necessary obtain an urgent haircut(TJ). We are told that it is in Jennings' opinion about fifteen miles from Haywards Heath, but other than the fact that it is reasonably near the sea, and linked thereto by the River Dun, we are given no other clues as to its whereabouts. We do know that it is well-served by bus and rail. The town has a District Council, as well, apparently, as a Borough Council(JD, AG), but it is the former that Miss Thorpe persuades to provide environmentally-friendly facilities in Linbury(AG). Dunhambury has a colourful history, founded by the Romans, pillaged by the Jutes, besieged by the Saxons, looted by the Danes, destroyed by the Normans and rebuilt by the Tudors. It has been ravaged by fire, flood, plague and death watch beetle. It also boasts a Mayor; historical features include the 16th century castle walls, the 17th century Market Cross, the 18th century town hall, and the 19th century fire station; it also contains a museum and art gallery some distance from the town centre. It is well-endowed with a shopping mall, supermarkets, showrooms, and department stores, and boasts a municipal library, Memorial Park and Gas Works, although is not without its dingier establishments and the odd fly-blown cafe(SO). Creature comforts are catered for by Ye Olde Tudor Bunne Shoppe, established 1969, with watery welsh rarebits and hard buns apparently serving as the house specialities(TJ, JR, TY), as well as the Red Lion and the Bell Hotel, the latter offering a choice of jelly and ice-cream, sultana roll and rhubarb and custard for dessert(EJ); it is in the Bell Hotel that Mrs Atkinson fulminates about her son's horde of accompanying ants(JR), and from the window of that Hotel that Jennings sees what he believes to be the theft of Mr Wilkins' car(EJ). Memorable moments can be recorded courtesy of the photographers Scuttlewell & Openshaw(AG). Clean washing is assured by the Float Iron Laundry(JF), the Express Dry Cleaning Company(JO), and, as for launderettes, the Launderama in Station Road(pop music laid on) and the Washataria in the High Street, complete with hot-drink vending machine(JR). Entertainment may be provided at the Empire Cinema(OF). Tidy torsos are maintained by, among others, Walton's Men's Hairdressing Saloon(established 1929) with the helpful Mr Hales(TJ). Bargains can be picked up from the Dunhambury Auction Mart, which for Jennings yields an oil painting and primitive cooking stove for the princely sum of 25p after the town's sports shop spurns his offer of the 25p for a tennis racket(TY). Pets can be obtained from the Dunhambury Pet Stores, owned by H. Fagg; it is from this shop that Mrs Atkinson senior obtains F.J. Saunders, the guinea-pig later to wreak havoc on school routine(TT). Motorists, who may have had their car serviced by the town's Star Garage(EJ), must beware of parking in the High Street near the town hall on odd dates, as Mr Wilkins finds to his cost(TT). Our first visit to the town takes us to the town's fire station(JG); there follows an expedition to a second-hand bookshop to flog two priceless Latin grammars(JA); a trip to the town's museum when Jennings and Darbishire, by being told to dispose of their wheel, get to know the town rather better than they had bargained for(JD); a trip to the cricket ground to see a county cricket match, one of only a couple played there each year(AT); a big meal at the Red Lion followed by an illicit afternoon at the Empire Cinema(OF); an organised outing for the Camera Club which climaxes with Mr Wilkins changing a wheel using Jack Carr's car jack(TT);   a shopping expedition involving the purchase of a music stand from a junk shop from a man Jennings wrongly believes to be French(TW); a secret visit to the Express Dry Cleaning Company in the High Street which culminates in a request for elastic-sided gumboots and extra large ear-trumpets in a nearby hardware store(JO); an unsuccessful mission to try and locate the owner of Swing-Wing, the racing pigeon, at the town's post office(JB); the unsuccessful attempt to sell a honky-tonk piano to the town's shop which results in a visit to the Youth Club in the dingy Denton Street and an impromptu street concert party(TJ); in the same book, a trip to town for a Guy Fawkes mask and some emergency hairdressing following an accident with a can of aerosol(TJ); an emergency cleaning operation after paraffin is spilt on Jennings' overcoat, followed by a failed mission to find the hedgehog expert Robin Laxton and an afternoon spent counting TV aerials(JR); a search for bargain tennis rackets(TY); and Darbishire's fruitless search for fishing tackle, but accidental sighting of Jennings' missing half-sovereign in a back-street coin dealer's(SO).

Dunhambury & District Gazette The Linbury and Dunhambury area local paper, with its office in Dunhambury, and by all accounts a fairly uninspiring read; Mr Wilkins claims there is nothing worth reading in it, and even Johnny Gray, its ace reporter, can think of nothing that fills its pages other than **"fires, baby-shows,(and) council meetings**(JB)**."** It is the possible inclusion of Jennings' alerting of the fire brigade after his disastrous, and strictly secret, pigeon mission which causes the boys to try and divert the paper from the masters - but they have no need, as the paper ends up in a bucket of soapy water(JB). It is, however, the existence of a nature column in the paper, written by Robin Laxton, which prompts Miss Thorpe to make a suggestion to Jennings about how to find more information about his hibernating hedgehog(JR).

Dunhambury Weekly Echo The newspaper which tells of the arrest of the thief of R.J. Findlater's possessions following a day's play in a county cricket match in Dunhambury(AT). This journal is not otherwise referred to in the series at all; perhaps the Dunhambury & District Gazette superseded it.

East Brinkington Village about three miles from Dunhambury, where Jennings goes in search of Mr Goodman and information about the owner of Swing-Wing. We are told it nestles in a fold of the South Downs, boasting a church with a spire, the finest scenery and the worst bus service for many miles around(JB). It is the home of alleged pigeon expert Stan Goodman(JB); Peter Nutt who is prepared, as second prize winner in the Linbury fete, to exchange his bath salts for Jennings' pig(JI); the brother-in-law of Gracie Hepplewell, suspected of being without a dog licence(JR); and Robin Laxton, author of the weekly nature column in the local paper, with whom Jennings tries to make contact regarding the welfare of his hedgehog(JR).

Edna See entry for Hepplewell, Gracie.

Elmer Pet fish of Bromwich major whose adventures include a confrontation with Mr Wilkins amid the murky water of the school swimming bath(JL).

Epaminondas Donkey who strays into the company of Jennings and fellow campers. As a result, Jennings is introduced to its keeper, Mrs Hockin, owner of the Retreat(JE).

Especially Jennings!(EJ) Fifteenth book in the series, first published by William Collins in 1965, 192 pp. Dedicated to John Henry Ainley.

Illustrated by Douglas Mays. The series was now comfortably back in its one-book/one-term cycle, with several clear indications that this book is set in the spring term, and a direct sequel to JO, with the new cook appointed at the end of that book featuring on several occasions in this book. Gilbert & Sullivan aficionados will be delighted with one exchange in the book: **"You see, between you and me, I don't eat sweets."** He stared at her, appalled. **"What, never?" "Well, hardly ever."**

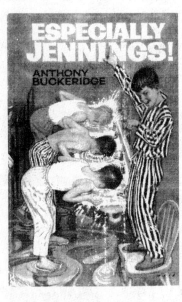

Synopsis

Chapter 1 - Flood Warning - Matron's refusal to "shop" the boys to Mr Wilkins after their latest flood escapade make them determined to repay her.

Chapter 2 - The Membership Club - The repayment is in the form of helping to get school breakfast ready - hence the discovery of free cereal packet gifts, and the formation of the Club.

Chapter 3 - Something For Nothing - An ideal aim for the Club appears to be the ordering of space guns advertised on the cereal packet - which Jennings believes are free.

Chapter 4 - Outdoor Aerial - The discovery of a crystal set gives the Club yet more to do - after dark too - until the aerial is unfortunately thrown into the night.

Chapter 5 - Night Operations - Jennings and Darbishire, trying to retrieve the aerial, find themselves locked out. How can they alert their colleagues before they are discovered?

Chapter 6 - The Key to the Mystery - Mr Wilkins is also on the prowl, believing there to be an intruder in the grounds. Eventually the truth emerges. The crystal set is a write-off.

Chapter 7 - Contact - Jennings should have known better than visit the sick-room just before half-term; luckily the only patient merely had an ankle injury.

Chapter 8 - Wholesale Distribution - Aunt Angela's chocolates were of course meant for Matron - if only Jennings had realised before handing them round...

Chapter 9 - Costly Mistake - Jennings realises the space guns are not free, but by lucky chance they have just been banned by the Head so no-one will want one after all.

Chapter 10 - The Mixed Assortment - Jennings' appeal for substitute fare for Matron's chocolate box does not get quite the response he had hoped for.
Chapter 11 - Gift Horse in the Mouth - Jennings gets away with it - just - and goes off for half-term with Aunt Angela and Darbishire with a clear conscience.
Chapter 12 - False Alarm - Mr Wilkins' car gives him trouble and he arranges for a mechanic to drive the car to the garage - Jennings gets the wrong idea.
Chapter 13 - Hold Up - The supposed theft is duly reported; Mr Wilkins is flagged down for allegedly driving a stolen car; and Jennings drops Mr Wilkins' car keys in the post box.
Chapter 14 - La Plume de sa Tante - Jennings' expertise in French is outweighed by his inability to draw well, write neatly, or pass potatoes down the lunch table.
Chapter 15 - The Gift of Tongues - Jennings' chance meeting with Henri Dufour opens up a whole new world of matchbox tops.
Chapter 16 - The Fellow Phillumenist - Mr Wilkins misinterprets Jennings' conference with Henri, but all is forgiven, especially as Henri is enrolled for Linbury next term.
Chapter 17 - Account Rendered - Mr Carter finds use for the dormant monies in the Jennings Membership Club coffers - and Jennings comes top in French.

"Or if you don't want that, you can have it a la carte. That means they bring it round on a trolley."

"She wouldn't say. She doesn't want to be bothered with trifles."
"There isn't any trifle; only jelly and ice-cream."

Evans Participant on Jennings' side in the football match played to see if Jennings was to blame for being scalded with hot tea(AG). Also see entry for Parslow.

Fagg, Herbert Arthur Caretaker of Gaitskell Court in south-east London, and stern enforcer of house(or flat) rules. It is his discovery, through Jennings' tactlessness, of Emma Sparrow's animal menagerie which prompts the flight of the animals to Mrs Hockin's Retreat. However, he later reveals a more caring side as he assists in the smooth running of the Animal Fair(JE).

Findlater, R.J. Sussex and England cricketer who offers a lift to Jennings and Darbishire for the county match in which he is playing, after the boys were left behind as a punishment. Through Mr Findlater they are offered seats in the Members' Enclosure at the ground. After the match, Jennings assists in apprehending the man who has stole Findlater's possessions from the changing room(AT).

Fliplugs A tall, beaky-nosed 13 year-old Bracebridge student, with large ears and large feet, real name Hodges, who lends Jennings some house shoes and then gleefully reveals that Jennings' attempt to get himself a warm shower may have resulted in the draining of the school swimming pool. He seems strangely disappointed when informed that Jennings' actions have not, after all, had that effect(TJ).

Flittonborough major Also known as Flybow, the clumsy Sports Day relay runner(JF).

Food The appetites of the boys are, as one might expect, fairly sizeable. They will think nothing of consuming three helpings of shepherds pie(JR, JA), or baked beans on toast between courses of a meal out(OF); and when there is the enticing prospect of free space-guns on the horizon, they are happy to tuck into double or even treble portions of Krunchie-Whispies(EJ). A satisfying meal at a neighbouring school is ample reason for wanting to be picked for the school football team, even as linesman(TJ, SO) - particularly when we are told that the boys' normal Sunday teatime fare is oily pilchards, beetroot and desiccated lettuce(TH). A number of school picnics are organised, always to the delight of the boys; indeed for some of them the wait for the arrival at the picnic site is too much and picnic food is consumed before the boys leave the premises(FI). The most eventful picnic combines explosive attempts to brew tea for the masters, and Darbishire's vain bid to fool his chums into believing that they have discovered prehistoric cave paintings(TY). The lure of sponge cakes encourages boys to enter poetry and handwriting competitions(JA). It is the prospect of substantial refreshment at the Linbury fete which keeps the boys there longer than they should have stayed, resulting in their ill-fated entry for the "Bowling For A Pig" competition(JI). It is the thought of being deprived of milk-and-biscuits which make the prospect of a night's imprisonment in the attic even less palatable(JI). It is only natural that the boys should be allowed village leave to buy sweets, as the boys for the majority of the series have no tuckshop on the premises - although we are told that Mr Russell dines there on his visit to Linbury(JF); it is even more natural that they should baulk at being served with only two prunes as second helping of pudding(TT), and should want to wolf down the Christmas ham and tomatoes in order to catch up with others on Christmas jelly and custard(AU). It is Darbishire's enjoyment of Miss

Matthews' ice-cream which partially prevents him from recording Jennings' first ever House match half-century on the scoreboard, although it would have helped if he had not drawn a fictional cafe menu on the side of the scoring box first(JB). Popularity for a boy is guaranteed if he has a food parcel from home, and it is expected that there will be a share-out, even if on one occasion Jennings comes unstuck by sharing out chocolates meant for Matron - he has to cobble together a none-too-appetising substitute selection(EJ). Allegations, subsequently proved to be false, that staff members are indulging in extra lunches leads Dormitory Four to organise its own midnight feast, although the ambitious menu is reduced to sausage and potato when the post office refuses to accept Temple's two-shilling postal order(TT). Midnight feasting again crosses the boys' minds when Jennings receives cake and lollipops from his aunt, but it takes a sleepwalking escapade and an unscheduled nocturnal fire-drill to get the provisions from the tuckbox room to the dormitory(TW). Jennings believes that plying masters with food will find favour with them, hence an elaborate food-smuggling operation prior to an "At Home" party for the staff which Mr Wilkins believes to be another midnight feast(TW). It is only the following term when a midnight feast is successful(see entry for Dormitories above); what Mr Wilkins later that term believes to be a further feast is in fact a dormitory cleaning operation(LI)! The departure of Mrs Cherry, the school cook, means that the school must temporarily suffer the rigours of cold fish fingers and beetroot, served up by the reluctant Mrs Hackett, before a school jumble sale indirectly leads to the appointment of a replacement(JO). However, even she goes out of favour with the boys, by preparing **"ghastly old boiled beef - we call it pink hippo(EJ)."** No wonder they tuck so keenly into the roast lamb and potatoes at the Bell Hotel at Dunhambury when allowed out at half-term(EJ)!

Incidentally, Buckeridge, who claims he was always hungry when he was at boarding school, insists that no school food is ever as bad as it is made out to be in books. As he says **"There's a tradition in all schools that you have to say the food is terrible. You're letting the side down if you admit that you enjoy it."**

****

"We sell postage stamps - we don't buy them. Certainly not dirty-looking specimens in this condition."
"But they've never been used. You'd be able to sell them again ever so easily if you cleaned them up a bit and put some more sticky stuff on."
(TT)
****

Form Three The class of 17 boys in which Jennings, Darbishire, Venables, Temple and Atkinson remain throughout the series. Mr Wilkins has little to say in their favour: **"I tell you, frankly, they're turning my hair grey. There are more half-wits to the square yard in that form than in any other in the school**(TT).**"**

Fouracres, Mr See entry for Barney.

Fox, Mr Fierce and uncompromising Bracebridge teacher who is reluctant to dismiss Darbishire from the detention class over which he is presiding. His brief cameo appearance is not allowed to pass without some delicious examples of his dry humour:
"We appear to have caught an unusual-ah-specimen in our net," he said. "I don't recollect having seen that face about the premises before; the loss, of course, is mine. But tell me, dear boy, to what are we indebted for the honour of this most delightful visit(JA)**?"**

Freeman, Alderman Connie, Mayor of the south-east London suburb in which Gaitskell Court is situated. She is, we hear, a local legend - a well-loved figure who works with tireless devotion in her community. She agrees, at Mr Fagg's suggestion, to open the Animal Fair in aid of Mrs Hockin's Retreat. As a result of her agreeing to come, the event wins the support of the busybodies Mesdames Pratt and Plumrose(JE).

Frost See entry for Marshall.

Furnival, Dr. The youthful, sandy-haired school doctor who, we are told, always visits Linbury Court on Mondays, and is disposed to chatting with the headmaster; he is also generous, giving the sick Darbishire a first-day cover stamp after Jennings has broken school rules to obtain one(JI). His kindness is repaid by being invited to the school's charity firework party(TJ). His absence on holiday means an eventful trip to Linbury for Dr Wooderson(JR).

George See entry for Perce.

George The Third Matron's large ginger tom cat, the name derived not from royal connections but because he is the third generation of a feline family Matron has adopted. Although we are told some boys try to obtain his pawprint for Form Three's Natural History museum(JD), his first appearance in the series is in the kitchen garden where the boys are searching for F.J. Saunders the guinea pig, and so concerned are the boys that the cat might attack FJS that they shut the cat in Mr Wilkins' room and remove FJS - which makes Mr Wilkins jump to the wrong conclusion(TT). It is the necessity to purchase a half-crown tin of Puss-Ee-Kins cat food for GTT which brings Mr Wilkins into unwelcome confrontation with Jennings and Darbishire who are on a secret dry-cleaning operation(JO). After being frightened by Miss Thorpe's playful pup Jason(JR) the cat's last appearance in the series sees him keeping guard over the charred remains of ruined school breakfasts which Jennings and Darbishire have left for the birds - the breakfasts, thus left, are witnessed at first hand not only by the Headmaster but some prospective parents(SO).

Gerald With William, one of Venables two gerbils; inevitably Ger and Bill for short. Panic ensues when their disappearance coincides with the disappearance of some allegedly poisonous toadstools(SO).

****
"Why don't they teach grown-ups to write so people can read it." He frowned over the next line and said: **"This bit looks like `your hatter swerved to jog my fairy melody.'"**(FI)
****

Getting Around With much of the action of the stories taking place beyond the school gates, the boys and masters rely upon various means of transport to convey them to their destinations. Besides public transport(for which see separate entry), the boys make use of the school minibus(TY), roller skates both with and without the aid of keys to free them at the end(AU), tractor and trailer(JI), bicycles, including the new one presented to Jennings by his aunt(FI)(although it is some time before boarders are allowed to keep bikes at the school, and it helps if Jennings, having borrowed a bike, does not then damage it(SO)) and also enjoy having lifts in masters' cars. Mr Wilkins' car is the butt of many unkind comments(FI) and he is not the most hospitable of lift-givers particularly when his car keys end up inside a locked postbox(EJ) but that does not stop the boys engaging in competitions to see who can have the most lifts, enduring in the process journeys in Mr Hind's car, with swirls of tobacco smoke wafted back from the driver's seat(TW). As Darbishire points out **"So far this term I've had three rides in Mr Carter's car, two in the Head's, two in Mr Hind's and one in yours. Lucky old me! If I go on like this, I shall soon break the Form Three record(LI)."** An invitation by the Headmaster to take two 2nd XI players home from Bracebridge results in a flood of hopeful applicants, the chosen two being Jennings and Darbishire who had in fact made the journey to Dunhambury by car after hitching a lift with an attractive young woman. Venables is right to exclaim **"Some chaps get jam on everything**(JO)**."** A number of hair-raising bicycling exploits are recorded, such as the infamous occasion when bikes were hired to reach the Fair(JD) and Jennings' being forced to ride a death-trap of a machine to reach a phone box to call the fire brigade to extinguish a potentially disastrous fire - his reward is a lift home with a journalist(JB). In one book, Jennings secures transport either to or from Dunhambury by school coach, where he naturally wants the much-coveted corner seat(TJ), bus, Mr Wilkins' car, Miss Thorpe's car, together with trailer laden with piano(TJ) and the Headmaster's car! It is the train which is used to convey Jennings, plus Emma and animal menagerie, to Mrs Hockin's Retreat(JE).

Gladys See entry for Clough, Mrs Bertha.

Goddard, Mr Like Mr Topliss, mentioned merely as a Linbury teacher but without anything to say. Apparently his specialities are Geography and Art.

Goodman, Mr & Mrs Stan Couple who live at a whitewashed cottage in East Brinkington, to whom Jennings is referred in trying to find a home for Swing-Wing. The expert, Stan, is out when Jennings arrives; Mrs Goodman can do little to help except tell Jennings how to get an early bus back to Dunhambury and sympathise when Swing-Wing shoots out of his basket(JB).

Grandma See entry for Jennings, Mr and Mrs.

Gray, Johnny Reporter with the Dunhambury & District Gazette who inadvertently shocks Jennings with the revelation that the latter's heroics in alerting the fire brigade to a blaze will be published in that paper; and subsequently upsetting the boy by informing him that it never got there after all. From the composition of the paper his job does not sound wildly interesting - see entry for Dunhambury & District Gazette(JB).

Grimshaw, Dr. Author of a Latin grammar which Jennings wants to sell to raise money for a prize for Venables, and a lecturer at Mr Pemberton-Oakes' university(JA).

Hackett, Mrs Connie Member of the ancillary staff at Linbury who comes in daily to do the washing-up. During the interregnum between the departure of Mrs Cherry and the arrival of Miss Matthews as school cook, she undertakes the cooking, and provides an array of unappetising dishes consisting mainly of tinned meat, boiled beetroot, rock-hard jacket potatoes, cold fish fingers and cold sardines. A stoutish, middle-aged lady of a normally easy-going disposition, we are told that **her chief interest in domestic work lay in those jobs which could be tackled with slap-dash vigour rather than skill** so that **plastic beakers crumpled under her heavy-handed grip.** She inadvertently succeeds in relieving herself of the burdens of her new office by inviting all the ladies of Linbury to Jennings' private jumble sale - one of whom accepts the vacant post on the spot(JO). She temporarily retains a high profile even after the appointment of the new cook, and having delegated to Jennings and Darbishire the task of dispensing cereals she is elevated to the rank of Junior Moon Cosmonaut by virtue of the free badges contained in each packet, despite being **"somewhat over the age and weight limit(EJ)."** It is partially through her being left in charge in the kitchen one Friday morning that breakfast is ruined and the burnt breakfasts are spread out for the Headmaster and prospective visitors to see(SO). However, she really comes into her own by agreeing to buy pigeon food for Swing Wing from the Linbury General Stores(JB) and supplying food both for Jennings' camp cookery(albeit in unsuitable form) and the school picnic(TY); and it is her failure to make a proper note of a telephone call by Miss Thorpe which safeguards the secrecy of the Plan of the Antique Piano(TJ).

****

"What's this nonsense about stamping wildebeeste making for the drinking hole?" Mr Wilkins demanded. "It sounds to me like Form 3 lining up for cocoa."(JE)
****

Hales, Ronald Alfred Men's hairdresser, and employee of Walton's Men's Hairdressing Saloon, Mr Hales is also Linbury Court's "official" barber, attending there on alternate Tuesdays. It is he who removes traces of aerosol from Jennings' hair and corrects Darbishire's amateurish attempts to do the same; he later on comes to Jennings' rescue even more heroically when he suggests a possible home for the honky-tonk piano Jennings is saddled with, and as a result Jennings enjoys a splendid concert party with the Dunhambury Youth Club(TJ).

Miss Haskins Secretary to the mercurial Mr Catchpole(JF).

Hawkins Linbury Court's night porter, also known as Old Nightie. A thin, elderly, flat-footed man with hunched shoulders, drooping head and stealthy glances in all areas, and normally dressed in dungarees, his thirty-nine-year-old routine of sweeping the boiler room out by 10.45pm and adjourning to the sanatorium is broken on the very night that Les Perks decides to visit the sanatorium himself(JF). The boys rarely see him; his night's work is virtually over when he emerges from the gloomy depths of the stokehold to sound the rising bell, although he is roused from sleep at 4.30pm on the afternoon before General Merridew's visit to dredge pellets of blotting paper from school ink wells(JL). He has strong views about boys being out of bounds and will report such behaviour to the masters. He is responsible for leaving Jennings and Darbishire locked in the boiler room after they have gone there to try and roast chestnuts(OF).

Hepplewell, Mrs Gracie   Short, dark-haired, gregarious 43-year-old housewife and occupant of 17 Marina Terrace in Linbury. She, together with her younger, taller neighbour Edna, mistakes Jennings and Darbishire, as they tour Linbury village counting TV aerials, for TV licensing inspectors, suspecting central bureaucrats of employing children to do their dirty work for them. As a result not only caution, but the statistics taken by the two boys, are thrown to the winds. She is in a more forgiving mood later on in the term, as she advises Jennings what to do with his evil-smelling overcoat(JR).

Higgins, H.   The balding, lugubrious and slightly deaf shopkeeper, jeweller and silversmith of Linbury village. Having retired from his Dunhambury jewellery business some years ago, he works purely for love, selling such items as screwtop pencils, butterfly brooches, tarnished watch-chains, fly-blown sugar tongs and spectacle screws, and engraves dog collars and silver. Indeed, his visit to the school to collect the sports cup for engraving provides the Linbury Court Detective Agency with its first assignment(JF). Later he sells an extremely delicate alarm clock to Jennings and Darbishire for what they believe is a leaving present for Mr Wilkins(AT) and agrees to display prizes for the village bazaar in his window(LJ).

Hind, Mr   Teacher of history and music throughout the school, and art as well as more general subjects to the lower forms. He is also known to escort school picnics, preside over swimming competition, and coach at the cricket nets. A tall, dark, thin, pale, resigned-looking, studious young man - Matron believes, unlike Mr Wilkins, that he isn't too old to celebrate his birthday(TT) - he has a dejected, long-suffering, look about him and speaks in a soft, purring, rather tired drawl which might suggest to some - wrongly - that he was only half awake. Out of school the curly stem of his short cherrywood pipe is clutched between his teeth and sprouts out of his chin like a goatee beard or even an artifical limb, leaving a lingering trail of blue smoke; the bowl is liable to be polished on the side of his nose! Casually dressed in well-worn clothing, and clearly somewhat bohemian in outlook, music is his great passion; he is unimpressed with Jennings' idea of making music by attaching elastic bands to tuck boxes(JO); he does not like Jennings to aim to "rattle off" a piece of music on the piano(AU); he insists that school orchestra members should participate in his informal concerts, allowing Jennings the perfect pretext to frighten Venables into returning Darbishire's recorder(TW); he is happy to entertain the boys with his jazz repertoire(TH); and he will think nothing of missing his apple tart to catch a radio symphony concert - and by doing so, is the first to witness Jennings' imitation of a sleepwalker(TW). His bohemian outlook does not stop him asserting himself when he needs to. He campaigns vigorously for hot food during the interregnum left by Mrs Cherry(JO); he renders Jennings' house-match fifty null and void because there is no scorer to record his feat(JB); and his powerful voice breaks up the party round the notice-board which leads to the horrifying suggestion that a drawing-pin has escaped into Matron's bath salts(JI). For all that, some things do elude him; he has a reputation for being somewhat dreamy at times, which allows Darbishire to lay a trail of green poster paint, borrowed from an Art class, round the grounds(LI), and which allows Jennings to embark on the plan of the Secret Haircut(TJ), to further his secret society to unearth the time capsule(TH), and to proceed with a conjuring trick in the end-of-term school concert when the item might have been better omitted(JO). Through the blue fog which surrounds him, many gems issue forth. His account of the Lascaux cave paintings so inspires Darbishire that the latter is encouraged to pursue his downland cave hoax(TY). He has a propensity for terrible jokes: when a boy offers him a light for a bonfire, he replies **"I have a flair for this sort of thing(TJ)."** Best of all is his description of Jennings as an **"illiterate nitwit...uncouth youth...a sub-human relic...in short...a miserable specimen(JF)."**

Hinkley's Farm See entry for Three Acre Marsh.

Hipkin, Dr Basil Featherstonehaugh D.Sc. F.Z.S. and Mrs Couple who play a prominent part in just one book as a result of an accident between the boats being incompetently manoeuvered by Jennings and Dr. Hipkin, with Jennings saving the Doctor from possible drowning. His wife insists on driving the boys back to school but, because the expedition giving rise to the incident was contrary to school rules, the boys take her to Bracebridge instead, mistakenly thinking no Linburians will be present. Mrs Hipkin is a forceful and one cannot help thinking rather domineering lady, unimpressed by the boys' lack of recall of their own school and headmaster; it is her insistence which forces Dr Hipkin to accept an invitation to speak at Linbury's speech day. Since he is a zoologist and shares Form Three's enthusiasm for natural history, he is a resounding success(FI). By way of compensation he is invited to the school's charity firework party(TJ).

Hobden, Dick(i) Customer of Mrs Lumley whose appearance at her establishment for his regular Friday order of two dozen eggs provides a pretext for Jennings to evacuate the premises of his colleagues so that he and Darbishire can eat in peace(JR).

Hobden, Dick(ii) Genial and sympathetic porter at Southcombe Station who looks after Emma Sparrow's animal menagerie, en route for Mrs Hockin's Retreat, whilst Ben the dog goes walkabout(JE).
Presumably to avoid confusion with his namesake above, he was renamed Jack Hobden in the 1992 Macmillan reprint.

Hockin, Mrs Owner of the Retreat, an animal sanctuary at Southcombe in Surrey, close to where the boys are enjoying a summer camp. She is befriended by Jennings, who asks for her help when his Aunt Angela's neighbour Emma Sparrow needs to shift her animal menagerie out of her London flat. Hustled by Major Rudkin, her none-too-friendly neighbour, she is faced with having to replace her fencing, at vast cost, or lose her animals. The boys' fund-raising fails to produce the necessary cash, but Mrs Jane Seymour comes to the rescue(JE).

Hodges See Fliplugs.

Holidays It is one of the features of the Jennings series that we hear very little about what the boys do in the holidays. Buckeridge actually said: **"I don't follow them outside school. If school is your background, you've got them captive for 24 hours a day and you concentrate on that bit; if you don't do that, if you follow them for the rest of their lives outside school and that sort of thing, you're enlarging your background to such an extent that it's all much more difficult."** Holidays are more likely to be referred to either in retrospect, when a prized posssession obtained in the holidays, such as a space helmet(LJ), is flaunted by a pupil towards his colleagues, or in anticipation, when crossing off the days and sometimes hours is a popular end of term hobby(JG). The only serious school holiday activity that is described involves Jennings' stay with his aunt and his collaboration with Emma Sparrow to save her animals and Mrs Hockin's Retreat(JE).

Homesickness   Those who object to the principle of boys and girls as young as ten years of age being made to forsake home comforts and being forced to face up to life in a boarding school will derive little support for their cause from the Jennings books, which present a wholly acceptable picture of life as a prep school boarder. It is only in Jennings' and Darbishire's first week at Linbury Court that our heroes are allowed to indulge in yearning for home life, leading to their bold plan to escape from the school; Darbishire is the only one to succumb to tears, however(JG). It should be pointed out that the end of term and return home is also eagerly anticipated, to the extent whereby Darbishire as self-appointed Official Calendar Compiler creates a calendar demanding hourly crossing-out of figures throughout the last week of term(JG). Occasionally the end of term is celebrated in verse(See also entry for Poetry below):

This time tomorrow, where shall I be? Miles away from Linbury.
No more spiders in my tea, no more sleeping in the dormit'ry.(JD)

Goodbye lumpy mattress in my freezing dormit'ry.
Goodbye my school dinner and goodbye to my school tea.
Bullet-proof potatoes and bomb-proof hard-boiled eggs.
And goodbye to cocoa made from Diesel dregs.(JE)

Honeyball, Police Constable Herbert Stanley   Linbury's beat bobby, and none-too-willing recipient of information from Jennings concerning alleged thefts and losses of property. His first confrontation with Jennings is one February afternoon when he is called away from his poached egg to be regaled with Jennings **"blethering about atom bombs and secret plans and spies with unpronounceable names(JD)."** A few terms later, Jennings is apprehended upon suspicion of theft of his own bicycle, reported by Venables, and he must again indulge in lengthy and painful dialogue with the long-suffering constable(FI); and, moving on to the next summer term, Jennings presents the officer with Pyewacket the cat, for the recovery of whom Mr Wilkins has promised a reward of ten shillings - a fact PC Honeyball feels constrained to announce to Mr

Wilkins when master and pupil meet in his office(LJ). A not dissimilar occurrence takes place a few terms later when Mr Wilkins is apprehended by PC Honeyball for driving a car which the police, on Jennings' information, believe is stolen, and Mr Wilkins is only allowed on his way after routine procedures have been rigorously complied with(EJ). When PC Honeyball's patience, of which he has only a short supply, is exhausted, he is apt to exclaim **"Cor, stone the crows!"**

Houses Linbury has two houses, Drake and Raleigh. Jennings and Darbishire are both members of Drake house. There is far more emphasis on inter-house rivalry early in the series, Drake usually winning any sporting contest, e.g. school sports(JF), cricket(JL), and junior swimming(AT). However, much later in the series we hear of Jennings making 51 runs for Drake in a junior House cricket match - a personal best - but it does not count, because Darbishire has abdicated his scoring duties by kind permission of Mr Wilkins(JB). House rivalry is resurrected right at the end of the series; a cricket match ends in disaster for Drake when Darbishire, acting as Bromwich's "runner," forgets to run at the crucial moment. As a result the match is lost and Bromwich says under no circumstances will he lend Darbishire his father's metal detector to try to find the time capsule(TH).

Hoyle, Adrian Curator of the Dunhambury museum, whose knowledgeable, suave and courteous manner is tested to the limit by the discovery, in the Roman gallery, of a piece of equipment that he has only just informed its temporary custodians was an old wheel belonging to a sand and gravel cart owned by the Borough Council. His courtesy hides an assertive streak which is deployed to ensure that Mr Wilkins does not leave the museum without taking it with him(JD).

Sergeant Hutchinson The efficient officer responsible for tracking down the thief of the school sports cups and whose success is at least partially owed to Jennings and Darbishire(JF).

I Love You Too The series is rich in insults of a particularly damning kind:

"You're a gruesome hornswoggler, Jennings."(OF)
"You shrimp-witted bazooka, Darbi!"(OF)
"Honestly, Darbishire, sometimes you're as thick-skulled as a crash-helmet!"(LJ)
"You great clumsy hippopotamus, Darbishire!"(LJ)

"Honestly, Jen, I've met some crazy maniacs in my time, but I reckon you take the silver medal for beetle-headed lunacy against all-comers!"(FI)

"You're not fit to be in charge of an oil-fired gumboot, let alone somebody else's tennis-racket."(TY)

"You clumsy great grid-iron. Look what you've done!"(TY)

"T't, t't! You ARE an ignorant clodpoll, Darbishire!"(JD)

"Everybody knows he plays like a flat-footed starling."(JI)

"You're a rotten chizzler, Venables."(LI)

Illness The pupils of Linbury Court are as prone to ailments as any other set of schoolboys, and the chaos caused to the school can be considerable. A bilious attack causes Jennings to miss his first big football match(JG); an outbreak of mumps enables Darbishire to become an unlikely cricketing hero(JL); another bilious attack confines Jennings to the sick-room when he should be in detention, much to Mr Wilkins' annoyance(JD); Bromwich's illness leads to Darbishire being picked to swim for his House, despite his inability to swim at all(AT); Matron is called upon to cure a bad case of twisted belt-buckle-itis(AT); illness of Jennings' colleagues is yet another nail in the coffin of their ill-fated home-made play(OF); Atkinson's tonsilitis results in the appearance of F.J. Saunders within the walls of Linbury(TT); Jennings' blister enables him to miss the 2nd XI cricket and go on an illegal bike ride and boat trip with Darbishire(FI); Bromwich's indisposition leads to Jennings being appointed dormitory captain, with dire results(AU); Temple's sneezing fit causes Mr Wilkins to seek out Jennings at Lumley's Cafe, finding him under a table(LI); Bromwich's ankle injury causes panic when Jennings, who has made contact with him in the sick-room, believes he has caught something contagious(EJ); Darbishire tries to make his headache on the morning of Mr Wilkins' maths test convincing, and puts the thermometer under the hot tap(JI); Temple's illness causes huge confusion for Dr Wooderson, who instead of being taken to his patient is referred to a hedgehog(JR); Bromwich's summer influenza leads to Jennings borrowing his pocket radio and having it confiscated(TY); and Mr Wilkins' illness prompts Form Three to provide a gift of a rhubarb plant in an evil-smelling peanut butter jar and a card saying "Happy 80th Birthday Grandad(TH)."

Ivy The sewing maid whose careful routine for arranging the school laundry basket provides Leslie Perks with what he thinks is a foolproof opportunity for burglary(JF).

Jason Miss Thorpe's playful honey-coloured boxer puppy who causes chaos in her home, on Farmer Arrowsmith's land, and at school, where he causes the spillage of paraffin which is to prove costly to Jennings when he tries to clean his paraffin-soaked overcoat(JR). He reappears towards the end of the series, his unruliness extending to disruption of the maple-tree planting and thinking that **"all visitors to the cottage had come for the express purpose of lying on the floor and playing tug-of-war with his mistress's wellington boots(AG)."** He also alerts Miss Thorpe to the digging being carried out by Mr Carter and Robinson, which Miss Thorpe erroneously believes to be the work of badger baiters(TH).

****

"Why not help me to find it instead of standing there diddly-dee-ing and diddly-dum-ing like a half-baked potato."
Darbishire wrinkled his nose and said: "Baked potatoes don't make that sort of noise." (LJ)
****

Jennings Abounding(JB) - BOOK   Seventeenth book in the series, first published in 1967 by William Collins, 160 pp. Dedicated to Toby Price. Illustrated by Douglas Mays. Reissued in the new Macmillan edition in 1993 as **Jennings Unlimited** to avoid confusion with the stage play which was also named **Jennings Abounding.** This was the first "post-compilation" book, the first new Jennings book for two years, and as with JL and LJ, the first of a "pair" of books set in the summer term, the next being JI.

Synopsis

Chapter 1 - French Cricket - The boys try unsuccessfully to teach their new French friend, Henri, the laws of cricket.
Chapter 2 - Feathered Guest - Jennings gains closer acquaintance with a pigeon nestling near the attic, and spells out his name in drawing-pin holes on a beam in the attic.
Chapter 3 - The Writing On The Wall - Darbishire's attempt to liven up the cricket scoring box meets with a frosty response.
Chapter 4 - On The Record - An even frostier one comes from Jennings whose 51 in the junior House match cannot count because of Darbishire's neglect of duty.

Chapter 5 - A Bird in the Hand - The feathered guest is christened Swing-Wing and plans are laid to re-unite him with its owner, starting with a trip to Dunhambury.

Chapter 6 - Operation Swing-Wing - Jennings is directed to Mr Goodman's in East Brinkington, but on arrival at his home the bird escapes without warning.

Chapter 7 - Emergency Call - As Jennings heads back to Dunhambury, he is suddenly co-opted into calling the fire brigade to deal with a blaze.

Chapter 8 - News Item - Jennings is aghast to learn that his heroism, arising from his breach of school rules, may be reported in the local paper.

Chapter 9 - The Worm In The Wood - Jennings' antics in the attic are mistaken for woodworm activity. Swing-Wing has returned to Linbury.

Chapter 10 - The Two Pronged Plan - An elaborate plan is concocted to prevent the local paper being seen by the staff.

Chapter 11 - Front Page Splash - The plan fails, but Robinson's bucket of soapy water, placed right under the letter box, saves the day - not that the offending story was there anyway!

Chapter 12 - Punishment Deferred - Jennings' presence in the attic is discovered and retribution looms.

Chapter 13 - Reprieve! - The woodworm expert, called apparently needlessly, does discover woodworm activity in the attic and Jennings escapes punishment.

Chapter 14 - Bird on the Wing - Mr Carter has got to hear about Swing-Wing and arranges for its safe return to its owner.

Chapter 15 - Outlook Unsettled - Despite the bird escaping from the basket again, it is re-united with its owner who helps to start a bird-watching craze amongst the Linbury boys.

"Pigeons eat peas and beans and things."
"I've got a tin of <u>baked</u> beans," Atkinson said doubtfully. "They might be all right if I washed the tomato sauce off."

"In a geometry lesson when Old Wilkie says `Draw two identical triangles.' Well, you know how one triangle always comes out a bit different from the other, however hard you try - that's variable geometry."

Jennings Abounding! - PLAY Described as a "comedy with music" and not strictly part of the series, this dramatic version of Jennings' adventures was premiered at New College School, Oxford, on July 7th 1978, and performed again at the Little Theatre, Lewes, on December 28th 1978.

JENNINGS
ABOUNDING!

A comedy with music

Book and lyrics by
ANTHONY BUCKERIDGE

Music by
HECTOR CORTES and
WILLIAM GOMEZ

Additional music and arrangements by
NIGEL CARVER

Samuel
French

It starred Danny Marshall as Jennings, Nicholas Cory-Wright as Darbishire, Anthony Buckeridge as Mr Wilkins and Tony Potter as Mr Carter. In the play, Linbury Court is a co-educational school. As well as Jennings, Venables and Temple, the play features Rowena Binns, Christine Archer and Emma Walker, together with Mr Carter, Mr Wilkins, the Headmaster, Matron and Irving Borrowmore. The play consists of a mixture of dialogue lifted directly from the Jennings books, and brand new dialogue, all supplied by Anthony Buckeridge. There are also several songs, the music for which was written by Hector Cortes and William Gomez: School Song, Famous First Words, Earthman Go Home, Three Boos for Sir, The Things They Do, Rhubarb, Fire Drill, Crossing Off the Days, I Can See Myself, Unmusical Mob, I Never Knew Matrons Had Birthdays, No Room in the Profession, It's Not Easy to Forget. All the action in the play is based on plots used in the Jennings books:

The Space craze(AT)
Rehearsal for the end-of-term concert(JO)
Leadup to, and performance of, scene from Henry V(OF)
Mr Wilkins' allegedly leaving(AT)
Attempted midnight feast(JL) and (TW)

The playscript was published by Samuel French in 1980.

Jennings Again!(AG) Twenty-fourth book in the series, first published in 1991 by Macmillan, 151 pp. Dedicated to Eric Rosebery. Illustrated by Rodney Sutton. Macmillan had already re-published several of the Jennings titles, but succeeded in persuading the author to add a brand new title to the list after a drought of 14 years. The characters are the same, but this book is much more topical than any of the others with its stress on environmental issues. Whilst the author was clearly directing a strong message to youthful readers, the material throughout is disappointingly thin.

Synopsis

Chapter 1 - The Aim of the Game - The Headmaster battles to improve environmental awareness as the boys play Space Invaders.

Chapter 2 - Global Football - Mr Wilkins' talk on deforestation is interrupted by Jennings, chained as he is to a roller.

Chapter 3 - Miss Thorpe Goes Green - The boys are despatched to clear up Linbury village.

Chapter 4 - Marina Gardens Gets the Message - Marina Gardens is littered with leaflets exhorting them to Keep Linbury Green.

Chapter 5 - The Tea Pot Trophy - A game is played to decide whether Jennings was to blame for being scalded with hot tea.

Chapter 6 - The Miser's Mattress - The boys are introduced to Miss Thorpe's fish and agree to feed them during her absence.

Chapter 7 - The Niggling Doubt - Did Jennings accidentally turn off the immersion heater in the fish tank?

Chapter 8 - Out of Bounds - No, he did not.

Chapter 9 - Facing the Camera - The school has its photo taken and Jennings manages to get in the panorama twice.

Chapter 10 - Lost In Transit - Jennings gets separated from the party going to an ecological exhibition in London.

Chapter 11 - Underground - Jennings is re-united after meeting a climatologist whose stolen wallet Jennings recovers.

Chapter 12 - The Maple Tree - The climatologist's reward is a maple tree which is duly planted in the grounds.

Chapter 13 - Photo Finish - Mr Wilkins is not pleased with Jennings' double appearance in the photo.

"Oh, for goodness sake!" stormed Jennings. "You're about as much use as an oil-fired gumboot."

Jennings and Darbishire(JA) Fourth book in the series, first published in 1952 by William Collins, 256 pp. Dedicated to M.J.S.
Not illustrated. Dustjacket and frontispiece by S. van Abbe.

JENNINGS and DARBISHIRE

Anthony Buckeridge

Synopsis

Chapter 1 - Happy Returns - Jennings' birthday is marked by the receipt of a camera and a printing outfit, which inspires him to establish a Form Three newspaper. An accident with some pellets causes him to write a letter without using the letter "e."

Chapter 2 - The Unwelcome Gift - In an attempt to get a good story for the Form Three Times, the boys go to Linbury Cove where a French fishing vessel is sheltering. Their ineptitude in French results in a misunderstanding which leads to their being presented with a parcel of raw fish.

Chapter 3 - Continental Breakfast - Jennings decides to cook the fish in the darkroom whilst developing his first photos. The cookery ends in disaster, and Mr Wilkins intervenes.

Chapter 4 - Conjuring Trick - Jennings, who has managed to conceal the existence of the fish parcel from Mr Wilkins, hides it up Mr Wilkins' chimney.

Chapter 5 - The Form Three Times - The first issue of the paper appears, including a competition which helps to arouse interest. Jennings constructs an elaborate plan for recovering the fish parcel which is wrecked by the arrival of the headmaster.

Chapter 6 - The Incomplete Anglers - The only option left is to fish the parcel out from above. This too is a failure, which is hardly surprising as Venables has already recovered the parcel.

Chapter 7 - Sponge Cake Substitute - The discovery that Jennings has forgotten to post a letter to Aunt Angela requesting sponge cakes as prizes for the magazine competition leads to hasty discussion about what can be provided instead.

Chapter 8 - The Brilliant Forgery - Jennings' attempts to sell first editions of Latin text books belonging to Venables and himself collapse in ruins but it appears that Venables, the potential prize winner, has cheated.

Chapter 9 - Jennings Presents The Prize - A book inspection, prompted by a shortage of Latin grammars, panics Venables into demanding his Latin book back. Once he establishes he has NOT been cheating, he is only too happy to accept it as his prize.

Chapter 10 - Destination Unknown - The football match at Bracebridge is less remarkable than the events preceding - when Darbishire is held in a detention class by mistake - and following, when Jennings and Darbishire find themselves stranded in the countryside round Pottlewhistle Halt.

Chapter 11 - The Search Party - A search party is convened to find the missing boys.

Chapter 12 - The Shades of Night - The boys are discovered, but having returned to school and been punished, they are already working on new ideas for the next issue of their paper.

Chapter 13 - The Initial Difficulty - A decision to do a feature on Famous Lives leads the boys to try and find out what Mr Wilkins' first name is - a quest which meets with a frosty response.

Chapter 14 - Venables Stands Treat - Venables entertains Jennings and Darbishire to tea at Mrs Lumley's only to find he has forgotten his money. On his return to school he finds himself being bundled into Mr Wilkins' detention class, where Jennings and Darbishire should be. Meanwhile, all they can do is to keep eating....

Chapter 15 - The Paying Guest - Margaret Wilkins arrives at Lumley's Cafe, and the boys, unaware of who she is, takes her into their confidence. After she has paid the bill and they have returned to Linbury, the penny drops...

Chapter 16 - Visitor For Mr Wilkins - Margaret charms her brother into letting the boys off the grim reprisals he may have had in store for them, and provides much material for the FTT about his past.

Chapter 17 - Here Is The News! - Mr Wilkins' past heroics provide the highlights of the second issue of Form Three Times.

He had spent some time in compiling the rules and had gone to the trouble of adding: The Editor's indecision is final. It was therefore understandable that he resented these flippant remarks.

Jennings wasn't convinced. "But how can this book have been written by a dead man?"
"Well, perhaps he wasn't dead when he wrote it, but he is now," came the logical answer.

"Has any boy got a torch to lend Mr Wilkins?"
"Yes I have sir. Here you are, sir; you can have this one," said Temple generously.
"Thank you," said Mr Wilkins. "Are you sure you won't need it yourself?"
"Oh, no, sir, that's all right. It's no good to me, sir - it hasn't got a battery."

Jennings as Usual(AU) Tenth book in the series, first published by William Collins in 1959, 256 pp. Dedicated to Geoffrey Anderson. Illustrated by Douglas Mays.

This is a curious Jennings book for three reasons. Firstly, it is extremely economical in its use of characters. No new character is introduced to the series for the first time, and nobody appears in the book who does not appear in at least one other story. Secondly, it is by far the most parochial of the stories. The whole of the action takes place on the school premises, without a single foray into the outside world, and without even a mention of a person outside the school. Thirdly, the narrative is in places considerably more serious and thoughtful than any to be found in other Jennings stories; the author takes a whole chapter out to explore the dilemma of a schoolboy torn between loyalty to his colleagues and a desire to be trusted by his teachers.

Synopsis

Chapter 1 - Message Received - Mr Wilkins is baffled and none too pleased by the boys' craze for ingenious methods of telecommunication.

Chapter 2 - Jennings Makes His Mark - Jennings is responsible for turning a routine book inspection into a fiasco as he sets his bungee alight.

Chapter 3 - Trouble After Dark - Dormitories 4 and 6 plan a telephoning session, which is temporarily abandoned when an intruder is allegedly seen to enter the building.

Chapter 4 - False Alarm - The intruder is Mr Wilkins, but that does not stop the staff abandoning their dinner in search of the supposed unlawful visitor.

Chapter 5 - Morning Music - Mr Wilkins' moves his bedroom next door to the music room where he can check up on Jennings' progress with Beethoven's Minuet in G.

Chapter 6 - Unwelcome Promotion - Jennings is made dormitory captain, moments after he has effectively sanctioned Venables' breaking dormitory rules.

Chapter 7 - Jennings Takes Charge - Jennings' efforts to keep Venables on the straight and narrow are doomed, and the Head's intervention results in Jennings' demotion from the post.

Chapter 8 - Tangled Web - A full inquest into the latest events results in Mr Wilkins agreeing to give Jennings responsibilities in another sphere.

Chapter 9 - The Mobile Man Trap - Jennings is unable to cope even with his new duties after Venables' roller skate becomes wedged to him.

Chapter 10 - The Assistant Masterpiece - Jennings draws a caricature of Mr Wilkins in an exercise book, which he believes Mr Wilkins to have collected in at the end of a test.

Chapter 11 - Autograph Hunt - Subtle efforts by Jennings and his colleagues to recover the offending book are unsuccessful.

Chapter 12 - Record Performance - With a little help from Beethoven Jennings tries again - only to find he need not have bothered as the book is safely inside his desk all the time.

Chapter 13 - Token of Goodwill - As Christmas draws near, Jennings prepares a jet-propelled card for Mr Wilkins in the hope of recovering his confiscated penknife.

Chapter 14 - The Misguided Missile - The card is delivered but when Mr Wilkins finds that a full exercise book has been used as decoration, Jennings is banned from the end of term party.

Chapter 15 - False Whiskers for Two - Whilst carrying out the punishment imposed instead, Jennings finds Mr Wilkins' lost pen and decides to deliver it in traditional Christmas style.

Chapter 16 - The Christmas Spirit - Both Jennings and Mr Wilkins appear at the party as Father Christmas and all ends in a cascade of ham, tomatoes, jelly and ice cream.

"But you great addle-pated clodpoll, Darbi, they don't have to be cocoa tins! Any old tins would do just as well."
"Atkinson's got a golden syrup tin."
"There you are then. It'd be just the job."
"I doubt if you'd hear much through it, though," Darbishire went on. "You see, it's still half-full of golden syrup."

"I wouldn't mind living in Australia, Darbi," he remarked. "I mean, you'd be able to play cricket when everyone else was playing football, wouldn't you."
Darbishire glanced up. "There'd be a bit of a hoo-hah on the pitch if you did that," he observed. "You might get the balls mixed up."

Jennings at Large(JE) Twenty-third book in the series, first published by Armada, the paperback imprint of William Collins in 1977, 157 pp.

Dedicated to Nicola Suzanne. Not illustrated. Cover illustration by Michael Brownlow. This is the great "oddity" in the Jennings series. It is the only title to have appeared for the first time in paperback. Hardly any of the action takes place at Linbury Court or even Linbury village. There are only brief appearances of Jennings' friends at Linbury, or the Linbury staff. Aunt Angela is revealed, not as a benign lady of leisure in a smart suburban house which previous books might have led the reader to suggest, but a social worker living in a London tower block. For the first time in the series we meet a girl - indeed three girls - of Jennings' age. No titles are given to chapters, which follow on one after the other without even a fresh page. In 1992 the revised Macmillan edition appeared, this time with chapter titles, and these are set out below.

Anthony Buckeridge

JENNINGS AT LARGE

An Original Armada

Synopsis

Chapter 1 - Crossing off the Days - The boys look forward to the end of term at Linbury.

Chapter 2 - Stormy Weather - Mr Wilkins makes heavy weather of erecting the tent at summer camp.

Chapter 3 - Right of Way - The boys meet animal sanctuary owner Mrs Hockin and irate neighbour Major Rudkin.

Chapter 4 - Scene Change - Jennings, staying with his aunt in London, meets animal-lover Emma and her menagerie.

Chapter 5 - The Best Laid Plans - The busybodies, Mrs Pratt and Mrs Plumrose, discover the menagerie as it is smuggled into Jennings' aunt's flat.

Chapter 6 - Heated Argument - Mr Fagg, the caretaker, gives Emma a deadline to get rid of her animals.

Chapter 7 - Change of Plan - The animals are moved by train to Mrs Hockin's Retreat at Southcombe.

Chapter 8 - Mrs Hockin's Dilemma - Mrs Hockin reveals that the Retreat may have to close as she cannot afford a new fence.

Chapter 9 - Boxing Clever/Sitting Pretty - Emma and Jennings decide to hold a fund-raising fair to help Mrs Hockin.

Chapter 10 - The Fun of the Fair - The Fair takes place.

Chapter 11 - Mr Fagg Mounts Guard - The Fair proceeds, both helped and hindered by the Pratt/Plumrose double act.

Chapter 12 - Return to Linbury - The sum raised is not nearly enough, and other methods must be devised.

Chapter 13 - The Sponsored Trot - A sponsored relay run is organised to raise more cash.

Chapter 14 - Journey's End - The relay run is a success, but still the money pledged is not enough.

Chapter 15 - Last Night of Term - The boys learn that Mrs Seymour's intervention, with her riding school, has saved Mrs Hockin.

"Oh, but we ARE observing wildlife and stuff," Jennings assured him."It's going in through our eyes all the time we're asking our riddles, sir."

Jennings' Diary(JD) Fifth book in the series, first published by William Collins in 1953, 253 pp. Dedicated to Martin. Not illustrated. Dustjacket and frontispiece by S. van Abbe.

<u>Synopsis</u>

Chapter 1 - The Start of it All - Jennings' efforts to stop his dormitory colleagues stealing his diary from him - his aunt has promised him ten shillings if he writes an entry for each day of term - wreck the smooth running of the first evening of the spring term.

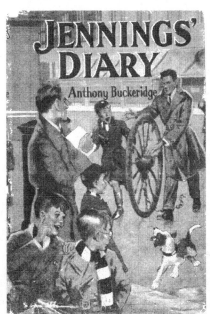

Chapter 2 - Top Secret - Jennings invents a code to record events in his diary, involving the spelling of crucial words backwards.

Chapter 3 - Jennings Finds An Ally - Jennings' illness is perceived by Mr Wilkins to be a ruse to escape a punishment. Matron stands up for Jennings, and the boy decides Matron must therefore be given a present.

Chapter 4 - The Scarlet Runner - Jennings and Darbishire, with the aid of five shillings from his uncle, hire bikes to go to Dunhambury to buy Matron a present. Darbishire is unable to mount his machine.

Chapter 5 - So Long At The Fair - The discovery of a fair, and the consequent expenditure, leave the boys with just 6d - which they then use on the Wild West Commando Range and win a vase for Matron, only for Darbishire to smash it on the way home.

Chapter 6 - The Present For Matron - Jennings gives Matron a bunch of snowdrops from his garden, and records in his diary that Mr Wilkins has lost a cuff link. His diary is confiscated by Mr Wilkins when the master sees that he has been described in the diary as the "missing link."

Chapter 7 - Assorted Fossils - Jennings, inspired by his holiday visit to the Natural History museum, establishes a collection of his own, beginning with what he believes to be a petrified fang but is actually Atkinson's old knife-handle.

Chapter 8 - The Rattling Relic - Jennings and Darbishire, on a "dig" at the nearby Roman encampment, unearth an old wheel and chain. Believing it to be a chariot wheel, they bring it back to school where it causes considerable damage to a staircase.

Chapter 9 - The Root of the Trouble - Jennings, having been allowed his diary back temporarily to update it, is unable to find it to return to Mr Wilkins.

Chapter 10 - Wrong Side of the Law - Worried that the coded information in the diary may be misinterpreted, Jennings goes to PC Honeyball in the village to report the loss. PC Honeyball is not amused either by the explanation or Jennings' sudden recollection as to its whereabouts. In recovering it, he finds Mr Wilkins' link and is allowed to keep his diary in exchange.

Chapter 11 - The Genuine Fake - The boys take the bus to Dunhambury museum. Mr Carter thinks the wheel, which Jennings wanted to take with him, has been left behind. He is wrong...

Chapter 12 - On View to the Public - Jennings and Darbishire are unable to find a home for the wheel and end up lodging it in the museum, despite it having been confirmed to them that it is totally valueless except as scrap metal.

Chapter 13- Mr Wilkins Rides Alone - Mr Wilkins is left to brave the wrath of the museum curator. Jennings and Darbishire, once again reunited with the wheel, sell it to a scrap metal dealer which provides money for a taxi for Mr Wilkins.

Chapter 14- Knotty Problem - It is the last evening of term. Mr Wilkins fastens Jennings' trunk so that it is all but impossible to undo it - and is then told he must undo it again himself.

Chapter 15 - Jennings Tries His Hand - To add to Mr Wilkins' troubles, he finds that his mark-book has been mislaid, containing the entire term's marks for Form Three.

Chapter 16 - Pack Up Your Troubles! - The mark book is discovered to have been reposing in Jennings' trunk, but thanks to Matron, bloody reprisals are avoided and term ends happily.

"Hurry up, hurry up! Question One for the last time; write down the date..."
"Yes, sir, I've done that," Darbishire announced brightly. "I've written the date, sir."

"Now, if it was J.C., we'd definitely know it had once belonged to Julius Caesar. I expect they were just as fussy in those days about having their private possessions properly marked as Matron is now."
"I say, Atki, they've got an antique iron comb here, with only three teeth in it."
"What about it?"
"Well, it looks just like the one you lent me to do my hair with before lunch."
"Don't be such a coot - it's nothing like mine. My comb's got <u>four</u> teeth in it," Atkinson pointed out.

Jennings Follows A Clue(JF) Second book in the series, first published by William Collins in 1951, 255 pp. Dedicated to the author's elder son Timothy John. Not illustrated. Dustjacket and frontispiece by S. van Abbe. Unlike most of the other books in the series which consist of a number of different adventures loosely connected with one or more linking themes, there is a much stronger storyline running right through this book, concerning the efforts of Jennings and Darbishire to solve the mystery of the light in the sanatorium and the theft of the Linbury sports cups.

Synopsis
Chapter 1 - Mr Carter Reads Aloud - The reading of Sherlock Holmes' exploits to Jennings one wet afternoon inspires Jennings to take up a career as a detective.
Chapter 2 - Ln. Ct. Det. Ag. - The Linbury Court Detective Agency is formed, and an order placed for some essential equipment for the task.
Chapter 3 - The Green Baize Bag - Mr Higgins' routine visit to the school to collect the sports cup for engraving is misconstrued by the Ln. Ct. Det. Ag.
Chapter 4 - Darbishire Keeps Watch - Darbishire's first assignment, keeping watch while Jennings goes to recover the sports cup, ends in confusion.

Chapter 5 - Triumph and Dismay - The sports cup is safely recovered and Jennings realises that his recovery work was not as heroic a feat as he believed it to be.

Chapter 6 - Further Outlook-Unsettled - Jennings' preoccupation with detective work incurs the wrath of both the Headmaster and Mr Wilkins, and the derision of his classmates.

Chapter 7 - Jennings Sees The Light - Jennings' first discovery of the light shining in the sanatorium late at night arouses his suspicion, but neither he nor Darbishire can remain awake long enough to detect the cause.

Chapter 8 - Mr Wilkins Grows Curious - Mr Carter explains to Mr Wilkins the real - and lawful - reason for the light in the sanatorium - the night porter.

Chapter 9 - Jennings Makes An Entrance - Jennings' has his first meeting with Les Perks, the laundryman, who is carrying out daytime reconnaissance on the sanatorium. Jennings' order, on behalf of the Agency, for a camera is treated seriously by the camera company.

Chapter 10 - Alarming Excursion - Jennings' sighting of the sanatorium light prompts him to make a nocturnal visit there with Darbishire. When they arrive, they find they are not alone.

Chapter 11 - Mr Wilkins Answers The Phone - There is another intruder in the sanatorium who locks them inside. Mr Carter and Mr Wilkins go to rescue them and find that the night porter, for once, was NOT that night responsible for the light being on.

Chapter 12 - The Empty Mantelpiece - The theft of the cups from the library, including the sports cup, is discovered, and the police are alerted.

Chapter 13 - Alibi For Old Nightie - The Ln. Ct. Det. Ag. mulls over its theories as to the identity of the burglar, and both members receive a caning from the Headmaster for their trouble.

Chapter 14 - The Headmaster Is Not Amused - Jennings incurs the wrath of the Head again, this time for misbehaving in class, and is told he cannot run in that afternoon's sports.

Chapter 15 - The Friend of the Family - Mr Russell visits Jennings to sell him a camera, and is somewhat disconcerted to find that Linbury Court is a school and not Jennings' own stately home. The 95 guinea cost of the camera is somewhat greater than Jennings, with his three and sevenpence, is able to afford. The Headmaster's concerns over the visitor are allayed when Mr Russell tells him he is merely a family friend. On that pretext, Jennings is allowed to compete in the sports after all.

Chapter 16 - Darbishire Runs A Race - The Headmaster is persuaded to buy the camera, which proceeds to record Darbishire appearing to beat Jennings in a race - in fact he was coming in last, in the race before.

Chapter 17 - The Vital Clue - Jennings realises he may have a clue to the identity of the burglar - a coat button - if only he knew where it was.

Chapter 18 - Perilous Journey - The coat button is traced to the laundry van, which in turn reveals the missing cups and the guilt of Leslie Perks.

Chapter 19 - Wednesday Evening Masterpiece - The Ln. Ct. Det. Ag, is wound up, courtesy of Mr Carter, but the Agency's finest hour is inadvertently recorded on camera to provide a lasting record for posterity.

"Jennings," he said, "when the author wrote this admirable book, he saw fit to call it A NEW LATIN GRAMMAR. Had he wished to call it A NEW EATING GRAMMAR, I have no doubt he would have done so."

"Don't quibble. You've made a frightful bish and you're about as much use as a radio-active suet pudding."

"The only way you could win would be if Mr Carter accidentally shot everyone else in the foot with the starting pistol. Dash it all, Darbi, you couldn't beat a performing seal running on its flippers."

Jennings Goes To School(JG) First book in the series, first published by William Collins in 1950, 255 pp. Dedicated to the author's daughter Jennifer Sally. Not illustrated. Dustjacket and frontispiece by S. van Abbe(although Douglas Mays provided a new dustjacket for a 1960's reprint). The book, Buckeridge's masterpiece, appeared as a response to the demand for the Children's Hour radio plays to be issued in book form. This book contains much greater use of slang and nicknames than any of the other titles; the slang was toned down significantly both in subsequent titles and in reprints of this book, of which there were many.

Synopsis

Chapter 1 - Jennings Learns The Ropes - Jennings arrives at Linbury Court

as a new boy, meets Darbishire and has seven attempts at writing an acceptable postcard home.

Chapter 2 - Trouble Looms Ahead - Jennings incurs the wrath of his Dormitory 4 colleagues by washing out of turn, while Darbishire is cowed by the threat of massive magisterial impositions for failing to meet required standards.

Chapter 3 - Jennings Gains A Reputation - Jennings and Darbishire try to run away from school, are apprehended by Mr Carter and prove their escapological skills by buying a stick of Valenti's rock.

Chapter 4 - Jennings Arrives Late - a spilt inkbottle and a confrontation with the headmaster conspire to reduce the meaningfulness of Jennings' contribution to his first school football.

Chapter 5 - The Bells Go Down - Jennings' decision to enliven a fire practice - of which he has been put in charge - by calling the fire brigade, does little for the blood pressure of Archie Cuppling and his crew who are hopelessly ill-prepared.

Chapter 6 - The Indian Rope Trick - As the firemen struggle to reach the school with a dodgy carburettor and an excess of left boots, Darbishire makes a mockery of the Pennetra Fire Escape.

Chapter 7 - Suspense and Suspension - The firemen are put to good use after all as Mr Wilkins is entangled in some ivy, after endeavouring to show the boys how to use the Escape. Darbishire has problems in his Cake List compilation.

Chapter 8 - The Literary Masterpiece - Half-term sees Jennings' parents baffled by his son's progress; Jennings' First Eleven debut is ruined by illness; and Darbishire's first attempt at detective fiction is consigned to the waste-paper basket.

Chapter 9 - Mr Wilkins Has An Idea - The happy coincidence of a lawless outbreak by Form Three, and a period of quarantine by Bracebridge, allows Mr Wilkins the chance to inflict a novel form of punishment - cancelling a First Eleven football match.

Chapter 10 - The Poisonous Spider - Jennings discovers a spider which

Darbishire firmly believes to be lethal. Mr Carter pronounces it safe, unbeknown to Darbishire. Mr Wilkins is embarrassed by Bracebridge's announcement that the quarantine is over.

Chapter 11 - Beware of the Thing - Mr Wilkins finds the perfect pretext for rescinding the cancellation of the Bracebridge match when Jennings removes the spider, which the master believes to be poisonous, to safety.

Chapter 12 - Jennings Uses His Head - The long-awaited match against Bracebridge sees Jennings miss a sitter, score a spectacular own goal and head one of the flukiest winning goals ever witnessed.

Chapter 13 - Mr Carter Makes A Suggestion - Mr Carter rejects Darbishire's revised attempt at a detective story, and suggests that stories about Jennings himself might be more successful.

Martin Winthrop Barlow Pemberton-Oakes, Esq., M.A.(Oxon), Headmaster, was not normally a devotee of the ballet, but on this occasion, he executed a number of pas de chats and grands jetes that would have done credit to a prima ballerina.

"I know, what about Flixton Slick?"
"Wizard prang! That'll be super."
"Don't be so wet, Darbi. If a chap was called Wizard Prang he'd be a conjurer, not a detective."
"Perhaps they won't come, sir," he said, "'cos Darbishire says they have baked beans on toast at fire stations, and it has to be a super-important fire before they'll let it get cold - the baked beans I mean not the fire."

Jennings In Particular(JI) Eighteenth book in the series, first published by William Collins in 1968, 192 pp. Dedicated to Corin, the author's youngest son. Illustrated by Douglas Mays. Although this book, like the preceding one(JB) is set in the summer term, it does not follow directly on from it as LI did from LJ; JB contains an incident which took place on June 29th, this book contains an incident on June 16th. Like all the later William Collins titles, this is one of the rarer books to obtain in its original form.

Synopsis
Chapter 1 - Roof-Top - The deposit of a ball on to the roof during an impromptu cricket match sends Jennings and Darbishire up on to the roof but leaves them stranded there.

Chapter 2 - Refuge - The two boys are able to get into the attic but no further. Mr Wilkins, when informed of the situation, goes to the rescue.

JENNINGS
in
particular

Anthony
Buckeridge

Chapter 3 - Rescue - Jennings' dormitory colleagues effect a rescue of their own but Jennings is still imprisoned - in a dodgy sleeping bag he thought he would need in the attic.

Chapter 4 - Retribution - Jennings is freed from the sleeping bag and after punishments follow, with suitable restrictions on liberty, he begins to think about a new issue of stamps.

Chapter 5 - On Target - As part of their punishment, the boys miss the junior picnic and have to help at the fete instead. Jennings enters the bowling competition and wins a pig.

Chapter 6 - Pig In A Poke - The boys, at Miss Thorpe's suggestion, take the pig to Mr Arrowsmith's and receive a somewhat frosty response.

Chapter 7 - Pig In The Middle - The pig ends up at the school and causes massive disruption to the quiet Sunday afternoon timetable.

Chapter 8 - Security Risk - Jennings and Darbishire make plans to secure their first-day covers, and receive terse words from Binns and Blotwell after the pig ruined their jigsaw.

Chapter 9 - False Alarm - A swop of prizes is arranged. Jennings gives his newly-acquired bath salts to Matron, and is then informed that there is a drawing pin in them. Or is there?....

Chapter 10 - Change Of Plan - Jennings acquires the perfect pretext to get to Linbury for the new stamps after Pettigrew has let him down. Darbishire goes on the sick list.

Chapter 11 - Cycle of Events - Jennings eventually obtains one stamp, leaving Pettigrew bemused, as his bike has been used for the purpose, without his consent.

Chapter 12 - Gesture of Goodwill - The bike misunderstanding is sorted out, Darbishire is presented with a second stamp - but the all-important postmarks are never put on the envelopes!

Chapter 13 - The Squaw on the Hippo - Jennings receives a letter from his aunt, with new stamp AND postmark - a shame, then, that Robinson should think the envelope was rubbish.

Chapter 14 - Full Circle - The envelope is retrieved from the bonfire, plus lots of old cricket balls. As one is smashed on to the roof, the boys realise they have come full circle.

It was your rotan old pig that did all the damage and we think Darbishire is a rota and Jennings is a bigger one so what are you going to do about it? With best wishes...

"And he could have had a fast car waiting at the end of the drive to make his get-away," said Rumbelow.
"He wouldn't need a car; he'd got a bicycle," Bromwich pointed out.

Jennings' Little Hut(JL) Third book in the series, first published by William Collins in 1951, 255 pp. Dedicated to G.A.B. Not illustrated. Dustjacket and frontispiece by S. van Abbe.

Synopsis

Chapter 1 - The Squatters - Hut-builders abound, each property developer asserting that their individual construction is the best. Bromwich Major wins the prize for the originality - his hut is to be inhabited by his goldfish Elmer.

Chapter 2 - Last Wicket Stand - Desperation reigns as Darbishire finds himself playing a key role in the House match with most of his colleagues stricken with mumps.

Chapter 3 - Operation "Exercise" - Bromwich's illness leads to Jennings and Darbishire taking charge of Elmer, which in turn keeps Jennings' mind so occupied that he antagonises Mr Wilkins in his geometry class.

Chapter 4 - Elmer Finds A Loophole - Elmer escapes into the murky waters of the swimming pool, giving Mr Wilkins a nasty surprise when he takes a dip.

Chapter 5 - The Kettle of Fish - The search for Elmer ends happily when Robinson discovers the fish and places him in the night watchman's kettle.

Chapter 6 - Maiden Voyage - Attempts to sail a model yacht on the pond near the huts end up with Jennings falling into the pond himself.

Chapter 7 - The Best Laid Plans... - Venables' attempts to cover for Jennings' misfortune end in detection for Venables and even greater discomfort for Jennings.

Chapter 8 - The Small Back Room - The Headmaster's tour of inspection of the huts ends in disaster when he finds himself inextricably wedged in the annex to Jennings' and Darbishire's edifice. The huts are placed out of bounds.

Chapter 9 - England Wins the Ashes - Banned from using the huts, Jennings and Darbishire play cricket instead. Jennings manages to break one of the headmaster's cucumber frames in the process.

Chapter 10 - Absent-Minded Aunt - Jennings concocts a plan to replace the frame without the headmaster finding out about the accident. All depends on Aunt Angela...

Chapter 11 - The Visitors Arrive - Angela's postal order fails to arrive, but General Merridew does, bringing with him a potential Linbury recruit, his difficult grandson Roger. Jennings decides to use glass in some old photo frames to put the damage right.

Chapter 12 - Shortage of Glass - The movements of the General's party make the repair mission harder but the job is done, not undetected by Mr Carter.

Chapter 13 - The Difficult Guest - The headmaster entrusts Jennings and Darbishire with Roger whose black mood is only relieved when he hears about the huts and runs out to them.

Chapter 14 - Hue and Cry - Roger emerges from the huts in a state which bodes no good for his temporary guardians. The headmaster's wrath is compounded by Roger's mother's decision not to send him to Linbury as a pupil.

Chapter 15 - Mr Wilkins Hits A Six - Jennings and Darbishire avoid a caning only when Roger's mother reverses her decision on the strength of the hut escapade - which in turn leads the headmaster to rescind the hut ban.

Chapter 16 - Happy Ending - Mr Wilkins' cricket stroke, which also smashes a cucumber frame, goes unpunished, but resentment at this is short-lived as the boys return to the joys of primitive living once more.

"The General's a very important character," Brown Major explained. "He's been in the army since about the time of the Wars of the Roses, and he's been a military attache as well. I didn't think a chap could actually BE a military attache until Mr Carter told me. I thought they were sort of despatch case things that you carry military secrets about in."

**"If one did climb a tree, it'd be all over the newspapers. Big headlines:
GOLDFISH'S AMAZING FEAT!"**
"Yes, it would be, if it had any, wouldn't it?"
"Wouldn't it <u>what</u>?"
"It'd be amazing if a goldfish had got any feet."

Jennings, Mr and **Mrs** Responsible as they are for having inflicted Master
J.C.T. Jennings on the unsuspecting Linbury community, we see or hear
little of our hero's parents; this despite the fact that they live in Haywards
Heath, which Jennings describes as only about fifteen miles away from
school. Early on, father, an engineer who is liable to be sent abroad by
his firm, expresses some concerns over son's ability to cope with boarding
school life, concerns which are heightened when son's first reunion
with parents yields a succession of monosyllabic replies and then a welter
of unintelligible school slang. This is then passed on, in even more
confused form, to Grandma(JG). Mrs Jennings does, we hear, write a
weekly letter to her son with news, inter alia, of the family cat, goldfish
and puppies(SO). We are also informed that Jennings' father has size 9
feet(SO).

**Anxious though he was to listen, Jennings was even more eager to talk,
which meant that his parents' account of their travels became mixed
up with his own account of all that had been happening to him.**(JE)

Jennings, Of Course!(JO) Fourteenth book in the series, first published
by William Collins in 1964, 192 pp. Dedicated to John and Andrew
Williams. Illustrated by Douglas Mays. After the "blip" in the "one book,
one term" sequence occasioned by LI, we move into what is clearly the
Christmas term, with the climax of that term being the events of 16th
December. With the radio broadcasts on Children's Hour having finished
a year before, and Children's Hour itself finishing in 1964, Jennings
enthusiasts now had to rely solely on the printed word for fresh "fixes"
of Linbury adventure. This story is unusual for the quasi-masonic ritual,
not repeated in any other story, of boys on a number of occasions pressing
thumbs together to seal an agreement.

Synopsis
Chapter 1 - Wrong Foot Foremost - Jennings' bid to get back from a
school walk in order to get to the ping-pong table ends in muddy disaster.
Chapter 2 - In Hazard - As a consequence, the boys arrange a secret dry-
cleaning operation, with Darbishire designated as a far from willing
accomplice.

Jennings, of course!

Anthony Buckeridge

Chapter 3 - Surprise Item - Jennings' indifference to the usual fare for the end-of-term concert prompts him to take up ventriloquism.

Chapter 4 - The Hitch-Hikers - The dry-cleaning operation starts well as the boys reach town safely - not knowing that the 2nd XI footballers are hard on their heels.

Chapter 5 - Web of Crossed Purposes - Mr Wilkins' discovery of Jennings and Darbishire, their mission safely accomplished, does not end in the retribution the two boys expect.

Chapter 6 - Gred and Gutter Practice - Jennings' early ventriloquial endeavours are not 100% successful.

Chapter 7 - Sale or Return - Miss Thorpe is aghast when she learns that some of the village jumble sale items have been appropriated from the school lost property cupboard.

Chapter 8 - The Unconsidered Trifles - The items, plus all the other unsold jumble, are duly returned to the cupboard, cleared so thoroughly by Mr Wilkins days earlier. He is not amused...

Chapter 9 - The Wooden Horse - Jennings is forced into a ventriloquism demonstration; long before Darbishire bails him out, he realises he simply is not up to it.

Chapter 10 - Vanishing Trick - As Jennings turns his attention to conjuring, Matron is desperate for a replacement for Mrs Cherry, the school cook-housekeeper.

Chapter 11 - Open Invitation - Jennings hits on the idea of a school jumble sale to clear the unconsidered trifles - never imagining that Mrs Hackett will invite the villagers too.

Chapter 12 - The Lure of the Jumble - The villagers arrive in force, and chaos quickly results.

Chapter 13 - It's An Ill Wind... - Jennings and Darbishire are only saved from Mr Wilkins' wrath by the announcement that a new cook has been found from amongst the female hordes.

Chapter 14 - Tricky Predicament - Mr Wilkins' quick thinking saves

Jennings, wearing his magician's hat, from becoming the laughing-stock of the Christmas concert.

Surely, he argued, any sensible audience would rather watch a conjuror sawing a lady in half than listen to old Rumbelow, or somebody, bashing out "The Merry Peasant" on a tinny old school piano.

"It's not a game, sir. It's terribly urgent. You see, he's going to talk to an imaginary little person inside the horse, so there's got to be a sort of squeaky voice coming out of it to answer him."

Jennings Report,The(JR) Twentieth book in the series, first published by William Collins in 1970, 191 pp. Dedicated to Karen Tracy. The last book to be illustrated by Douglas Mays, and indeed the last traditional hard-cover William Collins edition to be illustrated. There are three curiosities about the printing of it; the typeset used is unique to the series, individual chapter titles are not printed above the right-hand pages(merely the book title) and there is no text printed on the reverse side of illustrated pages. In addition there is either a mis-spelling or printing error in the chapter-heading for Chapter 7, with "odorous" being spelt "oderous".

Synopsis
Chapter 1 - The Discovery - An afternoon walk introduces Jennings to a hedgehog in distress.
Chapter 2 - Red Herring - Using a trail of red herrings, Jennings defies Mr Wilkins and recovers the hedgehog.
Chapter 3 - Thorny Hedgehog Be Not Seen! - Some dexterity by Jennings prevents the discovery of the beast by Mr Wilkins.
Chapter 4 - Report in the Offing - Mr Wilkins is not encouraged by Jennings' ideas for subject matter for Form 3's maths project.
Chapter 5 - Break For Refreshments - The boys' research into TV-watching habits of locals meets with hostility from the natives.
Chapter 6 - The Bounding Boxer - The boys' first confrontation with Miss Thorpe's dog Jason leads to fruitful discussion regarding the welfare of the hedgehog.
Chapter 7 - The Odorous Overcoat - Jennings' follow-up from the discussion - a visit to Mr Laxton the expert - coincides with Jason running amok at school causing a spillage on to his overcoat.
Chapter 8 - Darbishire in Charge - Darbishire is left to look after both Jason, and Jennings' aunt as she arrives to take her nephew out.
Chapter 9 - The Mixed-Bag Day - The overcoat is eventually dry-cleaned,

and the trio enjoy their afternoon in Dunhambury.

Chapter 10 - The Venables Plan - Consternation greets the news that Mr Laxton is planning to visit Linbury Court.

Chapter 11 - A Confusion Of Visitors - It so happens that Dr Wooderson is also expected to see to a case of tonsilitis...

Chapter 12 - The Awakening - With the respective practitioners finally reunited with the proper patients, Mr Laxton's hedgehog expertise attracts a wide audience.

Chapter 13 - Second Attempt - The hedgehog's awakening is found to be a more satisfactory subject for a report than TV aerials.

Mr Wilkins was not at all impressed with Jennings' mathematical research. "I never heard such nonsense," he complained, running his eye over the scholar's statistics. "Bicycles! Measles! Life on Mars! What sort of use can you possibly make of information like that?" Jennings wracked his brains for an answer. There must be some purpose for which his questionnaire could be used. Finally he said:"Well, sir, you can only catch measles once. So if you know how many chaps have already had it, you could work out how many sandwiches you'd need if we went for a picnic on bicycles during an epidemic. And if some of the chaps who had had measles but didn't think there was life on Mars couldn't ride bicycles either..."

Johnson The hastily-appointed substitute for Jennings in the match against Bretherton House, who scores in that match and then again in the following week's match against Bracebridge, after Jennings' failure to convert at the first attempt(JG). When not excelling on the football field or in the long-jump pit(JF) he supports Oxford University, Charlton Athletic and Middlesex in no particular order. Jennings is invited to stand between Johnson and Nuttall when it is believed that Jennings is suffering from a contagious disease, and Johnson is one of the first to run for cover(EJ). He also doubles up as caterpillar-collector, picnic food transporter and amateur wrestler(TY).

Jones, Mrs Winner of a tasselled lampshade, the second prize in the Home Made Cake competition at the village bazaar, for her appetising sponge cake, thereby helping to secure the coveted third prize for Aunt Angela's cake(LJ).

Just Like Jennings(LJ) Twelfth book in the series, first published by William Collins in 1961, 256 pp. Dedicated to H.H. Illustrated by Douglas Mays. The following book, LI, is a natural sequel to this book, relating events that took place in the same term. Thus for the first time, the "one term - one book" sequence is broken.

Synopsis
Chapter 1 - Hasty Departure - Jennings only just catches the train - then thinks he has lost his ticket - then leaves it lying on the floor.
Chapter 2 - Train of Events - His colleagues safely recover the ticket, and present it to the inspector, but not before Jennings has concealed himself under the seat to avoid detection.
Chapter 3 - Transport Problem - Jennings' punishment, being banished

to another part of the train, means he together with Darbishire must complete their journey by unorthodox means.
Chapter 4 - Mysterious Stranger - A kite-flying expedition which goes wrong brings Jennings into Miller's Wood, and his first encounter with a suspicious bearded character.
Chapter 5 - Chalk Dust Trail - Jennings' amateurish efforts to find evidence against the stranger meet with little success.
Chapter 6 - The Bird Watcher - The real identity of the stranger, an ornothologist, is established by Mr Carter and the Head. Jennings fails to impress his colleagues with his detective work.
Chapter 7 - Surprise Item - Jennings' need to prove his detective

capabilities coincides with a visit to school by the bird watcher - with bizarre results.

Chapter 8 - The Mountaineers - Jennings upsets Mr Wilkins with his questions in the geography class, but is inspired to lead an expedition of his own. Pyewacket the cat comes to stay.

Chapter 9 - The Abominable Snow Cat - Pyewacket is discovered by the explorers and the expedition is disbanded.

Chapter 10 - The Vanishing Footprints - Mr Wilkins finds that Pyewacket has disappeared and determines to find him.

Chapter 11 - Errand of Mercy - Mr Wilkins is re-united with Pyewacket after a somewhat embarrassing session with PC Honeyball.

Chapter 12 - The Secret Plan - Mr Wilkins' reward for looking after Pyewacket is a pair of hideous vases. Jennings obtains some goodies from Aunt Angela which are consumed after lights-out.

Chapter 13 - The Unique Antique - Jennings smashes one of the vases, and, believing Mr Wilkins is genuinely upset, decides to find a replacement.

Chapter 14 - The Astounding Co-incidence - Jennings finds an identical replacement, little knowing that it is in fact the intact vase which Mr Wilkins has donated to the bazaar.

Chapter 15 - The Unlucky Winner - Jennings has put in Aunt Angela's cake for a bazaar competition in order to win the vase. The trouble is, the Headmaster is presenting the prizes...

Chapter 16 - Fair Exchange - Miss Thorpe ensures that Jennings gets the vase; Mr Wilkins generously donates his vase to Aunt Angela; and Jennings shares the cake round before going off to have his fortune told.

"Eccentric, that's it. It's like ex-service and words like that. It means they used to be centric but they're not any longer."

"It'll make a jolly good tent - especially with this air vent in the side."
"That's not for ventilation. That's where I put my foot through it the other night."

Laxton, Robin Tall, young East Brinkington man, and writer of the nature column for the local paper. Jennings is referred to Mr Laxton by Miss Thorpe because of his concern for his hedgehog. Following some correspondence, and an abortive trip to Dunhambury to try and see him, Jennings entertains Mr Laxton at the school. Mr Laxton, having initially been mistaken for someone else and told that the patient is **"sitting up in bed, writing his diary,"** provides both advice and assistance regarding the hedgehog's awakening from hibernation and thereby much valuable material for the revised Jennings Report(JR).

Leave It To Jennings(LI) Thirteenth book in the series, first published by William Collins in 1963, 192 pp. Dedicated to Spikki. Illustrated by Douglas Mays. This is a "landmark" title in two ways. Firstly, it was the first Jennings book to contain less than 200 pages and signalled the end of the traditional 256-page Jennings book. Secondly, it was the first book to follow on from where the previous title, Just Like Jennings, left off; we pick up the action in the same term rather than starting afresh.

Synopsis

Chapter 1 - The Shape of Things To Come - Jennings explains to his dormitory colleagues what Madame Olivera has prophesied.

Chapter 2 - False Witness - Jennings has to take responsibility for Venables carelessly putting Jennings' socks on after cricket.

Chapter 3 - Washing Instructions - Jennings' command to Venables to wash the socks produces disastrous results.

Chapter 4 - The Pleasure of His Company - Venables makes amends by inviting Jennings to eat with him at Lumley's Cafe - but without expecting to pay for him.

Chapter 5 - Jennings Weathers The Storm - Mr Wilkins has to seek out Jennings, who is required to play cricket against Bracebridge.

Chapter 6 - The Camouflaged Text Book - Mr Wilkins' displeasure with the state of Jennings' atlas forces Jennings into desperate measures when he finds his maths text book missing.

Chapter 7 - The Snake In The Grass - Jennings' enthusiasm for Form Three's geography project results in an unusual breakfast gift for Mr Wilkins.

Chapter 8 - In Case Of Fire - Delegated the task of collecting rainwater for said project, Jennings has to deploy the water for a more urgent task - putting out a staff room fire.

Chapter 9 - Aunt Angela Blunders - Not only does she send the replacement maths book instead of her postal order, but Angela also errs by sending the "with answers" edition.

Chapter 10 - The Great Rainfall Mystery - Jennings cannot work out why a dry spell should yield three inches of rain. Mr Wilkins has his own ideas...

Chapter 11 - The Smugglers - Dormitory 4 decides to hold a major clean-up operation in the hope of winning Matron's Dormitory Cup - after lights-out.

Chapter 12 - The Inedible Feast - Mr Wilkins mistakes the clean-up for something else but is forced to backpedal, even more so when the loss of the arithmetic book is found to be his fault.

Chapter 13 - The Seer of the Bacon Counter - Madame Olivera, the prophetess, is exposed as Miss Tubbs, a shop assistant. Jennings is unamused. The rainfall mystery is traced to the cricket hose.

Chapter 14 - The Wind of Fortune - A succession of happy events - Compensation from Mr Wilkins, the winning of the Cup and the promise of a river crossing - restore Jennings' faith in Miss Tubbs' psychic powers.

Chapter 15 - A Present For Miss Tubbs - Miss Tubbs is met on the field trip and Jennings, anxious to fulfil the prophecy in her tea-leaves, gives her a box of chocolates.

Chapter 16 - Leave It to Jennings - A happy discovery in the valley of the Dun brings the field trip, and the summer term, to a triumphant conclusion.

"Good morning, Professor Temple! $a2 + 2ab + b2$, don't you think?"
"Oh, definitely," Temple agreed pompously. "In fact, seven eighths are fifty six plus the square root of minus one and take away the number you first thought of."

"I'm extremely grateful, and I withdraw the remarks I made a few minutes ago."
Jennings beamed. "You mean, my head doesn't need seeing to after all, sir?"
"Well - er..." Mr Wilkins wasn't prepared to go quite as far as that.

Lewis Day-boy and associate of Marshall and Pettigrew. Indeed he helps the latter with his school maths project in the agricultural fact-finding deparment(JR). He is also an unwitting helper in escorting Jennings away from the premises for a secret haircut(TJ), and takes part in the football match to decide whether Jennings brought a hot-tea scalding on himself(AG).

Linbury The village half a mile from Linbury Court Preparatory School, population at last count 398. Surrounded by agricultural land, it straddles the main Dunhambury road from north to south, and straggles along it from east to west, and is linked to Dunhambury by an hourly bus. A disused railway line, now used as a rubbish tip by residents, until Miss

Thorpe helps to turn it back into a nature reserve(AG), is a reminder of earlier means of communication between Linbury and the rest of the world. Its features include an early Norman church at the far end of the village; a vicarage containing a garden large and rambling enough for the annual church bazaar; a village hall which serves as an ideal function for jumble sales and whist drives; a late Victorian horse trough ; a petrol filling station; a modest police station which is variously described as a semi-detached and a detached redbrick villa; and a cove, referred to most infrequently, containing a wooden jetty and shingly beach. Streets include Church Lane,a winding thoroughfare of small cottages facing the churchyard wall, and Marina Gardens, scene of a serious leaflet-scattering episode(AG). There are three shops in the village, at which the boys of Linbury Court are allowed to spend their money after a brisk walk across the fields or along Linbury Lane. Although the village contains the businesses run by Mr Higgins, jeweller and silversmith, and the Lumleys, the hub of the village is the Linbury General Stores. This shop is at the end of the main Linbury village street not far from the bus stop. It lives up to its name, serving a vast array of produce, with separate counters for bacon, stationery, tinned food, hardware including mouse-traps, cornplasters and egg-whisks(JI) and even corn-chandling(JB), as well as plenteous advertisements on the side wall(SO). It serves items which apparently could be hard to obtain in Dunhambury - paraffin by the pint, home-knitted bedsocks, cornplasters, rat-traps, foul-smelling substance for treating liver-fluke in sheep, caraway seeds, patent folding tin-openers, galvanised iron buckets, mouse-traps, mothballs, pot-plants and greetings cards(TH). Clearly Linbury has yet been spared the worst effects of out-of-town superstores!

Although we know that Linbury is in Sussex, and close to the Downs, it is difficult to place it on a real map of that county. We do get some clues; Jennings asserts that it is about fifteen miles from Haywards Heath(JG) and it does appear to be within walking distance of not only the Downs but also the sea, judging by the adventures of some of the boys in the earlier books(especially JA). This would place Linbury somewhere near the town of Lewes and indeed there is evidence to suggest that Dunhambury was modelled on Lewes, Buckeridge's own home town. However, a glance at the map shows that there are few villages in the Lewes region where both the sea and South Downs are within easy walking distance; moreover, Buckeridge has asserted that Dunhambury is modelled on a number of locations.

Linbury Court Preparatory School   The school of 79 boys, mostly boarders, and both male and female staff, which forms the central venue for all the Jennings series. Built on sandy subsoil and standing in 40 acres of grounds, there is in front of the main building a tarmac playground bounded on two sides by an L-shaped block and on a third by outbuildings. A gravel drive, passing playing fields, tennis court, gardening plots and the Headmaster's garden, links the school with Linbury Lane and the outside world. At the far end of the grounds across the playing fields is a coppice and a pond. The school includes a chapel, to which the boys may go on Sunday morning or Sunday evening; a spacious, oak-pannelled library; a swimming bath; a gymnasium containing a rostrum with curtains that never quite meet in the middle; common rooms for both boys and staff; an attic which sees a number of adventures; staff quarters and dormitories; a dining hall adjoining kitchens with thermostatically controlled dishwasher; tiled bathrooms with heated towel rails; self-closing bootlockers; and overhead ventilation. The boys do compare facilities at Bracebridge favourably against the paint-scratched woodwork and rough wooden benches of Linbury's dingy basement changing rooms!

Fireman Long See entry for Archie Cuppling.

****

"Don't be so bats, Binns! Why should any one want to pinch just one boot?"
"He might have been a chap with only one leg." (JA)
****

Lumley, Mr & Mrs Nothing sums up the rural yet vibrant character of the Linbury community better than the establishment run by this couple in the village, Mrs Lumley waddling around her assorted cats to dispense teas("High Class Teas A Speciality" she claims), cakes and soft drinks in the parlour, and Mr "Chas" Lumley repairing bicycles and offering bikes for hire. He also has a pigeon loft, and Mr Carter uses him as a valuable contact in tracing the owner of Swing-Wing(JB). Evidently the shop has long opening hours - Mr Wilkins is able to buy provisions for the "At Home" party from the cafe after the shops have shut(TW). The sweet-toothed Linbury Court fraternity will always have Mrs L's shop high on the list of priorities when a postal order arrives from home, as a much-needed break from the rigours of Mr Wilkins' maths project(JR), or when a treat is owed to one boy by another,even if the beneficiary is still expected to pay for his cream doughnuts and bottles of fizz(LI). Despite frequent visits by the boys, business is not brisk: **"On the rare occasions**

when customers called in for refreshment, they would sit round the little table in the window, after carefully shoo-ing a cat from each chair and removing Mr Lumley's spare waistcoats from the chair-backs(JA)." Our first meeting with this establishment is when Venables treats Jennings and Darbishire only to find he has left his money at school and has to hurry home for it. As a result, the boys end up eating far more than is good for them(JA). Jennings and Darbishire return to the Lumleys in order to hire bicycles from "Chas" to take them to Dunhambury to buy Matron a present, but soon regret their decision. As we are told, **It was a long time since anyone had hired one of his bicycles. Trade was not brisk in Linbury; and this was not surprising, for any luckless cyclist who had once spent an uncomfortable afternoon astride one of Mr Lumley's saddles was not likely to repeat the experience, if he could help it**(JD). Mrs Lumley's popularity in the community takes something of a battering when she is allowed to enter, and then wins, the cake-making competition at the village bazaar which strictly speaking is for amateurs: she collects an electric toaster for her beautiful cherry cake, even though her house is the only one in the village not to be wired for electricity(LJ)! Mrs Lumley is one of the many unwelcome guests at the school jumble sale and fails to endear herself to officialdom when she picnics in the library(JO).
In the opinion of the seventy-nine boarders of Linbury Court School, there was no one who could poach a tastier egg, bake a lighter cake or serve a jammier doughnut than Mrs C Lumley(LI).

Macready, Michael Denis M.A.(Lond.) School inspector who has the misfortune to visit Linbury on a day on which both Venables and Mr Wilkins have reason to believe inspectors of other kinds wish to visit them. At least the indignity of being addressed as a bus inspector and a police inspector is not as bad as being taken by Temple for the gasmeter reader and being treated accordingly. Thankfully, Jennings saves the situation with his masterly rendition, at Mr Macready's invitation, of six pages of late 13th century English history(TT).

MacTaggart There is an athlete by that name, also referred to as MacBonk, who is one of Jennings' Linbury contemporaries and who features early in the series as a fellow-competitor with Darbishire and Clarke, among others, in the half-mile run in the school sports(JF). However, right at the end of the series we meet a man by the same name(first name Tim) who was at school with General Merridew(and therefore must be some 50 years older than Jennings). His nickname, when at school, was Jumbo! Tim MacTaggart, at first mistaken for a badger baiter by the boys, tells them of the time capsule left by himself and General Merridew containing various Linbury artefacts from the 1940's. The discovery of the time capsule forms the basis of a slot in the school Drama Evening and re-unites the two Old Boys(TH).

Maggie A red-headed, serious-minded 12-year-old girl who is a talented clarinettist and class-mate of Emma Sparrow. She is enlisted to assist at the Animal Fair to raise money for Mrs Hockin's Retreat(JE).

Malapropisms Jennings' command of the English language, as well as that of his friends, is not always above reproach, particularly when it comes to long words. Anthony Buckeridge makes just as much humorous capital out of this as Richard Brinsley Sheridan in "The Rivals:"
"Please, sir, do you know anything about taximeters?"
"No, practically nothing."
"But I thought insects were your hobby, sir?" (JG)

"You're quite all right."
"Not even bucolic plague?"(JG)

"Oh, I don't mean its <u>really</u> killing me," the poet explained. **"You have to take the poem meteorologically, sir."**(JF)

"When you get past a certain age, you go bats. All grown-ups do; it's called, er -something like sea-lion." (JL)

"Anyway, no-one's voted against us, so that means Darbi and I are carried anonymously-er-umanimously-well, anyway, we've won twelve-nil, so that settles it."(AT)
Darbishire picked out a few of the coins for closer study.
"It's my latest hobby. It's called - er - what's the word. Something like rheumatics." (SO)

Markham, Cleo A West Indian girl from Trinidad with an **"irresponsible sparkle in her eyes and a happy knack of laughing her way through most of the problems of life."** A school colleague of Emma Sparrow, she masquerades as a fortune-teller in order to help raise money, at the so-called Animal Fair, for Mrs Hockin's Retreat. Her antics are fiercely condemned by Mrs Pratt(JE).

Marriott, George Area inspector of the London & Provincial Timber Preservation Company Limited, who having driven forty five miles to be

asked about woodworm in the attic and being told that a boy called
Jennings was the woodworm, still decides to inspect the attic; it is a
grateful Headmaster who is informed that there is still plenty of
woodworm about, and it should be seen to without delay; inadvertently,
Jennings has saved the day(JB).

Marshall A day-boy in the fourth form at Linbury, commuting to school
by bicycle with his friend Pettigrew. He plays a small but not insignificant
part in the catalogue of misunderstandings which infuriate PC Honeyball
when Jennings calls on him one evening(JD), and probably unwittingly
helps to provide camouflage for Jennings as he slips away, disguised
as Pettigrew, to have aerosol removed from his hair(TJ). Somewhat
confusingly, there is a boy named Marshall - we know not if it is the
same Marshall - in Form Three, who with his friend Frost chooses
roof insulation as his subject for Mr Wilkins' maths project(JR). See
also the entry for Pettigrew.

Martin-Jones, A.L. There is some uncertainty as to which form this
Linbury boy is in; one book has him as a sandy-haired fourth
former(AT) whereas other books(TJ) suggest he is one of Jennings'
colleagues in Form Three. He is a close friend of Parslow, has a
hearty appetite, demonstrated by his fear that their late arrival back
at school will deprive them of tea(LJ), and is cynical about the value
of bazaars(LJ). He enjoys football; this manifests itself in his playing
for the 2nd XI - which means he is also part of a subsequent search
party and rather peeved when the search for Jennings is over(JA)!
His enjoyment of football extends to his selecting a World Football
Eleven to play Mars(AT), and his giving Bromwich an injury which
leads to Jennings believing he has contracted an infectious disease
from Bromwich(EJ). He is at various times Honorary Secretary of the
Firework Fund(TJ); a keen cellist, to the extent of wanting to take his
cello on a camping trip(JE); a pop music enthusiast(JO); an enthusiastic
home-made-telephone creator(AU); officer in charge of "Beetles and
Small Stuff" in the Natural History Club(FI); a stamp-collector,
especially of stamps from South Africa because his uncle went there
once(OF); proficient long-jumper, coming in second in the school
sports(JF); with his friend Paterson, a tree-house-creator wishing to
supplement his new dwelling with rope ladder, air cushion and string
hammock(JL); and inky blotting paper flicker(AT). Only on rare
occasions does he play a prominent part in the action. He is the
owner of a pair of field glasses through which a coypu is apparently
"nearly" seen(LI); he rescues Matron's cat following a night-time fire

alarm(TW); he is the prompt for the ill-fated "Miser's Secret(OF);" he leads the demand to know what is happening to the Jennings Membership Club subscriptions(EJ); and he agrees that the destruction of the school is too big a price to pay for missing a history lesson(LI). He has his moments of imbecility; his essay on milk yield turns into an account of Battling Broadside, the rampant bull(LI) and he carries on a senseless conversation with Temple in the "language of Maths(LI)."

Mary The housemaid with a penchant for giggling who interrupts the Headmaster's lesson with Form Three to inform Jennings that Mr Russell has come to see him(JF).

Matron The Matron we meet early on is described as **"brisk and business-like....had little sympathy with junk-filled pockets and hair that would not be parted**(JG)**"** and with her customary energy and vigour stops Jennings playing against Bretherton House school in the First Eleven(JG). In the third book in the series(JL) she is replaced by a much friendlier, more tolerant woman - a young, attractive nursing sister who has a caring and understanding manner and who is sympathetic towards the boys in her care. Because of this, the boys, especially Jennings, will often turn to her in a crisis for advice and guidance. She is more concerned for Jennings' welfare than annoyed about his conduct when she finds he has fallen into the pond(JL); she provides cold cream for Jennings after he has wedged a bowl over his head while pretending to be a spaceman(AT); she successfully intercedes on Jennings' behalf to prevent punishment for losing Mr Wilkins' markbook(JD), and on Dormitory 4's behalf when Mr Wilkins wants to disqualify them from the "tidy dorm" competition she has instituted for cleaning up after lights-out(LI); she cures Jennings' twisted-belt-buckle-itis(AT); she helps remove Darbishire's false moustache(OF); she provides costumes for Jennings' Henry V scene in the end-of-term entertainment(OF); she takes responsibility for disciplining Dormitory 4 herself after one outbreak of disorder, rather than handing them over to Mr Wilkins and inevitably more severe punishment(EJ); she provides dry socks for Jennings after Venables' amateurish and disastrous attempts to wash another pair for him(LI); she willingly accepts Jennings' bath salts even though she cannot stand their verbena scent(JI); she takes a tolerant view of the chanted end-of-term slander about the standard of food provided(JD); she helps clothe the boys' guy(TJ); she provides a clinical thermometer to help monitor Old Sleepy's journey out of hibernation(JR); she convinces a doubting Mr Wilkins that Jennings has a genuine excuse for poor performance in a history test(JD); she comforts Jennings when he believes a bicycle shortage will prevent him going on a school picnic(FI); and she helps Mr Wilkins to see the funny side of driving his car to Linbury to report a lost cat when the animal is sitting in his car all the time(LJ). The boys are always anxious to repay her kindness. They may cycle out towards Dunhambury to buy her a present with a postal order from home(JD); they may present her with a temperamental alarm clock(AT); they will feel intensely guilty about having to deceive her, and will wish to shield from her any particularly nefarious activity they have indulged in for fear of losing her sympathy, hence, for instance, the secret dry-cleaning expedition(JO); they may offer to help sort out her medicine cupboard(EJ); and when Aunt Angela's present to her for caring for her nephew is prematurely consumed, they may club together to provide an interesting mixed assortment(EJ). She plays a pro-active role in Linbury Court life, serving meals, running the sewing room, organising a coffee party for Mr Hind's birthday(TT), ensuring that the boys are smartly turned out with bags properly packed before they are allowed to leave the premises at half-term and at the end of term(EJ, JD) and dealing with the gap left by the departing cook Mrs Cherry(JO). She is nobody's fool; she can tell a genuine illness from one designed to dodge a maths test(JD); even though she seldom punishes boys, she will report misdemeanours to masters when occasion demands; she is not taken in by dubious claims of virtuous conduct designed to help win the competition she has instituted for the tidiest dormitory(LI);and she is unimpressed by Darbishire's medical casework, particularly his diagnosis of a twisted buckle as housemaid's elbow(AT). With Mr Carter, she is the best-loved character in the series.

Matthews, Miss A school cook, and evidently the replacement for Mrs Cherry at Linbury Court, although evidently unlike her predecessor she does not double up as housekeeper(SO). Although she starts well, by preparing sausage and mash and pancakes for the boys within minutes of being appointed(JO), and allowing Jennings and Darbishire to assist in breakfast preparation which leads to the formation of the Jennings Membership Club, she later has to sack them for using dinner trolleys as chariots, and further antagonises her customers by her treatment of boiled beef(EJ). However, Darbishire forgives her when she provides him with delicious ice-cream after he has helped Mrs Hackett lay the tea(JB).

Merridew, Diana Daughter in law of General Merridew who only decides to send her son Roger Merridew to Linbury after seeing him caked with mud and covered in scratches after his pondside adventures with his hapless juvenile hosts(JL).

****
"Darbishire, you're the world's ozardest oik. You've got no more idea of how to be a detective than a cabbage!"
"D'you mean no more idea than a cabbage has of how to be a detective, or than I of how to be a cabbage?" (JF)
****

Merridew, Lieut. General Sir Melville, Bart., DSO, MC Linbury Court's most distinguished Old Boy. An ex-military attache, he is tall, elderly, thin, and very upright with snowy hair, bushy eyebrows and a white handlebar moustache. An attender at Linbury towards the end of the nineteenth century(and therefore well over 100 years old at the end of the series)he is a moody man of uncertain temper. He is unimpressed with Linbury's current regime and hankers after the days of uninterrupted maths, Latin and physical jerks. A notable figure at Speech Day and similar gatherings, his stock 25-minute speech recounts what a duffer he was when a Linburian and always ends with a request for a half-holiday. The time capsule he created with MacTaggart(who reveals his nickname at school was Mildew) and unearthed by Jennings and his friends reveals he was punished for fighting, impertinence and talking with his mouth full(TH); he is delighted to repeat the shutting of a master in the school library by tying the doorhandle to the school bell, although he is unimpressed when he himself is locked in the same room(AT). He is the unwitting foil for Leslie Perks' attempt to make off with the Linbury Court sports cups(JF); his gout allows Dr Hipkin to speak to the school and indirectly allows the Natural History club to display their creepy-crawlies(FI) and he is uncomplimentary about Mr Wilkins' sports jacket(TJ). The Headmaster eats out of his hand; it is the Head's desire to show his school as whiter than white which puts Roger, his grandson, off the idea of coming, and it is left to Jennings to save the day in his own inimitable way(JL).

Merridew, Roger Impetuous and boisterous grandson of General Merridew whose reaction to the spotlessly clean Linbury Court is "Huh!" In terms of temperament he is not dissimilar to Richmal Crompton's William. Jennings and Darbishire convert him to the joys of Linbury after a highly illegal journey to the huts which are then out of bounds(JL). Despite his mother's subsequent application for him to become a pupil at Linbury Court, he is never heard of again!

Miller's Wood This woodland, separated from Linbury Court by a meadow, is the scene of discovery of the mysterious stranger Dr

Tiddyman(LJ). Despite its possibilities for adventure, it is only mentioned in one other book, where its overgrown copses are mentioned as a focus for exploration for the boys on summer Sunday afternoons(TY).

Misunderstandings Anthony Buckeridge is a master at exploiting the pitfalls of conversational English:

"Bod's got a super-wizzo frog; it's got sort of yellow spot things all down its back."
"And is Mr Carter giving you your pocket money every week?"
"Yes...He keeps it behind the boot lockers."
"Behind the boot lockers?" echoed his father. "It doesn't sound a very safe place to me."
"Oh, it can't get away," Jennings explained. "It's in a cardboard box with moss and wet leaves." (JG)
"Wacko! There's a whole pile of letters for me," Jennings cried excitedly. "And three parcels. The big one's my cake and the square fat one's probably Aunt Angela."
Darbishire peered at the parcel through dusty spectacles. "Don't be crazy; she couldn't be that shape unless she'd been cremated."(JA)

"A plate of home-made cakes and doughnuts and three bottles of fizzy ginger-pop, please," Venables ordered importantly.
Darbishire followed Mrs Lumley's slow plod back to the kitchen with anxious eyes. "I hope she steps on it," he observed.
"There won't be much left of the doughnuts if she does. She's got shoes like violin cases," Jennings pointed out. (JA)
"I know enough to recognise a chariot wheel when I see one. I'd say this was a pretty old specimen - circa fifty-five BC."
Darbishire looked puzzled. "Circa?" he queried.
"Yes, that's Latin. It means round."
"Well, of course it's round. You don't have to be a brain at Roman history to know they didn't have square wheels."(JD)

"Yes, and we ought to have a fanfare, too, for when the king comes on."
Jennings looked puzzled. "What, roundabouts and coconut shies and things? You wouldn't find those at the Battle of Agincourt!"(OF)
"A second course, perhaps, that he was going to keep under his hat until after we'd finished the stew."
"Under his hat!" It seemed a queer hiding-place for a dozen fancy cakes.(TT)

"I've only got up to 'The Jolly Sailor Boy' in `Easy Pieces for Little Fingers."

"No-one's asking you to play it! What I'm trying to tell you is that there's a gramophone record of that piece in the music room."

"What, `The Jolly Sailor Boy'?"

"No, you clodpoll. Beethoven's Minuet in G."(AU)

"Yes, well I thought he might be a harmless old tramp last Sunday, just as the others did, but I've been thinking it over and I'm pretty sure he isn't one any longer."

Darbishire looked puzzled. "You mean he's given it up during the week?"(LJ)

"Passing off as his own work an essay in French written by a native."

"Oh, no, this boy isn't a native, sir. He hasn't got a tom-tom or anything like that."(EJ)

"Like old Wordsworth was nattering about."

"Who?"

"Mr Carter read us one of his poems in English," Jennings explained.

"I didn't know Mr Carter had written any poems in English."

"Not Mr Carter's poems, you clodpoll - old Wordsworth's! And I didn't mean a poem in English, either."

"No? What language did he write it in then?"(JI)

"Thirty seven point nine recurring chaps believe that there may be life on Mars."

"What are recurring chaps?"(JR)

"I saw your overcoat and I thought it was my Head coming up the street."

The man was baffled. "You thought my overcoat was your head?"(SO)

Dear Mr MacTaggart

We think you will be surprised to know that the tin box you buried with General Merridew has been found as I think you will be surprised to know...

"You can't say that," Darbishire criticised. "He DIDN'T bury General Merridew. He's still alive."(TH)

Even the staff are susceptible to it:

"Robinson thought the woodworm was Jennings?" he queried.

"No, no! The other way about. Robinson thought Jennings was the woodworm. He wrote his name on the beam, you see."
"Who did - Robinson?"(JB)

Money Like Billy Bunter of Greyfriars School, Jennings often finds himself relying on generous postal orders to see him out of what would otherwise be insuperable financial difficulties - for instance, the availability of only fourpence to replace a glass cucumber frame(JL), only 25p to replace two tennis rackets(TY), and still less cash available to buy a present for Darbishire, after Jennings has found his bank balance stands **"at the depressing figure of minus sixpence(TW)."** However, when the supply of postal orders dries up, other more ingenious methods have to be called upon, such as the proposed sale of first editions of Form Three's Latin text book(JA); the use of empty lemonade bottles and grimy stamps to pay for goods in the village post office(TT, JI); the proposed purchase of a 50p fishing rod on HP, or, failing that, advertising of goods for sale at Linbury Stores, such as Jennings' football boots(SO); the bartering of prized possessions to obtain other items from colleagues(TW); or the sale of what Jennings believes to be a Penny Black to solve the problems caused by distributing all the stamps on the approval sheet provided by S & S Boddington(OF). Despite such ingenuity, generous cash gifts from home or even loans of half-sovereigns(SO) may be the only way to finance activity that would otherwise be impossible - e.g. purchase of a fishing rod(SO), foxing to Valenti's on the bus(JG), or the bicycle ride towards Dunhambury(JD); but Jennings is completely thrown when his Aunt Angela sends him a new arithmetic book instead of rather than as well as the postal order he is expecting from her(LI)! It is not surprising that when entrusted with the Jennings Membership Club subscriptions, Jennings has little idea what to do with them, and is only rescued by Mr Carter's suggestion that the surplus go for famine relief(EJ). The raising of money for famine relief, in many ingenious ways, from sale of copyright in an essay to flogging a honky-tonk piano, forms the basis of the whole of a subsequent book(TJ), and a large part of another book is devoted to raising funds for Mrs Hockin's Retreat, including an Animal Fair and sponsored Relay Trot(JE).

Mudd, Alfred Hubert See entry for Borrowmore, Irving.

Mummery's The individual or company responsible for providing the Mammoth Amusements which relieve Jennings and Darbishire of two shillings and sixpence for rides and refreshment, but make up for it by providing them with a cutglass vase as a prize to take back for Matron as a present(JD).

Nicknames There is a positive surfeit of nicknames in the early titles, but the craze tends to peter out as the series goes on, and those that remain tend to be simply the shortening of existing surnames. The only ones that stick are "Jen"(for Jennings), "Darbi"(for Darbishire),"Ven"(for Venables),"Atki"(for Atkinson), "Bromo"(for Bromwich), "Old Wilkie"(for Mr Wilkins) and the"Archbeako"(for the Headmaster). Temple's nickname,"Bod," appears early on(JG, JL)but does not last; neither does Mr Carter's nickname, "Benedick," derived from his use of the word "Benedicata" at grace before meals!(JG) Robinson temporarily becomes "Old Pyjams," to distinguish him from the night porter Hawkins - known as "Old Nightie," but before long Robinson becomes known as "Old Robo!" MacTaggart is "MacBonk," Flittonborough major is "Flybow," Binns major is "Binnski," Stoddington is "Hippo," Pettigrew is known as "Petters," Martin-Jones becomes "Jonah" in one story only(JD), and similarly, Rumbelow becomes "Rumbo" just once(EJ). Hodges, the Bracebridge pupil, answers to the name of "Fliplugs" and he in turn refers to his Bracebridge headmaster as "Pinky" Parkinson(TJ). When two Old Boys get together they refer to each other as "Jumbo" and "Mildew," and discuss a teacher they refer to as "Wiggy."

Nutt, Mr Peter Doubtless forever cursing his parents' insensitivity over their choice of initial for his first name, Mr Nutt of East Brinkington is the winner of the second prize in the Bowling For A Pig - a jar of bath salts. He kindly agrees to take the pig in exchange - an agreement which seems ideal until Jennings presents Matron with the salts and is then told a drawing pin has got mixed up in them(JI).

Nuttall Linbury Court pupil who one tends to meet out of class. He has a keen ear for harmony and is critical of Mr Wilkins' piano playing(JG); he takes the corner kick which leads to Jennings' winning goal in his first 1st XI game(JG); he is in the half-mile line-up with Darbishire(JF) and the 2nd XI football team which goes on a nocturnal search of Jennings(JA); he is a keen bug-hunter(TY); he suggests taking a few more bottles of fizzy drink on a school picnic so everyone can have 3 each(TY); his hut boasts two plastic mugs and a flag on a pole(JL); he enjoys chess; he joins Martin-Jones and Bromwich to scavenge for replacement chocolates for Matron's mixed assortment(EJ); and, with Johnson, is frightened of being infected by Bromwich's bruised ankle(EJ).

O'Connor, Dr Bernard PhD, FRMetS Climatologist whom Jennings meets on the London Underground. By co-incidence Jennings is on a school trip to the Metropolitan Museum to see an exhibition devoted to ecological matters. Jennings recovers the doctor's wallet from the umbrella where a thief has secreted it. He is rewarded with a meal from a take-away sandwich bar, and, later on, a maple tree for the school grounds(AG).

****

"I read a story once, where the police raided a jeweller's shop, but they heard them coming, and hid all the booty in a trice."
"Hid it in a what?"
"A trice," Jennings repeated. "I suppose it's a secret cupboard, or something."(JF)
****

Old Linburians The most famous Old Linburian, and the only one to appear regularly in the stories, is the crusty General Merridew, but there are allusions to several others, most of them being fondly recalled when the General tries to introduce his daughter in law and grandson to the joys of Linbury Court. These include "Tubby" Tickner, "Pie-face" Pottinger, "Bone-head" Blatterweather and "Tadpole" Fitzarchway, who appeared with the General in the 1895 school photograph, as well as "Pongo" Bannerdale whose long-hop caused the General to hit a cricket ball clean through the headmaster's study window. Jennings' recital of part of the school honours board to Roger Merridew reveals a number of high achievers in Linbury's past, including R.K. Blenkinsop, G.H. Johnson, C.L.N. Herbert-Jones and B.A. Dadds. Atkinson finds himself in hot water for trying on the General's black homburg hat, but when the General sees it, he recalls with considerable pleasure that a similar act was perpetrated by Blatterweather in 1897(JL)! We are told that the Old Boys receive a copy of the school magazine and thus get to hear, inter alia, about Jennings' conjuring exploits(JO). Memories of Linbury in days past are revived for General Merridew when he is locked in the library, and he recalls the day he did just the same thing to his Latin master in 1897(AT), and further memories are stirred right at the end of the series, when Jennings sees Tim MacTaggart searching for the time capsule he left buried in the school grounds. It is the discovery of the time capsule which prompts the boys to write a play involving the two Old Boys - Tim MacTaggart and also General Merridew - who prepared and buried the capsule(TH).

Old Sleepy Name given by Jennings to the hedgehog discovered by him and Darbishire whilst on a school walk. Jennings is so concerned for the animal's welfare that he recovers him and brings him indoors, and, as with Swing-Wing(JB) spends much time and effort keeping the animal's existence and whereabouts a secret from officialdom. It is the anticipated awakening of Old Sleepy from hibernation which provides a fascinating afternoon for the two boys in the company of Mr Laxton, and an enjoyable project with which to impress parents on Open Day(JR).

Olivera, Madame Anatolia Alter ego of Miss Tubbs(see separate entry).

Openshaw, Mr Photographer from the Dunhambury firm of Scuttlewell and Openshaw which specialises in weddings and studio portraits; however Mr Openshaw also visits Linbury Court to take a panoramic photo of the boys and staff for the annual school photograph. Jennings manages to appear in it twice(AG).

Our Friend Jennings(OF) Seventh book in the series, first published by William Collins in 1955, 256 pp. Dedicated to Geoffrey Wincott, **"whose skilful portrayal of Mr Carter in Jennings At School has delighted so many listeners to Children's Hour."** The first book to benefit from Douglas Mays' illustrations; Mays was to illustrate all but two of the remaining Collins publications in the series(not counting the compilation or paperback editions)as well as provide dustjacket and frontispiece illustrations.

Synopsis
Chapter 1 - Bargains By Post - Mr Wilkins' insistence that Jennings and Darbishire do something useful with their spare time leads them to take up stamp-collecting.

Chapter 2 - On Approval - Stamps, ordered by the boys from mail-order dealers, arrive. Jennings distributes them among his friends but fails to realise they need to be paid for if retained.

Chapter 3 - Cross Country - Jennings and Darbishire interrupt their cross-country run to help a cow back on to Arrowsmith's land. Mrs A does not appreciate the gesture.

Chapter 4 - Transport Problem - The

boys, having incurred Mr Wilkins' wrath for their slow progress, take the bus home and infuriate him even more.

Chapter 5 - Lucky Break - In attempting to retrieve the stamps, Jennings discovers what he believes to be a genuine Penny Black.

Chapter 6 - The Penny Black - The priceless stamp blows away after Jennings has promised vast rewards with the proceeds of same.

Chapter 7 - The Penny Red - The stamp, when recovered, is found to be red. Bromwich plus paintbox is the culprit.

Chapter 8 - Jennings Switches On - Mrs Arrowsmith's peace-offering - chestnuts - results in a disastrous cooking session in the school boiler room.

Chapter 9 - First Rehearsal - The boys' home-made play, the Miser's Secret, making use of Darbishire's new false moustache,suffers some early setbacks.

Chapter 10 - Half Term - Uncle Arthur's half-term treat consists of a trip to the cinema - which is strictly verboten.

Chapter 11 - Hide and Seek - The boys' efforts to first find their cinema seats, and then escape the gaze of their teachers, do not meet with unqualified success.

Chapter 12 - Treat In Store - Jennings returns to school minus cap, and finds the school half-term treat is to go back to the cinema two days later to see the same film again.

Chapter 13 - Doubtful Treat - The expedition is exposed to official eye, but the boys' nightmarish experiences are deemed to be punishment enough.

Chapter 14 - Change of Plan - The loss of Darbishire's moustache seals the doom of the Miser's Secret as far as the school's end-of-term entertainment is concerned, and Shakespeare goes on the menu instead, with Mr Wilkins playing the lead.

Chapter 15 - Panic Behind The Scenes - Mr Wilkins realises he cannot do the part but needs a pretext for dropping out.

Chapter 16 - Curtain Up - Such a pretext is found when it is discovered there is no suitable costume available - but special guest Irving Borrowmore, who Mr Wilkins forgot to cancel, saves the day.

"How about collecting foreign stamps?" he suggested.
"Yes, we'd like to do that, sir," Jennings agreed. "The only snag is we haven't got any and..."
"Well, don't waste time making speeches about it. Go and collect some at once!"

"Aha! I recognise you," he began woodenly. "I presume you are my deadly enemy, Mr Percy Robinson, who is hoping to steal the secret

hoard of banknotes which I have just hidden under the floorboards at 231 High Street, are you not?"

Parkinson, Mr Headmaster of Bracebridge School. A portly, genial, thinning man with sandy hair and a generous moustache, his mistake about the quarantine period for German measles causes Mr Wilkins to prematurely cancel the match which would have seen Jennings' First Eleven debut(JG). Later on he remarks jovially about Jennings' bizarre choice of footwear for his visit to Bracebridge, and disappoints Fliplugs by revealing that Jennings has not, as first thought, drained the swimming pool. We will thus never know if Fliplugs was exaggerating when he prophesied that "Pinky" Parkinson would do his nut, blow his top and jettison his booster, when he heard what had happened(TJ).

Parslow Major Goalkeeper in the match in which Jennings makes his debut for the school, threatened with punishment for losing his football socks that have not been name-taped by his mother(JG). He is also favourite for Throwing The Cricket Ball(JF), and a member of the 2nd XI side which has to form a search party to locate Jennings and Darbishire(JA). We learn that by coincidence he is on the sick list at the same time as two colleagues sharing his Christian name of Robin(TT). With his friend Evans he chooses a Linbury traffic census as his subject for Mr Wilkins' maths project(JR).

Paterson Form 4 boy and goalkeeper in Jennings' first practice match who graciously allows our more generously clad hero to take over in goal and thus begin the long path to the First Eleven(JG). We see him later on as a hut-dweller-cum-rope-ladder-maker(JL), cricket-bat oiler(JI), and together with Brown, a member of a fictional footballing side used by Darbishire in a vain bid to distract Mr Wilkins with a complex question about the laws of the game(JA). His rebuke to Jennings for posing with Form 4 boys for the panoramic school photo results in Jennings appearing in the picture twice(AG).

Perce Train driver who together with his younger colleague, fireman Cyril and brake-van custodian George, assist in conveying Jennings and Darbishire to Dunhambury after travelling in the wrong part of the train and finding themselves stranded just outside Southaven(LJ).

Perks, Leslie The criminal laundryman who makes off with the school sports cups and nearly ruins the school's sports day(JF).

Perry See entry for Alsop.

Pettigrew A third-former, but friend of 4th-former Marshall. Like Marshall, Pettigrew is a dayboy and cyclist. He is plump and frecklefaced. Pettigrew's dayboy status enables him to bring Jennings fishing tackle from home(SO); the availability of Pettigrew's bike, despite the fact that it has a slow puncture, enables Jennings to pay a visit to PC Honeyball regarding his lost diary(JD), and assists Jennings in obtaining a priceless first-day cover stamp, even if the bike is taken without his permission and he believes it to have been stolen(JI). Similarly, his bright cape and again his day-boy status help Jennings to disappear into Dunhambury one afternoon for an emergency haircut(TJ). Pettigrew is a member of the Drake House junior swimming team of which Jennings is captain(AT) and is also no mean cricketer, going in with Jennings as opening batsman for Drake House in one Junior House match(JB)and with Martin-Jones in another(TH). Inevitably, his nickname is "Petters." Although he is admonished by Mr Wilkins for not keeping his cap on straight(LI), he wins the Form Four prize for General Progress and has a slight mishap as he leaves the rostrum, kicking his prize into the audience(FI) and in the same book together with Marshall saves the picnic outing by producing the correct hamper. With Marshall he helps to create an impressive Guy Fawkes Night bonfire with the contents of all the waste-paper baskets(TJ). Whilst not engaged on other matters, he enjoys taking part in space games(AG) and practising handstands(TY).

Pink, Walter, and Mrs Wally Pink, of 3 Church Lane, Linbury, a be-spectacled, red-haired, heavily tattoo-ed man in his late twenties, is the only named "villain" in the whole series, and even then he is described as a **"willing worker for good causes."** However he is known as somebody not to be trusted with cash, and he is also guilty of the theft of two new tyres and a two-gallon tin of paint. It is unfortunate that his ad for a fishing rod, which he has also stolen and which he is offering for 50p, should be read by the naively trusting Jennings and Darbishire. They are unable to pay 50p immediately to him, so they provide a valuable half-sovereign as security - a silly thing to do, as that is soon converted to cash. Eventually, the intervention of Richard Rodgers, from whom the rod has been stolen, and Mr Donaldson the water-bailiff, spurs Wally to take steps to recover the all-important coin and determine to go straight in future. By contrast, we hear that his mother, with whom he lives, is a respectable, hard-working member of the community, and Wally is a constant worry to her(SO).

****
"Yes, I remember you; name of Copeland? ...Campbell?
...Culpepper?...Something like that."
"Carter."
"That's it! Never forget a name or face." He nodded approvingly at his
own remarkable powers of memory.(AT)
****

Pinmill, Mrs Ethel   One of the gang of bargain-hunters which
unexpectedly descends on Linbury Court; as one who normally resented
the threepenny entrance money, a free jumble sale is too good an
opportunity to miss. She proves a valuable right-hand man(or woman?)
for Bertha Clough(JO).

Plackett   See entry for Alsop.

Plumrose, Mrs Ada   Together with Prudence Pratt, an occupant of
Gaitskell Court, the south-east London block of flats in which we meet
animal-lover Emma Sparrow. Both women are professional busy-bodies,
constantly complaining to Mr Fagg about the sins committed by fellow
tenants, and are also experts at moaning, gossip and scandalmongering.
However, they are gracious enough to attend the Animal Fair, largely
because the Fair is being graced by the presence of the Mayor(JE).

Poetry
"A merry Christmas with lots of good cheer
From yours truly C.E.J. Darbi-SHIRE."(AU)

"Hark how the feathered songster sings,
As it flies on rumpty-tumpty wings."(FI)

"We're tired of Maths and we're tired of French
Leaving Latin will be no wrench
No more of Wilkie's super bates
When once I'm out of these prison gates."(JG)

'Excuse our breaking into song
Believe you me, it won't last long.
We'll let off steam and then we'll stop.
Either that or we'll blow our top."(JE)

Pottlewhistle Halt   The remote downland railway station at which

Jennings and Darbishire leave the train after Jennings erroneously thought he had lost his glove. Despite its remoteness, the station is staffed and information provided by the porter enables the search party to gain a rough idea where the missing persons are. The author does not miss out on the humorous possibilities of the station name:

"It's either Whistlehalt Pottle or Pottlehalt Whistle," he muttered to himself.

"Oh, hullo, Enquiries! Can you put me through to a station called Whistlepott Hortle, please? What's that? There's no such place? Well, try Haltpottle Whistle, then(JA)."

The village of Pottlewhistle is only mentioned once more in the series, as being near the place of residence of one of Linbury's dayboys, Pettigrew(JD).

Pratt, Mrs Prudence See entry for Plumrose, Mrs Ada.

Pringle See entry for Stoddington R.K.

Public Transport Jennings seems to reserve some of his most infamous escapades for occasions on which he must travel by bus or by train. He starts as he means to go on, by antagonising a bus conductor on the way into Dunhambury during his attempted escape from the school(JG). The suspected loss of a glove on the way home from a football match causes Jennings and Darbishire to fail to alight from the train at Dunhambury and results in their discovering the delights of Pottlewhistle Halt and a full-scale search initiative by their colleagues(JA). A bus journey to Dunhambury to view the town's museum is enlivened by the presence on the vehicle of Jennings and Darbishire's rattling relic, an item they firmly believe to be an ancient chariot wheel(JD). It is the omnibus which enables Jennings to get out to East Brinkington to pursue enquiries about Swing Wing(JB); which conveys him, plus odorous overcoat, into town in search of Robin Laxton(JR); and which helps Jennings and Darbishire, much to the fury of Mr Wilkins, to complete their cross-country run in reasonable time, even if the bus takes them two stops too far(OF). The first quarter of one book is entirely devoted to Jennings' return to school by train(it is interesting to note that he started from London when we know that he already lives in Sussex where Linbury is also situated!) and the hair-raising consequences of banishing himself to a part of the train that is destined not to complete the journey, resulting in a free ride on the brake van - all this after he has hidden under the seat to avoid being apprehended for travelling without possession of a valid ticket(LJ).

Jennings travels with his classmates by train to see an ecological exhibition in London - how could an environment-conscious school party take a motor coach! - and is responsible for a heroic act on the London Underground(AG). Incidentally, in the same book we learn that Linbury has a disused railway line; we must assume the Beeching axe fell before the series started(AG).

The Company's Regulations did not say how one should deal with passengers who folded themselves up and mouthed at you and hoped to know their destination in the near future(JG).

Pudworth Station on the other side of Dunhambury from London and collecting point for milk-wagons, where Jennings' and Darbishire's "special train" is bound(LJ).

Pullen, Mr Dunhambury man who comes over to Linbury Court once a week to teach woodwork. He tells poor Rumbelow that **"you don't know one end of a screwdriver from the other"** and refuses to allow him to take his bird-table home at the end of term after ten weeks was spent creating it(TH).

Punishment The misdemeanours of Linburians frequently result in punishment. Anthony Buckeridge, unlike Angela Brazil, does not treat wrongdoing as so morally reprehensible that it threatens the honour of the school, although Jennings is on occasion susceptible to a red stripe in the conduct book against his House. Corporal punishment is applied in one book(JF)and the boys come within a hair's breadth of it in another(JL), but in such a circumspect manner that the reader might be forgiven for missing it altogether. On at least one occasion Jennings is said to have spent an uncomfortable time in the headmaster's study, and one can only speculate as to what form that discomfort might have taken(TW)! Although confiscations of property, bans from games and other treats, and/or detentions are frequently used, some punishments are ingenious to say the least, such as Mr Wilkins' cancellation of a school football match which rudely backfires on him(JG), and making Jennings learn six pages of history, which turns a lesson observed by a school inspector into an unexpected success(TT). Some are humiliating, such as Jennings being made to eat his meals in silence for a week following a prune-hunting expedition(TT), and partakers of an illegal Sunday afternoon adventure being made to join the Form I crocodile every Sunday for the rest of term(JL). Some are commendably imaginative, such as the probation order imposed on Jennings and Darbishire by Mr Carter(JL), or the community service orders handed down by the

Headmaster in the form of garden weeding, leaf-sweeping, litter-scavenging, tree planting and pitch-rolling(AG, JI). An illicit visit to the cinema results in Jennings being punished by having to miss what for him would be a third helping of the same film, and Darbishire being punished by having the third helping inflicted on him(OF). Some hit the pocket; orders for compensation following the defacing of a text book(JF) or soiling of a suit(JL) do Jennings' bank balance few favours. Margaret Wilkins would argue that sitting in Mrs Lumley's parlour eating endless quantities of doughnuts and pop consititute a much worse punishment than any detention(JA). Buckeridge never moralises, however, and does not use the books as a vehicle for trying to instil impeccable behaviour into his readers; as he says, **good conduct was an attitude of mind, rather than blind obedience to a list of rules**(JL). Even Mr Wilkins acknowledges **"It's got to stop somewhere**(AG).**"** On his first night at the school, Darbishire is terrified at the spinechilling punishments Temple inventively attributes to the masters at his new school: **"Don't you know that the angles at the base of an isosceles triangle are jolly nearly equal? Write it out a hundred and fifty million times before tea**(JG).**"** Jennings' first of many punishments is being made to stay in during football, although the sentence is soon remitted in full(JG). Darbishire succeeds in persuading Mr Wilkins to let Jennings off a punishment as his birthday present to his friend(JA). When Mr Wilkins seeks to reward Jennings for a rare good deed, his suggestion that **"the next time I do anything wrong you could agree not to say anything about it"** is not well received(TT).

* * * * * * *

"And how long have you been here?" Jennings wanted to know.
"Me? Oh, I've been here donkeys' years. Ages and ages," said Atkinson, and his voice came from the mists of antiquity. "Well, two terms, anyway," he compromised.(JG)
* * * * * * *

Pyewacket Margaret Wilkins' Siamese cat, entrusted to her brother for a few days. One wet afternoon Jennings discovers it on the premises and believes it to be a stray, thus precipitating the involvement of the police. Mr Wilkins helpfully drives Jennings into Linbury not knowing the cat is in the basket that Jennings is holding(LJ).

Religion The Jennings stories are not "preachy" and are not underpinned with any religious premise. Nonetheless, we are made aware at both ends of the series that grace is said before meals(JG, TH); and that the pupils and staff of Linbury attend chapel;it is also said that the boys knew Linbury's Norman church well for the school often attended services there in term time(LJ). Indeed the school feels able to invite the vicar of Linbury to their charity firework party(TJ). Vainly the boys hope that having sung hymns of mercy and forgiveness, the Headmaster will see them after chapel and sympathise with the presence of a pig in the potting shed one Sunday morning(JI).

Robinson, Henry Otherwise known as Old Pyjams(to distinguish him from the night porter, Old Nightie) or Old Robo, Robinson is the general factotum at Linbury Court - cleaner, caretaker, odd-job man and dogsbody, often to be found either in his cottage or his toolshed. Jobs he is called upon to carry out include window cleaning, watering the cricket square(water which the boys believe to be rainfall(LI)), preparing baggage for transporting at the end of term(JG), changing the water in the swimming bath(JL), repainting the woodwork round the swimming bath(AT), seeing to the attic ballcock - which leads to the discovery of Jennings' activities with Swing-Wing(JB), cleaning the floors and thereby allowing newspapers to fall into his bucket in the process(JB), drainpipe painting - the required ladder being used by the boys to get on to the roof to search for cricket balls(JI), and struggling with combustible rubbish for his monthly bonfire (JI). We meet him in the very first chapter of the series, telling the boys there is not yet any soap in the washroom(JG). Introduced to us as a man in his early twenties, he is a methodical worker who prides himself on doing exactly as he is told. Although a kindly man always ready for a chat, he treats the boys with mistrust and is critical and suspicious of their behaviour and their motives. He tends to lock rooms when he is cleaning them; he will not hesitate to report suspicious behaviour to the master on duty. That is not to say that he does not bail the boys out on occasions; he provides paint for Darbishire to touch up the swimming pool cubicle he has inartistically smeared(AT); he provides paraffin for the boys to brew tea for the masters on what proves to be a highly temperamental cooking stove(TY); he rescues Venables' gerbils after they have gnawed their way out of captivity(SO); he provides replacement glass for a cucumber frame Jennings has shattered(JL); he helps Mr Carter unearth the time capsule left by Tim MacTaggart(TH); he provides a shuttle service of refreshments when the huts are re-opened(JL); and he creates paraffin flares and provides bonfire material for Guy Fawkes Night celebrations(TJ). Sometimes his devotion to duty produces problems for the boys. His assertion that the spider in the bunch of bananas is poisonous puts the boys on red alert(JG); his lack of understanding of First Day Covers puts the boys' stamp-collecting endeavours in peril(JI); and his tidying-up leads to the temporary disappearance of all the letter E's in Jennings' printing outfit(JA), as well as prompting the belief that Jennings has been eating poisonous toadstools(JO) and a tankful of tadpoles has hatched into a crowd of frogs(FI).

Rocker See entry for Barney.

****

Half-way through the second lesson Mr Wilkins began to send out tremors indicating that an earthquake might be expected at short notice. Form Three regarded this as a promising sign; it meant that the rest of the morning would teem with interest, always provided, of course, that someone else received the brunt of the attack. (JG)
****

Rogers, Richard Frederick Angler of a stout and pompous nature, whose fishing rod is stolen by Wally Pink and who discovers the rod, at that time in Jennings' custody, whilst out for the afternoon with Mr Donaldson. With Mr Donaldson, he traces the true thief(SO).

Ronnie Miss Thorpe's young blue-jeaned assistant at the Linbury fete who produces the pig which Jennings so thoughtlessly won, to be conveyed to Mr Arrowsmith's farm(JI).

Rudkin, Major Obnoxious and cantankerous landowner at Southcombe. His property adjoins that of Mrs Hockin at the Retreat, and whilst she is busy caring for animals he is busy shooting them, barring lawful rights of way, and insisting on Mrs Hockin's erecting a fence she is in no position to finance(JE).

Rumbelow, D.W. Podgy, red-haired, freckled Form Three boy, nicknamed Rumbo, who frequently pops in and just as quickly out of the Linbury Court action. His hut is called the Cosy Nook and a hole therein is blocked up with a school text book(JL). He is responsible for Odd Jobs and Fodder in the Natural History club(FI). His deployment of his newly acquired space gun prompts a ban on such items which gets Jennings out of a tricky predicament(EJ). He is a 2nd XI footballer and one of the party searching for Jennings and Darbishire on the South Downs(JA), and he searches for Jennings down the coal-hole when the latter goes missing after being named in the 2nd XI cricket team(LI). He enjoys improvising, creating binoculars out of 2 lemonade bottles with sticky tape(LI), table-tennis, impromptu darts, using Jennings' pen which causes a broken nib and hence trouble for the owner(TT), leather work, piano-playing, teaming up with Atkinson on violin to perform the Fairies' Lullaby at the school concert(JO), impromptu cricket, sending a hard leather ball down which Darbishire's tennis racket cannot cope with(TY), model railways, being keen to take his railway set to camp(JE), photography, capturing Binns storming the ramparts of Dunhambury castle with his water pistol(TT), and after-dark telephoning from dormitory 6(AU). He has little understanding of the greenhouse effect(AG) but believes there is life on Mars with **"special little men with eight arms and legs**(JO)**."** He is not a good woodworker; Mr Pullen, the woodwork tutor, will not allow him to take his birdtable home and it thus becomes available for Jennings and his secret birdwatching society(TH).

Russell, Mr Salesman with a laugh like a railway engine, sent by Mr Catchpole to sell a 95-guinea movie camera to Jennings and somewhat taken aback to find his prospective client's credit balance is three and sevenpence. He sells the camera to the headmaster instead(JF).

Saltmarsh, John D. Experienced pigeon breeder, show judge, authority on different types of wildfowl, and birdwatcher, from Old Mill Farm, near Swaffham, Norfolk; it is the arrival of his racing pigeon at Linbury Court which causes excitement among the boys as they do their best to fend for the bird. The bird having obligingly returned to him, he provides the boys with a signed copy of his book,"Birds in their Habitat(JB)."

****
"I think there's a bus-stop somewhere along here."
For fifty yards they stumbled uncertainly; then Jennings bumped into
an obstruction which loomed up suddenly before his hazy gaze.
"I beg your pardon," he apologised to a post marked `Bus Stop,' and
again they moved on. (JG)
****

Saunders, F.J. The guinea pig which Atkinson receives as a present from his grandmother. Mr Wilkins rashly agrees to adopt it, but its voracious appetite and wanderlust bring Jennings and Darbishire into contact with it, culminating in adventures involving Matron's cat, cabbage-leaves and a parrot cage(TT).

School Life Temple was twanging soft notes on a guitar made from **elastic bands stretched across his pencil box; Atkinson was dredging**

pellets of blotting paper from his inkwell and using them to block up the cracks between the floorboards. Bromwich major was making a watch chain with paper clips and Venables was contorting his facial muscles in an effort to look like a slant-eyed oriental. It was, in short, an ordinary class waiting for the lesson to begin(JA).

Scuttlewell & Openshaw Dunhambury photographers entrusted with the Linbury Court school photograph(AG). See entry for Openshaw, Mr.

The Sea Early books leave us with little doubt that the sea is within walking distance of Linbury; one Sunday afternoon the duty master is told that some boys are walking to the sea(JL) and one of Jennings' more exotic adventures is a meeting with some generous Frenchmen in Linbury Cove(JA). However none of the Jennings stories use the sea as a source of schoolboy adventure and there are no references to the sea in later books.

Seymour, Mrs Jane Not the third wife of Henry VIII, but the Good Samaritan who assists the Sponsored Trot when the official accompanying transport breaks down,and who offers to bring her riding school to the Retreat to save Mrs Hockin from disaster(JE).

Fireman Short See entry for Archie Cuppling.

Similes Like P.G. Wodehouse before him, Buckeridge was a master of the simile. In the compilation volume, a whole section of the book was devoted to the more colourful ones.
At the moment, however, there was no sign of the golden streak, and he clumped down the stairs with the ill-humour of a bull in a cattle truck.(AT)
Angry now, Mr Wilkins heaved at the door-handle like the anchor-man of a tug-o'-war team.(AT)
Before they could stop, the leader of the hot-footed chargers had skidded on to the slippery oil-bath where he floundered crazily like a clown in an ice-pantomime.(AT)
For as he opened the door, the misguided missile struck the lintel above his head, dropped neatly on to his right shoulder, and left him choking and gasping in a blinding blizzard of chalk dust, as thick as a snow storm on the South Col of Mount Everest.(AT)
"You look about as cheerful as a corncrake with chilblains."(AT)
Why, it was scarcely half an hour since she had treated their efforts to round up her livestock with the hostility of a sharp-shooting sheriff

dealing with wild west cattle rustlers!(OF)

The deep booming voice belonged to Mr Wilkins, and it appeared to be coming from below ground level, like some angry volcano giving warning of explosions to follow.(FI)

Mr Wilkins paused and took a deep breath. "I shall pounce! Suddenly, without warning- just like that - I shall pounce!" There came into Mr Carter's mind a fantastic vision of Mr Wilkins leaping out of the common room cupboard with a deep-throated roar, like a panther pouncing on its prey.(TW)

With shrill cries in the local dialect they advance upon the merchandise laid out upon the tables with the determination of the Assyrian coming down like a wolf on the fold.(JO)

Darbishire was so frightened that his knees trembled like a blancmange in a railway dining-car.(EJ)

Mr Wilkins emitted a sound like a medieval fowling-piece being discharged at the Battle of Agincourt.(JG)

Her voice, which was usually the trill of a thrush on a spring morning, now shrilled out like a myna bird protesting at the quality of the food in its feeding-dish.(TJ)

Slang   One of the most appealing aspects of the series is the unique schoolboy slang, devised by the author specially for the stories, and never to be forgotten amongst Jennings fans everywhere. Buckeridge said: "The slang is my own, in the main. When I wrote the first radio play I did make a terrible mistake of using current slang. If you can remember that far back, people were talking in sort of RAF wartime slang, `wizard prangs' and things like that, and I used some of these - and of course a few years later it was so dated it was embarrassing to read, so I cut out all that sort of thing and made up my own. `Clodpoll' is an Elizabethan word - Shakespeare uses it - so that can't very well date. `Fossilised fish-hooks,' that sort of thing, I make up myself, so it can't really date in the way that if you say something is `brill,' the next year it's going to be `great.' We don't have `decent chaps' any more, we have...well, I'm not quite sure what the modern equivalent is, but you don't have ordinary current slang because you know that it's going to date in a very short time."

Some examples:

"Temple and Atkinson were creating like blinko all through lunch."(AT)

"Oh, gosh, this <u>has</u> bished it up!" (JL)

"Don't be such a bogus ruin, Jen. You can't take a fish for a walk."(JL)

"One minute, they're in a supersonic bate and there's a hoo-hah going on..."(JL)

"He came stonking into the tuck-box room like a square dancing cart-horse just now and blew me up because I didn't know where you were."(JD)

"If you mean Venables and all that crush, they went stonking upstairs like a tribe of hippopotamuses about five minutes ago."(AT)

"You great, crumbling, addle-pated ruin, Jennings. You've forgotten to post it!"(JA)

"Of all the prehistoric clodpolls I ever met, you get the bronze medal for beetle-headedness," he said warmly.(JA)

"Oh, fish-hooks, this is frantic!"(JD)

"Pass down to Jennings that Old Wilkie's got him in his gunsights and he's going to action-stations after tea for a roof-level attack."(JD)

"Petrified paintpots! Hide, Jennings!" gasped Darbishire.(AT)

"Oh, how supersonic! This is going to be lobsterous fun."(AT)

"If you ask me, Jen, you've gone and landed yourself feet first in the most lobsterous hoo-hah since the Wars of the Roses."(AT)

"But Mr Wilkins hasn't <u>got </u>a model railway, you bat-witted clodpoll!"(AT)

"Honestly, Darbi, I've met some bat-witted clodpolls in my time, but I reckon you win the silver challenge cup for addle-pated beetle-headedness, against all comers!"(AT)

"Oh, fish-hooks! Some gruesome specimen has pinched my laces!"(OF)

"Oh, don't talk such dehydrated eyewash," Jennings answered impatiently.(OF)

"What a ghastly catastroscope," lamented his fellow-author. "Why do those gruesome hoo-hahs always have to pick on us to happen to?"(OF)

"Crystallised cheesecakes! I've got it!" he cried. "A supersonic brainwave, if ever there was one!"(TT)

"Go by boat! Wow, what a lobsterous wheeze!"(FI)

"Old Wilkie's in a ghastly bate."(TW)

"Just think what would happen if you went waltzing back to school, driving a massive great porker, all alive and kicking. The Archbeako wouldn't half create."(LJ)

"What! And get another dollop of punishment for leaving the room without per!"(LI)

"Honestly, Jen, you're the most shrimp-witted troll I ever met."(JO)

"What a ghastly shemozzle," he lamented.(EJ)

"We might have known we couldn't expect much help from a bat-brained, shrimp-witted clodpoll like Petters."(JI)

"You're crazy! I've heard some bat-witted wheezes in my time but this one takes the certificate of merit for genuine copper-bottomed lunacy."(JR)

"Don't talk such addle-pated eyewash."(AG)
"You're as beetle-headed as a cockroach!"(TH)

The earlier titles contain far more use of schoolboy slang than any of the other titles. As regards Buckeridge's admission that the language in the very first book became embarrassing to read, here are some examples from this book which were rarely, if ever, to re-appear:
"Oh, ozard egg!" he groaned.
Oh, prang! Oh, jolly g.! Oh, hefty ziggety door knobs!

"Witch prang!" exclaimed Jennings.
"What do you mean, which prang? There is only one."
"No, I don't mean which prang. I mean Witch Prang...It's the feminine of Wizard Prang."

Ironically, "hefty ziggety door knobs" was incorporated into the emasculated adaptation of JG the BBC Radio Collection, as a rare concession to the Buckeridge style(see separate section relating to Jennings in Sound and Vision).

Southaven Junction Railway station between London and Dunhambury where Dunhambury-bound trains are wont to divide, with the rear portion being detached and not completing the journey - as Jennings discovers to his detriment(LJ).

Southcombe Surrey village, less than 30 miles from London but successful in retaining its rural character. It is the venue for the boys' camping holiday, and the home of the good Mrs Hockin, the owner of the Retreat, as well as the unpleasant Major Rudkin(JE).

****
Mr Pemberton-Oakes went on to say that the practice of bombarding visitors with blackboard wipers and choking them in blizzards of chalk-dust was not, in his opinion, the best way of making people feel welcome in new surroundings.(SO)
****

Sparrow, Emma, Jane and Mr G.J. Family who live in 72 Gaitskell Court in south-east London, in the same block as Aunt Angela. Jennings befriends Emma, a thin, wiry, dark-haired, brown-eyed girl of roughly his age, when staying with his aunt, and discovers that she is the proud owner of a collection of animals she has rescued from neglect. She goes as far as to save a rabbit who she feels is suffering in a nearby pet shop. When Jennings inadvertently reveals to Mr Fagg that she keeps animals, she loses no time in evacuating them, at Jennings' suggestion, to the Retreat at Southcombe, and with Jennings' help organises a fair to raise funds for the Retreat. Her mother Jane, a nursing sister at the local hospital, is a friendly woman in her late thirties, and her father is a sub-officer at the fire station(JE). Emma Sparrow, with her friends Maggie and Cleo, are the only girls of Jennings' age or even Linbury Court School age to appear in any of the Jennings stories.

Speaking of Jennings!(SO) Twenty-second book in the series, first published by William Collins in 1973, 157 pp. Dedicated to R. & W. Corke. Not illustrated, but there is a colour photograph on the cover of the first(and only) hardback edition showing some of the action from the story, which might(wrongly) lead readers to believe that the book was filmed. The very last Jennings book to be published by Collins as a hardback, and the last Jennings book for four years.

Synopsis

Chapter 1 - Financial Problem - Jennings purchases a stolen fishing rod from Mr Pink and leaves a valuable old coin as security.
Chapter 2 - Assorted Hobbies - The boys succeed in smuggling the rod into school.
Chapter 3 - False Alarm - There is fear, luckily allayed, that Jennings may have eaten poisonous toadstools.
Chapter 4 - The Wildcat Scheme - Mr Pink reveals that he has not got the old coin any more.
Chapter 5 - Errand of Disaster - Darbishire, sent to buy fishing tackle, discovers the coin has been sold to a dealer.
Chapter 6 - The Stowaway - Darbishire tries, needlessly as it turns out, to conceal his presence on the homegoing school bus.
Chapter 7 - Burnt Offering - Prospective parents are put off Linbury when confronted with a heap of burnt breakfasts.
Chapter 8 - Trouble in Store - Jennings is told, to his horror, that the old coin was never his to keep.
Chapter 9 - The Well-Planned Non-Event - Jennings and Darbishire take

their new rod plus tackle to the river.
Chapter 10 - Guilty, but Ignorant - The water-bailiff and the true owner of the rod call the boys to account.
Chapter 11 - Mr Pink's Headache - The villainy is traced to Mr Pink who is told he must recover the coin or face court action.
Chapter 12 - Welcome Return - Mr Pink manages to recover the coin, returns it to Jennings and vows to go straight.
Chapter 13 - This Term, Next Term...-(at 4 pages, the shortest chapter in the series)Mr Pink is found to be offering more dubious goods for sale...

Fantastic Bargain!...Must be Seen! Yours for only 50p. Suit 11-year old with ordinary feet. Discreet inquiries to J C T Jennings, Linbury Court School.
"It might have helped if you'd said what we were trying to sell," his companion pointed out.

Sport and Exercise There is not in the Jennings books the obsession with sport that one would find in earlier boys' schools fiction, and the "Well hit, sir!" and "Played, Biffy!" school of writing seems a world away. Indeed it is only very occasionally that sporting encounters are described in any detail, and if one of the major protagonists in the series helps his side to a victory, it is a matter for passing comment rather than a major event in the life of the school. However, a balanced picture of Linbury Court life would be incomplete without some reference to the ways in which the boys let off steam. As has been stated in the section devoted to principal characters, Jennings is keen on all sports, and frequently picked to represent his school at sport. Darbishire, however, boasts no sporting prowess at all, and it is hardly surprising that a trial football match should see him as goalkeeper, with science fiction novels scattered about his person, and speculating about the likely consequences of an invasion from the planet Mars(TJ). Football is indeed the dominant game in the autumn term, and Jennings' first taste of representing his school at football is graphically described; his creator, in true Boys' Own style, allows him to head the last-minute, albeit very lucky, winning goal(JG). Curiously this is for the First Eleven; later we hear that Jennings is considered more suitable for the 2nd XI and that is where he stays. Other 2nd XI football matches against Bracebridge are given only cursory treatment, with more eventful aspects of the day being accorded greater prominence, such as a dry-cleaning expedition(JO), Darbishire's foxing into Dunhambury to procure fishing tackle(SO) or Darbishire's ineptitude with Jennings'camera and the unfortunate consequences of Jennings' carelessness with his gloves(JA). The most infamous afternoon's inter-school football, inevitably at Bracebridge, begins with Jennings arriving at the latter school clad in one shoe and one gumboot; both Linbury teams fail to win; and Jennings then interferes with the plumbing to such an extent that he believes he has drained the swimming pool(TJ).Occasionally watching a football match is a mere inconvenience to be endured before being allowed village leave(JA). Rugby takes over in the Easter term, together with the school athletic sports, purposely held in March, partially so as not to interfere with the boys' cricket(JF).The theft of the Merridew Sports Cup co-incides with the school sports day which, with Jennings' house squeezing home, is described in some detail, including such important events as the egg-and-spoon race(JF). In the summer it is, naturally enough, cricket which dominates. There is something of a glut of cricket in the same term that Swing-Wing is adopted by the boys, the most significant episode being Jennings' attainment of a half-century in a House match, even though Darbishire's gluttony makes a nonsense of his heroics(JB); another junior House match sees Darbishire disgracing himself by neglecting his duties as runner(TH). On one occasion, however, thanks to the Drake House junior cricket XI being decimated by mumps, Darbishire is promoted to the team and his important contribution to Drake's success is fully described(JL). As well as representing the junior section of his House, Jennings represents his school as a 2nd XI cricketer, although on the day that an injury keeps him out of the side for a game against Bracebridge, far more coverage is given to his illicit activities that day than the action of the game he is missing(FI). Cricket at a higher level certainly appeals to the boys, but the boys have no objection to going to Dunhambury to watch a county cricket match(AT) or tuning in to Test Matches on the television or radio even when a junior school match or one of Mr Wilkins' lessons is in progress(TY). One summer term, the emphasis changes from cricket to swimming, as we hear of the various events which result in Drake winning the junior swimming relay, and Darbishire learning to swim(AT). Throughout the year, sedentary and indoor sport is not neglected; chess is played(JF), shooting lessons take place(JF) and there is keen competition for the table-tennis table one wet afternoon(JO). Impromptu sport is popular too, such as the football match played with an old globe to decide whether Jennings was to blame for being scalded with hot tea(AG). During the summer term, impromptu cricket is popular, notwithstanding the disintegration of composition cricket balls during the World Cricket XI v Outer Space match(JI), the ending of a Test Match between England (Jennings) and Australia (Darbishire) because the players have broken the headmaster's cucumber frame(JL), and the enforced ending of an impromptu tennis session because of broken rackets. This incidentally prompts a whole chain of events not the least of which is the discovery of the Downland cave(TY). Even outside those parts of the timetable given over to sport, the boys are made to engage in health-giving exercise, of which the most notorious example is the cross-country run which sees at least two participants complete the run on four wheels(OF). Aside from that, there is some variation from book to book as to the freedom boys are allowed when made to go out for walks. On occasions this will consist of a strict organised crocodile led by a long-suffering master who has to endure not only idiotic prattle but various dodges to get home before anyone else(TW, JO) not to mention pleas to rescue hapless hedgehogs(JR). Some weekend afternoons see all but the most junior boys take walks of their own, away from the school premises(TY) although even then we are told that rules are quite strict and the boys will devise ruses to return to the more interesting coppice and marshland at the end of the school grounds(JL, TH). Some exercise can bring altruistic benefit, such as the Sponsored Trot from Linbury to Southcombe in aid of Mrs Hockin's Animal Retreat(JE).

"In the next para. I call Jennings the doughty pivot of the team. Here, look, just after this bit about the ball being literally glued to his flashing feet."

"What's a doughty pivot?" demanded Atkinson.

"I'm not sure," Darbishire replied: "but I got it out of a newspaper, so it's bound to be a pretty stylish way of saying he's spivish rare."(JG)

Stoddington R.K. House captain of Drake responsible for giving Darbishire his first taste of House Cricket(JL) and a runner in the Sports Day Relay alongside Pringle and Wyatt(JF). Also known as Hippo, he is the largest boy in the school, five-feet-nine, and growing rapidly.

****

"What you really want is an experienced cook-general like my friend Mrs Tebbut. Prepare a banquet fit for a king, she could."

"Really!" Matron's heart filled with rising hope. "Do you think we could persuade her to take the job?"

"Oh, no! She's been dead five years, come Pancake Day."(JO)
****

Susannah The Eighth, Kettlebridge Mr Arrowsmith's potentially prize-winning Landrace sow, whom Mr Arrowsmith claims he has been looking after as though she was his own daughter, and who he believes to be the finest sow that has been bred around the district for years, with her straight back, bright eyes, curly tail and forward ears. Her prospects of success in the County Show are not enhanced by having to share her sty temporarily with the pig Jennings has won at the village fete(JI).

Swing-Wing Name given to racing pigeon N 720 NU 67 by the boys when it arrives at Linbury after escaping the clutches of its owner, John D. Saltmarsh, during a training flight. Because the care of Swing-Wing involves making illegal trips to the attic, the boys go to great lengths to conceal the bird's existence to any of the masters. Whereas therefore it would probably have been easier to explain the situation to Mr Carter at the outset, an elaborate smuggling operation is set in motion, and Jennings goes on a difficult but secret mission to Dunhambury to try and trace the bird's owner, before a combination of events leads officialdom to discover what has been going on. On two occasions the bird causes inadvertent chaos by shooting out of its basket; fortunately on the second occasion it becomes reunited with its grateful owner(JB).

****

A notice in the cottage window said: Chas. Lumley - Home-made Cakes and Bicycles Repaired.
"Here we are," said Venables, pushing open the garden gate. "Of course, it's only a little place. If it was a smart restaurant they wouldn't bother about repairing home-made cakes." (JA)
****

Take Jennings, For Instance(FI) Ninth book in the series, first published by William Collins in 1958, 256pp. Dedicated to the "Jennings Club" of Warden House School. Illustrated by Douglas Mays.

<u>**Synopsis**</u>
Chapter 1 - The Naturalists - Form 3's interest in Natural History conflicts with the masters' interest in their personal cleanliness.
Chapter 2 - Future Plans - Mr Carter plans a picnic for the naturalists but Jennings has a transport problem.
Chapter 3 - Jennings Makes Amends - Without a bike, Jennings tries to win favour with Mr Wilkins by cleaning his car. Then his new bike arrives.
Chapter 4 - A Case of Obstruction -

Jennings' cleaning efforts have succeeded in immobilising the car and he is told he can stay behind.

Chapter 5 - Jennings is reprieved following a misunderstanding about laundry baskets, for which, unbeknown to Mr Carter, he is to blame. The picnic gives him ideas for future exploration.

Chapter 6 - Collision Afloat - The idea blossoms into an illegal bike ride and boat trip. A collision with Dr Hipkin's boat results, but Jennings pulls Dr Hipkin from the water.

Chapter 7 - Plan of Escape - Anxious that their exploits should not become known, the boys ask Mrs Hipkin to take them to Bracebridge - where Linbury's 2nd XI and teachers are!

Chapter 8 - The Plan Misfires - The whole sorry affair is revealed to the headmaster but the boys' lifesaving exploits save them from further punishment.

Chapter 9 - Blot on the Copy Book - Venables thinks Jennings has been disallowed village leave and takes his bicycle without consent.

Chapter 10 - Daylight Robbery - Venables' action, and Jennings' subsequent recovery of the machine, provide headaches aplenty for PC Honeyball. Jennings procures a bike lock and chain.

Chapter 11 - The Fateful Date - Jennings forgets the combination of his lock but happily is reminded of it not by the fact that the number - 1588 - is of historical significance, but that it is Linbury Court's telephone number!

Chapter 12 - Alterations to the Programme - General Merridew's indisposition forces the school to approach Dr Hipkin to give the end of term speech.

Chapter 13- Disappearing Trick - Mr Wilkins mistakenly believes Jennings' tadpoles have become frogs, and commands the boys to search for frogs.

Chapter 14 - The Scientific Frogman - Jennings meets Dr Hipkin again and helps him to write the speech.

Chapter 15 - Present For Mr Wilkins - Mr Wilkins is not pleased with the offerings of frogs - until Dr Hipkin reveals that frogs are a particular interest of his.

Chapter 16 - The Trouble With Grown Ups - None of the boys can understand the sudden about face which turns their collection of creepy-crawlies into objects of interest rather than disapproval.

"He didn't look much like a famous scientist to me," Venables complained. "He wasn't wearing a space-helmet - just a floppy old trilby hat as ancient as a school bun. I was hoping he'd have one of those plastic suits with zip fasteners and..."

Texas Dan An employee of Mummery's Mammoth Amusements whose encouraging cries inspire Jennings to indulge in some sharpshooting, resulting in a handsome prize(JD).

Thanks to Jennings(TT) Eighth book in the series, published by William Collins in 1957, 256 pp. Dedicated to **"Wilfred Babbage, who has earned the thanks and esteem of so many listeners to Children's Hour by his inimitable performance as Mr Wilkins in `Jennings at School.'"** Illustrated by Douglas Mays.

Synopsis

Chapter 1 - Mr Carter on Duty - Mr Carter agrees to provide extra school lunches for the auditors and organise an excursion for the Camera Club. These decisions seem harmless enough...

THANKS TO JENNINGS

ANTHONY BUCKERIDGE

Chapter 2 - The Furtive Feasters - Jennings' dismissal from lunch for misbehaviour results in his uncovering what he believes to be a major scandal - extra lunches for staff!

Chapter 3 - Food For Thought - The discovery of the scandal prompts Jennings and his colleagues to plan a midnight feast by way of compensation.

Chapter 4 - Small Game Hunt - Mrs Atkinson's present to her grandson - a guinea pig - temporarily escapes from Mr Wilkins' hands and is temporarily adopted by Jennings.

Chapter 5 - The Organised Outing - Jennings' attempt to photo a squirrel in a Dunhambury park leads to his being imprisoned in the park railings.

Chapter 6 - Darbishire To the Rescue - Darbishire uses a car jack to secure Jennings' release - but not before Mr Wilkins has called the fire brigade.

Chapter 7 - Emergency Call - Mr Wilkins eventually summons the fire brigade who are not best pleased when they find nobody who needs extricating.

Chapter 8 - Jack Carr's Car Jack - The car jack used to rescue Jennings is the property of who else but Jack Carr. Having persuaded the senile Mr Carr that the jack is his property, the least Mr Wilkins can do is change his flat tyre.

Chapter 9 - Assorted Pets - Jennings rediscovers F.J. Saunders but in an attempt to protect the pet from Matron's cat, he ends up locked in the attic.

Chapter 10 - The Last of F J Saunders - Jennings is rescued after sending messages with the help of a parrot cage. His punishment is to learn six pages from his history text book.

Chapter 11 - Contributions in Kind - Plans for the midnight feast gather pace, but the donations are not what Jennings had in mind.

Chapter 12 - Catering Arrangements - The donations prove useless, and the menu is modified. A coffee party for Mr Hind's birthday gives Jennings the excuse to visit Linbury to order the cakes - cakes Jennings' fellow-feasters believe are for them.

Chapter 13 - No Smoke Without Fire - The midnight feast goes literally up in smoke before the feast plans are properly discovered by officialdom - but Mr Carter recovers the cakes.

Chapter 14 - An Inspector Calls - An inspector visits Linbury just a short while after Mr Wilkins and Venables have each fallen foul of petty bureaucracy.

Chapter 15 - Confusion Below Stairs - Even though the inspector is a school inspector, Mr Wilkins and Venables each have cause for alarm.

Chapter 16 - Thanks to Jennings - The inspector's ruffled feelings having been calmed, Mr Wilkins redeems himself as Jennings recites his six pages of history in front of that inspector.

"The only edible object I could find in my room was a compressed-looking liquorice allsort that some wretched third-former had left between the pages of his history book. But the brute wouldn't look at it."

"Hullo? Fire Station? My name's Wilkins, and it's urgent!" he began. "Spell it? U-R-G-E-N..."

That's Jennings(TH) Twenty-fifth and, at the time of going to press, final book in the series, first published by Macmillan in 1994, 121pp. Dedicated to the Leeds section of the Old Boys' Book Club. Illustrated by Rodney Sutton. After taking us, in the last two books, on a tour of high-rise London suburbs(JE) and giving us a lesson on environmental issues(AG), this book is a welcome return to much more traditional themes and although it is not in the same class as the first twenty or so in the series, it has plenty of delightful incident and dialogue.

Synopsis
Chapter 1 - Softening Up Old Wilkie - With Mr Wilkins unwell, Form

Three wonders how to soften him up so that he will not give them a maths test on his return.

Chapter 2 - Plant In A Pot - The softening-up process takes the form of a rhubarb plant in a peanut butter jar, and a card saying Happy 80th Birthday Grandad. Mr Wilkins is unamused.

Chapter 3 - Badger-Snatcher? - Jennings and Darbishire see a man in the school grounds whom they believe to be looking for badgers.

Chapter 4 - Close Secret - The man is in fact Tim MacTaggart who is not, as they suppose, trying to find badgers but is looking for a time capsule containing old Linbury souvenirs.

Chapter 5 - Bird of Ill-Omen - The boys, determined not to let on to their colleagues, start a search for the capsule but pretend that their secret activity is to do with bird-watching.

Chapter 6 - Change in the Weather - Some wet weather prompts discussion as to the content of the end-of-term Drama Evening.

Chapter 7 - Plan of Campaign - The boys try to persuade Bromwich to lend them his metal-detector to help find the capsule.

Chapter 8 - The Runner - Bromwich refuses to help after Darbishire lets his House down badly in a junior cricket match.

Chapter 9 - Hide-and-Seek - With other Form Three colleagues now let in on the time capsule secret, the search for the capsule proves fruitful.

Chapter 10 - The Hole in the Ground - The time capsule is unearthed and Jennings is determined to tell Tim MacTaggart; meanwhile preparations for the drama continue.

Chapter 11 - Old Boys' Reunion - The creators of the capsule are invited to the Drama Evening. What it lacks in professionalism it makes up for in enthusiasm.

Chapter 12 - Curtain Down - The contents of the time capsule are examined with nostalgia by the Old Boys.

"Anyway, it's not my fault if Miss Thorpe doesn't label her plants properly. How was I to know it was rhubarb?"
"Pity she didn't put custard on it," said Martin-Jones. "That might have given you a clue."

"H'm! I'm afraid you'd have rather a job training a hawk to swoop down on an old bedroom slipper."
Jennings considered this. "It might think it was a rabbit, sir, especially if it was a bit short-sighted."

Thompson Minor Ginger-haired third former. With Brown Major and Rumbelow, one of the onlookers as Archie Cuppling and crew rescue Mr Wilkins from the ivy(JG). We are told that on the cricket field, where he represents his House at Junior level, he always plays the same stroke to every delivery he receives(JL). He is Darbishire's potential swimming opponent in the first lap of the House swimming relay(AT). We also hear that although he is not much good at cricket(JB) he is a 2nd XI footballer, and when not busy on the football field, he is known to spend the hobbies' hour bartering stamps(OF, TT), playing the guitar(JI), playing chess(TT), recording rainfall(LI), puppet-making or writing feeble poetry for Jennings' competition(JA), assisting in the construction of a bird sanctuary(JB), working keenly on the agricultural side in Mr Wilkins' maths project(JR) or perhaps practising the violin for his end-of-term solo(OF). He is one of the occupants of Dormitory Three when Blotwell, thanks to Jennings' antics, is unable to find a bed; his name is apparently difficult to say backwards(JD). Like Parslow and Atkinson, his first name is Robin; he suffers a football injury while Atkinson suffers from tonsilitis(TT).

Thorpe, Miss A small, sharp-featured, slightly-built, middle-aged spinster, she is the tireless organiser of almost every aspect of Linbury village life. She makes no appearance at all until halfway through the series(LJ) after which she is a fairly regular visitor to the stories. She is a brisk, perky bird-like woman with a piping laugh, who speaks(and sometimes twitters) in an eager, chirruping, occasionally high-pitched and penetrating trill which can be deafening to those speaking to her on the telephone. Her high-pitched voice is likened to a well-trained mynah bird demanding its breakfast(AG). Her many community activities include work with the village playgroup, the WI, the Mothers Union and the church choir, as well as organising outings for the elderly and the ladies of the village, not to mention carboot sales, jumble sales, whist drives and church bazaars with presumably charitable aims in mind. She is a warm-hearted champion of the "little man" and staunch opponent of bureaucracy and injustice. She helps the boys return to school the contents of the lost property cupboard which Mr Wilkins callously saw fit to dispose of(JO); she assists the cause of famine relief by helping the boys take her old piano into town with a view to getting a fiver for it(TJ); she helps to find a good home for the "sweet little piggy" Jennings has carelessly won at the village fete(JI); she allows Jennings to pick a plant from her garden as a present for Mr Wilkins(TH): she supports Jennings in his bid to enter Aunt Angela's cake for a competition with a view to winning a vase for Mr Wilkins(LJ); she reacts with horror when she believes Mr Carter, busy digging for a time capsule, to be hunting badgers(TH); she is critical of Mr Wilkins for his churlishness in objecting to his old sports jacket being used for the boys' guy(TJ); and she puts the boys in touch with Mr Laxton, the nature expert, when she hears about their newly-adopted hedgehog(JR). Not surprisingly, she turns out to be a model of environmental friendliness, being the proud owner and user of a bicycle, organising the boys into scavenging for litter one Saturday afternoon, printing(from recycled paper of course) leaflets on Keeping Linbury Green, campaigning successfully for more efficient litter disposal and collection, suggesting that the boys visit the ecology exhibition in London, and trying to persuade Mr Arrowsmith to take up organic farming(AG). She is on friendly terms with, and frequent visitor to, Linbury Court, and unstinting in her praise of assistance proferred by the boys, however great the breaches of school rules such assistance has occasioned. Her home, the very old, very small Oaktree Cottage, stands in a tidy garden near Linbury village centre. The cottage is noteworthy for its big expanse of sloping tiled roof, big bow windows, solid oak front door studded with nails, and absence of television. Miss Thorpe also owns a thatched barn which she has bought to store furniture she has no room for; this includes a mangle and honky tonk piano. She is the proud owner of an aquarium the care of which she unwisely entrusts to Jennings when she goes to visit her sister in Kent(AG) and an unruly boxer puppy Jason who will not respond to her daily obedience lessons(JR).

Three Acre Marsh Together with Boland's Wood and Hinkley's Farm, one of the landmarks between East Brinkington and Birchingdean which Mrs Goodman points out to Jennings as he wonders how he can get back to Linbury after his failed mission to return Swing-Wing to its owner(JB).

Tiddyman, Dr. Author and birdwatcher in Miller's Wood whom Jennings mistakes for a spy, and whose glove-wearing frustrates Jennings' attempts to obtain his finger-prints. Once he has forgiven Mr Carter and the Headmaster for frightening away the chiff-chaff, he comes to Linbury, gives a slide-show, and relays by way of a tape-recording the efforts of Jennings and Darbishire to expose him as a secret agent(LJ).

Time Time stands still for Jennings and his friends, but a look at the content of each story, as well as the year of publication, may give an idea as to the year in which the action of that story might have taken place. The space craze brings with it Jennings' belief that the age of Space Travel is only just around the corner, and in the same story General Merridew looks back on his schooling at Linbury in 1895, sixty years ago, which places that particular story into the 1950's(AT); but in other stories the time is less clear. Occasionally somebody will refer to a specific date which will narrow the choice considerably - for instance, P.C. Honeyball, on being asked the date by Jennings, proclaims it to be Saturday July 10th. July 10th fell on a Saturday in 1954, four years before this story appeared, but did not again so fall until 1965 by which time the story(FI) had been in print seven years. Because terms come and go, it simply is not possible to tie Jennings down to any year or indeed any decade; he moves with the times, staying forever young. All one can do is say that certain stories could not have been set BEFORE a given year - decimal currency arrives towards the end of the series, with Jennings proferring twenty five "p" for a tennis racket in a sports shop(TY), and Mr Hales is said to be on his way to a tea-shop established in 1969 (TJ). Similarly, certain stories could not have happened AFTER a given year - in one book direct-dial telephoning appears not to have arrived(FI) and in another steam locomotives are still very much in vogue(LJ).

The increased interest in environmental matters in the late 1980's and early 1990's prompted a book in the series devoted almost exclusively to environment-related issues; the same book refers to the possibility of an unheard-of phenomenon in the 1950's, a wheel-clamped skateboard(AG)! Other 80's and 90's expressions and fads creep into the last books in the series - we meet the "greenhouse effect(AG)," hear the expressions "over-the-top," "fast-forward" and "laid-back(TH)," and following the film Jurassic Park, it is suggested that the boys perform the Pied Piper of Hamelin with cardboard dinosaurs(TH).

Tomlinson, Albert Nurseryman and seedsman and surprised but more than willing recipient of ten shillings intended by Aunt Angela for Jennings, thereby depriving Jennings of the money which he desperately needs to replace the headmaster's cucumber frame(JL).

Tompkins, Mr Chiropodist in the Dunhambury area, and according to Gracie Hepplewell the best man for corns and chilblains(JR).

Topliss, Mr Alluded to as teacher of French and Latin at Linbury Court(TT), and shooting instructor(JF) but given no role in any of the action.

Translations As has been stated in the section devoted to the Story of Jennings, translations have been numerous, and large numbers of copies have been sold around the world. Jennings has become Bennett in France, Fredy in Germany and Stompa in Norway. The translators have coped bravely with the peculiarly English ambience of the stories, not to mention some of the language:

"Autrement dit, tu viens a Dunhambury avec nous."
"Hein? Oh! Supersonique!"(**Bennett et le General,** French translation of AT)
"Pi-ou-ouou!...Brrroum-brrroum!...Pi-ou-ou-ou...Ta-ca-ta-ca-ta...Boum!"(**L'Agence Bennett et Cie.,** French translation of JF)
"Ploink-tjasji-tjasji-ploink...ploink-tjasji-tjasji-ploink!: sang Stompas sykkel, hoyt og skingrende i dur.(**Stompa skriver dagbok,** Norwegian translation of JD)

Trouble With Jennings, The (TW) The Eleventh book in the series, first published by William Collins in 1960, 256 pp. Dedicated to the boys of Canterbury Cathedral Choir School. Illustrated by Douglas Mays.

Synopsis
Chapter 1 - The Start of the Trouble - Jennings is smitten with the snorkel craze and wants to buy a music stand for Darbishire. Hardly the recipe for disaster one might think...

Chapter 2 - The Handy Gadget - The snorkel certainly proves to be handy for cleaning the fish tank - but what else?

Chapter 3 - A Case of Obstruction - Darbishire is locked out of his bathroom with the tap running.

Chapter 4 - Flood Warning - Mr Wilkins averts one flood but not the second, caused by Jennings and his snorkel.

Chapter 5 - Overhead Expenses - Jennings' actions cause the music room ceiling to collapse - with a little help from Mr Wilkins.

Chapter 6 - Ici on Parle Francais -

Jennings procures a music stand for Darbishire and gets some French practice too.

Chapter 7 - Shakespeare Sets A Problem - Form 3's English prep, précising Macbeth, has intriguing possibilities.

Chapter 8 - The Planned Operation - Lady Macbeth's sleepwalking is re-enacted by Jennings as he tries to retrieve provisions for the midnight feast.

Chapter 9 - The Finishing Touch - Mr Wilkins' brilliant plan for calling Jennings' bluff works well - until he rings the bell.

Chapter 10 - False Alarm - The bell brings the whole school downstairs for an unofficial fire drill.

Chapter 11 - Exchange of Gifts - Darbishire has no use for his birthday music stand after he has given away his recorder to obtain a telescope for Jennings!

Chapter 12 - Musical Interlude - A bout of bartering means that Darbishire is able to delight the audience at Mr Hind's musical evening.

Chapter 13 - Good Resolution - An "At Home" party is planned so that Jennings might fulfil a resolution to be kind to old people and think of a treat that Sir etc. would like.

Chapter 14 - Heatwave - Food gathering for the party is complicated by Darbishire's provisions melting in his pocket.

Chapter 15 - Mistaken Intentions - As Atkinson produces a washing sponge instead of the sponge cake requested, the masters misinterpret the boys' good intentions.

Chapter 16 - The Old Folks' At Home - Mr Wilkins conducts a somewhat premature raid on the food supplies but realises his mistake and the party is a great success.

"Look at the ceiling, boy ; just look at it."
Jennings looked at it. "Yes, sir. It's on the floor, sir."

Aloud he quoted: "Dear Sir, you are invited to a party with toasts and refreshments. R.I.P."

Trust Jennings!(TJ) Nineteenth book in the series, first published by William Collins in 1969, 192 pp. Dedicated to Felix Otton. Illustrated by Douglas Mays. The first book to go decimal - more than a year before decimal currency came into being! After two books set in the summer term, we move here into the autumn term, with football and fireworks.

Synopsis
Chapter 1 - The Best of Both Worlds - After some sobering words by Mr Carter, it is agreed that the Form 3 Firework Fund will organise a charity school firework party.

Chapter 2 - Science Fiction In the Goalmouth - Darbishire's goalkeeping prowess is hampered in a manner Peter Shilton never had to worry about.

Chapter 3 - Wrong Foot Foremost - Jennings' desire to get prime place on the school coach leaves him with a bizarre selection of footwear.

Chapter 4 - Drainage Problem - Jennings' attempt to heat up Bracebridge school showers almost brings catastrophe.

Chapter 5 - Aerosol Accident - An illegal foray into Matron's cupboards looking for clothes for the guy, and a full can of silver paint conspire to bring calamity for Jennings.

Chapter 6 - Short Back And Sides - The only answer to Jennings' silver hair is a secret trip to the barber's. What a shame Mr Wilkins should decide to do the same...

Chapter 7 - In Hazard - Jennings is discovered, despite his best attempts at concealment.

Chapter 8 - Plan of Campaign - A misunderstanding means that Jennings escapes punishment for his exploits and can now concentrate on obtaining "Penny for the Guy."

Chapter 9 - Penny for the Guy - Miss Thorpe misconstrues the boys' street collecting, but comes to their rescue when Mr Wilkins lambasts them for appropriating his sports jacket for the guy.

Trust Jennings!
Anthony Buckeridge

Chapter 10 - Bonfire Night - Despite a misunderstanding with some young saplings, the bonfire night is a huge success.

Chapter 11 - Transport Problem - The discovery of an unwanted piano in Miss Thorpe's barn provides Jennings with another great fund-raising wheeze.

Chapter 12 - Double Yellow Line - The piano is conveyed to Dunhambury but Miss Thorpe's inability to park the car brings its own problems.

Chapter 13 - Honky-Tonk - The music shop refuses to

give cash for the piano, but Jennings' barber suggests an alternative buyer. Moments later, a concert party at the Dunhambury Youth Club is in full swing.
Chapter 14 - Copyright Reserved - Not only does the Youth Club accept the piano, but an outstanding piece of written work by Jennings leads to a grand total of £10 being raised for famine relief.

Sometimes there was a dedication. Perhaps he could adopt that as his personal trademark. How would it be if he dedicated his science prep - To Mr Wilkins - but for whose insistence this great work would never have been started, let alone finished!

"Yes, I know, sir. They were just a few odd books that I happened to have up my jersey and - er - in places like that."

Tubbs, Miss(AKA Madame Anatolia Olivera) The bacon-counter assistant at Linbury General Stores, whose fortune-telling at the village bazaar, under her assumed name, entices Jennings to her tent(LJ). Her prophecies, that her young client will make a journey over land and water, will come into some money, and will achieve an ambition he has set his heart on, are not meant to be taken seriously - it is all good harmless fun. But Jennings is determined to get his money's worth. When fulfilment seems unlikely, he burns with resentment, but three fortunate events(a field trip including a 300-yard boat journey, Mr Wilkins' re-imbursement of some money, and Dormitory 4 winning the Dormitory Cup) convince Jennings of the power of the supernatural(LI).

****
Mr Wilkins eyed the sorry-looking drawing without enthusiasm. "What's this splodge meant to be - a milk churn?"
"No, that's a sheep, sir - <u>un mouton</u>," the artist explained. "You can tell that because it's got legs at each corner." (EJ)
****

Typically Jennings!(TY) Twenty-first book in the series, first published by William Collins in 1971, 159 pp. Dedicated to Sarah Jane and Roger Ardley. Not illustrated. Dustjacket and frontispiece by Val Biro. Sadly this is one of the less appealing of the Jennings books. Apart from Charlie, the sale room porter, and Mrs Maverick, the straying Southdown sheep, we meet no new characters, the storylines hold few possibilities for humour and some of the dialogue lacks both humour and credibility.

Synopsis

Chapter 1 - The Rickety Racket - Both Jennings and Darbishire have their tennis rackets broken in an impromptu game, and vow to replace them.

Chapter 2 - The Umpire's Decision - Junior cricket comes to a standstill because of the Test match being heard on Bromwich's miniature radio.

Chapter 3 - Sale Price - Jennings, trying to buy two tennis rackets at an auction sale, comes away with a cooking stove and revolting oil painting instead.

Chapter 4 - The Hide-Out - The boys discover a cave on the South Downs, and assist a maverick sheep, whilst trying to find a suitable spot for camp cookery.

Chapter 5 - Quiet Commentary - The radio is confiscated after being used in Mr Wilkins' maths lesson.

Chapter 6 - Thunder in the Air - Jennings returns to the cave but has to return in semi-nudity as Darbishire has moved his clothes.

Chapter 7 - The Bogus Bug-Hunters - Jennings devises what proves to be a successful plan to recover his clothes as well as Darbishire's glasses which have also been left on the Downs.

Chapter 8 - Doubtful Security - Bromwich, furious at the radio confiscation, receives the oil painting as security for its safe return.

Chapter 9 - Blow-Up - The school picnic becomes explosive when the boys try to use the stove to make tea for the masters.

Chapter 10 - Prehistoric Joke - Darbishire fails to fool his colleagues with his cave paintings, but frightens them by enticing them into the cave where the maverick sheep is situated.

Chapter 11 - Restricted Access - Jennings pushes Mr Wilkins towards returning the radio by suggesting a way of freeing the school minibus which has got stuck in the garage entrance.

Chapter 12 - Full Circle - With the radio returned, and Mr Carter finding new rackets for the boys, all ends contentedly.

"Well, Venables, why do you think these primitive peoples felt an urge to express themselves by drawing on the walls of their caves?"
"I suppose it was because they hadn't got any decent drawing paper, sir," he said brightly.

Uniform The school colours are magenta and white. We are told that school uniform in the winter months consists of a flannel shirt and shorts and a heavy jersey; the regulation colour is grey, brightened only by a red tie and a band of the same shade round stocking-tops and sweater neck(JO).

Valenti's Sweet shop at which Jennings procures a stick of rock with which to impress Temple having foxed out of school following a severe attack of homesickness(JG).

Venables, Mrs The anxious mother of Jennings' Form Three colleague makes only one brief appearance, on the platform at Victoria station, when she bends Mr Wilkins' ear concerning her son's cough medicine and summer vests, and whether his new shoes are the right size(LJ).

Washbrooke Major Six and a half stone footballer who in Jennings' first practice football match causes our hero to make one of the more unorthodox clearance manoeuvres that the game has seen(JG).

Weston, Tom Like Mr Arrowsmith, a farmer and breeder of Landrace pigs, living a few miles from Linbury and thus easily able to visit Mr Arrowsmith when invited to look at the sow Susannah the Eighth and assess her chances of success at the County Show. The spectacular build-up Mr Arrowsmith has given the animal collapses into hilarity on Mr Weston's part, when a second, rather less prestigious occupant of Susannah's sty is discovered. The hilarity gives way to quieter amusement when Mr Weston realises that he himself was the donor of the miserable creature Jennings has ill-advisedly placed in the sty after winning it at the fete(JI). Mr Weston's help proves invaluable when students on Mr Wilkins' maths project wish to compare different farmers' crop yields(JR).

Wildsmith, Brian Gordon Mechanic and employee of the Star Garage to whom Mr Wilkins' car is entrusted when it develops trouble on a routine journey to Dunhambury. A young man of twenty, he is pale and thin with long black side-whiskers and a hairstyle like an old English sheepdog but is good with cars; later that term, M. Dufour also has cause to call upon his services (EJ).

****
"Yes, I'm much better, thanks. Matron says I'll be as right as a trivet by the morning."
"What's a trivet?" demanded Temple suspiciously. It sounded to him like some new dodge to avoid going back into school. (JD)
****

Wilfred A cousin of Jennings and the proud owner of white rabbits whose welfare is alluded to in Aunt Angela's letter to Jennings which ends up in the hands of Mr Tomlinson(JL)

Wilkins, Margaret Mr Wilkins' sister to whom Jennings and Darbishire are eternally indebted after she pays the bill for the excess of refreshment they have enjoyed at Mrs Lumley's tea shop, persuades her brother not to punish them for missing his detention class, and provides them with first-rate information about her brother for the Form Three Times. A London hospital nurse, she is, we are told, a very likeable person, without the turbulent manner, burly build, loud voice and heavy footfall of her brother(JA). One summer term she displeases her brother by firstly making him look after her cat Pyewacket, but then giving him a hideous pair of vases as a thank you present(LJ).

William See entry for Gerald.

Women Although the school is a boys' school, we are told there are women on the staff(JG) and a large number of women feature in the narratives. Besides Matron we meet, in one book only, the housekeeper Mrs Caffey, the mercurial maid Ivy and her giggly colleague Mary(JF). Other ancillary staff mentioned are Mrs Cherry, Miss Matthews and the fearsome Connie Hackett. Mrs Arrowsmith, the farmer's wife, appears on the scene when Linbury Court adventure spills over into neighbouring land(OF). General Merridew's daughter-in-law Diana is shown round Linbury Court but does not appreciate the show of neatness laid on for her(JL). Mr Wilkins' sister appears on the scene in two books, in the first taking tea with her brother(JA) and in the second entrusting her cat to him(LJ). In the village of Linbury we meet the bird-like Miss Thorpe, Miss Tubbs at the bacon counter of Linbury stores and Mrs Lumley selling home made cakes at her cafe; Mrs Lumley is part of a large posse of women, led by Ethel Pinmill and Bertha Clough, who mistakenly believe they will be welcome at Jennings' jumble sale(JO). They can cause problems without setting foot in the school; it is Rumbelow's grown-up sister who provides the boy with a space gun which shatters the

Headmaster's window, even if the breakage indirectly saves Jennings' bacon(EJ). Away from school, we meet Jennings' mother albeit only infrequently; we are far more likely to hear about Aunt Angela, Jennings' favourite aunt, who is mentioned in numerous stories. Jennings' encounter with the Gaitskell Court community puts him in touch with Emma Sparrow and her mother Jane, Alderman Connie Freeman the local mayor, Emma's friends Maggie and Cleo, and the busybodies Mrs Pratt and Mrs Plumrose(JE). Jennings, however, is far too young to have any romantic leanings towards the opposite sex. The culture and atmosphere of the books throughout is almost exclusively masculine.

Wooderson, Dr Kenneth Middle-sized, middle-aged man who is sent to Linbury to deputise for Dr Furnival during the latter's absence on holiday. Although the Linbury staff are confident that he will prove a more than adequate substitute, Dr Wooderson's bedside manner is tested to the limit when on a routine visit to the school to see Temple who has tonsilitis, Darbishire mistakes him for Robin Laxton the hedgehog expert and informs him that his patient is **"curled up in a ball without rolling"** and has been **"fast asleep since about last October(JR)."**

Work Bearing in mind that the purpose of a school is to educate, it would indeed be curious if the Linbury Court stories failed to give us glimpses into the classroom activity within the school, and although the action will often take us outside the classroom, Linburians could certainly not be accused of neglecting their studies. All the classroom glimpses we get are, naturally, into that of Form Three, where predominantly Mr Wilkins and, to a lesser extent Messrs Carter, Hind and Pemberton-Oakes endeavour to instil into the boys some academic knowledge. Commendably, written work and rote-learning are often sacrificed to make way for initiatives such as the maths project leading to the Jennings Report(JR) and a project spotlighting aspects of local life such as flora, fauna and rainfall(LI). The boys are too young to be studying for public examinations, and there is no mention made whatsoever of entrance examinations for public schools. That having been said, the teachers are often rendered speechless, perplexed or downright exasperated by the failure of their pupils to pay proper attention to their work or to think through their answers before committing them to paper:

"What have I just been saying, Jennings?"
"You said that if you knew all about similar triangles, it helped you to cross a river, sir."
"Quite right!" For a moment Mr Wilkins had thought that the boy had

not been paying attention, but it seemed that he was mistaken. "And how exactly would you go about it?" he inquired.

Jennings thought desperately. "Well, sir, I suppose you'd make big wooden ones, so that you could sit on one triangle and paddle across with the other." (JL)

"You haven't finished that exercise yet, have you, Jennings?"

"No sir, I haven't <u>quite</u> got to the end of it yet, sir."

"Why not?"

"Because - well, because I haven't quite got to the beginning part yet, sir."(JL)

"According to my figures he must have finished the journey after half past z, sir."

Mr Wilkins drew in his breath like a vacuum-cleaner coping with an obstinate fluff-ball.(JA)

He retraced his steps to the master's desk and opened the volume at what he judged to be the chapter on mixed fractions. His expression changed as he found himself reading...<u>and with one blow of his fist the enrag'd bosun sent the rascally sea-cook sprawling full-length upon the deck</u>.(LI)

"Sir, please, sir, what shall I do, sir? I haven't got my name on my algebra book, sir." (AU)

"Do we have to work it out in our books, sir?" inquired Martin-Jones.

"Of course. You don't imagine I want it embroidered on the lampshade, do you!" (JA)

"I tell you, Carter, that form's turning my hair grey. Can't behave; will talk; won't work; must fidget. I've been shouting myself hoarse in there all morning."

"That's probably the trouble," Mr Carter replied. "Have you ever tried talking quietly? You see, Wilkins, if you rampage round a class-room like a bull in a china shop, they just think it's most frightfully funny." (JG)

The teaching which is absorbed by the boys is, however, known to inspire some of their most impetuous adventures. The study of Tennyson's "Revenge" leads to the maiden voyage of the boys' own yacht in the school pond on a highly illegal Sunday afternoon enterprise(JL); knowledge of the date of the Spanish Armada helps Jennings remember the number of his combination padlock - until he tries to recall it with his bicycle safely locked(FI); study of Shakespeare's Macbeth leads to an unlikely sleepwalking venture in order to try and organise a midnight feast(TW); a geography lesson about the ascent of Everest leads to a mountaineering trip up the school staircase in full costume(LJ); the environmental study of Linbury Court prompts Jennings to present Mr Wilkins with a grass snake for his breakfast(LI); the Latin declension of "hic haec hoc" results in a fierce classroom battle(JF); and Mr Hind's instruction about the prehistoric Lascaux cave paintings inspires Darbishire to try some cave artistry of his own(TY).

Even if the intellectual development of the pupils is not quite as their teachers would like, their repartee will surely get them a long way in life:
"Three days to go a mile! Don't be ridiculous, you silly little boy! Why, a snail could do it in that time!"
"I was pretending it WAS a snail, sir."(JA)

The only subject in which we gather that Jennings attains academic excellence is French, in which during one term he comes top(EJ).

Wyatt See entry for Stoddington R.K.

****
"We stop the very next car that comes along and say to the driver: ` Quick, follow that car!' That's what ` Dick Barton' does anyway, and it always works."
Darbishire carried his objections a stage further.
"Well, supposing he catches a bus?"
"Then we stop the next one, and tell the conductor to follow the one in front." (JF)
****

5. COLLECTING JENNINGS

The complete set of the first editions of the twenty-five Jennings books, with dustjackets, and preferably signed by the author, is obviously the goal for the collector. There are marked differences, however, in the availability of the respective titles, as well as the prices which one must be prepared to pay for them.

Most secondhand booksellers with a reasonable proportion of shelf space devoted to children's books will carry at least a token selection of Jennings books, more often than not without dustjackets. The most comprehensive selection of first editions for sale, with dustjackets, known to this writer is kept by David Schutte, Myrtle Cottage, Stedham, Midhurst, West Sussex GU29 ONQ(tel. 01730 814654). This writer acknowledges David's assistance in providing the information set out below.

It should be pointed out that the valuations given below are not a guarantee that the books are available at all, or available at the prices suggested, or will be sold for the prices suggested.

The popularity of the Jennings books during the 1950's and early 1960's means that titles published during this period were printed in fairly large quantities. First editions of all titles up to TJ, bar the first six titles and the compilation, can be picked up for between £20.00 and £30.00, depending on its condition(say £20.00 for Very Good, £30.00 for really Fine). A lucky collector may stumble upon a very presentable copy for even less. However, it is more difficult to find the first third of the series in perfect dustjackets, and for this reason they command a higher price - between £35.00 and £50.00 in Very Good or near Fine condition, with a slight premium on JG. A really Fine edition of JG might fetch up to £80.00 or £90.00, and really Fine editions of the next half-dozen books could realise up to £60.00, particularly if signed by the author.

Print runs of the later Jennings titles, also the compilation, were smaller and those that are now out of print are much scarcer. £45.00 was at the time of writing being asked for a Very Good/near Fine edition of JR, £35.00 for a Very Good edition of the compilation, £35.00 for a really Fine edition of TY, £25.00 for a Very Good edition of SO, and £18.00 for a well-thumbed paperback first edition of JE(the cover price being 45 pence!!). It is these titles which the collector will have greatest difficulty in tracing, and where the real winners are the ones who paid the few shillings it would have cost to buy them new! The last two titles, AG and TH, are notionally still in print, commanding cover prices of £7.99 and £8.99 respectively.

The collector who cannot afford the £700-800 it will cost him to assemble a collection of Very Good/Fine first editions in dustjacket can take consolation from the fact that all the titles up to EJ were reprinted, and it should be possible to obtain most reprints, with dustjackets, for £10.00 or possibly substantially less. A 1966 reprint of JG was selling in December 1994 for £12.00, and a 1963 reprint of JF could be obtained for £6.00 in April 1995. All the reprints except some reprints of JG retained the original dustjackets, and the texts remained exactly the same. As regards the later books, the "reprint" collector will of course have to resort to first editions to complete his collection, and naturally will pay considerably more for those copies because they are few in number. It should also be borne in mind that many reprints did not incorporate the colour frontispiece illustration despite the fact that it continued to be referred to in the table of illustrations(which certainly caught me out more than once as, ignorant of the meaning of the word "frontispiece" as a child, I searched vainly for a picture that was not there!).

For those who are happy just to enjoy the Jennings books for their own sake(and why not?) there are plenty of copies without dustjackets which will usually be going for £5 or less(perhaps a little more for first editions) but their resale value will be negligible. The serious collector/investor should always ensure that his copies come with dustjackets. Failing that, the Puffin and Armada paperback re-issues, which began to appear towards the end of the 1960's and which then petered out during the mid to late 1970's, reproduce reasonably faithfully the inimitable language and style of the originals, although there has been some discreet editing down. Copies can be obtained for less than the price of a National Lottery ticket, and the colour covers are certainly worth seeing for curiosity value alone.

To be avoided, by the purist at any rate, are the John Goodchild hardbound and Pan Macmillan softbound re-issues of the Jennings books, deliberately aimed at the new generation of Jennings enthusiasts, rather than the nostalgic collector. The paperback editions are still widely available, costing £3.50 or thereabouts, but there are many changes from the original texts.(see also THE STORY OF JENNINGS)

" No, you clodpoll!" corrected Darbishire.

He attached it with stamp hinges.

"Thomas Henry was better known as the illustrator for the Richmal Crompton William stories; here however he has provided two iluustrations for a Jennings story which appeared in the BOYS BRIGADE OMNIBUS."

Other bookdealers, besides David Schutte, which always have a fair number of Jennings books in stock, are at the time of going to press:

Sarah Key, The Haunted Bookshop, 9 St Edwards Passage, Cambridge CB1 2PR(Tel 01223 312913)

Rose's Books, 14 Broad Street, Hay-on-Wye HR3 5DB(Tel 01497 820013)

West House Books, Broad Street, Hay-on-Wye HR3 5DB(Tel 01497 821225)

The Children's Bookshop, Toll Cottage, Pontvaen, Hay-on-Wye HR3 5EW(Tel 01497 821083)

Ripping Yarns, 355 Archway Road, Highgate, London N6 4EJ(Tel 0181 341 6111)

The Fifteenth Century Bookshop, 99/100 High Street, Lewes, East Sussex BN7 1XH(Tel 01273 474160)

6. JENNINGS FOR EVERYONE

Sunday, 25th December 1966. My grandfather pressed into my seven-year-old hand a small rectangular shaped parcel which when unwrapped was found to contain a small hardbacked book with a colourful dustjacket illustration depicting two small boys exchanging pleasantries with a friendly train crew.

Tuesday, 23rd May 1995. A brisk drive through the tranquil Sussex countryside led me to East Crink, Barcombe Mills, near Lewes, to meet for the first time the creator of the series of books of which that small hardbacked book was a part.

In between; a passionate love for that series of Jennings books which has persisted undimmed and which has at times bordered on the obsessional. A series of books must be special to a fan who, like this one, has dreamed on many occasions of entering a bookshop to discover a new title in the series on the shelf, only to be bitterly disappointed upon waking the next morning!

I shall not easily forget my meeting with Anthony Buckeridge; the enormity of his achievement in creating such a popular well-loved schoolboy, whose adventures are enjoyed by children and adults right across the globe, has not spoiled him. Those who have to travel long distances to work would envy his own workplace; a cosy upstairs study lined with bookshelves, looking out on to glorious downland scenery. Quentin Blake's drawings, spurned by William Collins, adorn his staircase; a glassfronted bookcase on his landing contains the first editions of all the Jennings books, and another room contains large quantities of presumably remaindered paperback editions and translations. There is the French:
"Brrloum brrloumpff! Reveillez-vous, mon garcon."
Or the Norwegian:
"D-d-dette er jo LATTERLIG! D-d-det er....umph!"
Or even the Indonesian:
"Kalian bergurau!" ia berkata. "Lihat apa yang baru saja terjadi."
In the midst of what is a veritable museum of Jennings, Anthony Buckeridge is a delightful, helpful man who is pleased to talk of the characters and the places he has created. He makes no secret of his whereabouts to those who look him up in the telephone directory; he

and his charming wife offer splendid hospitality to those who come to see him; and any visitor who has spent time in his presence, with the glorious South Downs countryside forming a spectacular backdrop to his rural residence, cannot fail to leave it truly enriched by the experience.

Nearby is Lewes, the county town of East Sussex, and the second-hand bookshop at the top of the town is, appropriately enough, full of copies of the Collins hardback editions of the series. Jennings books are collectors' items, as has been stated earlier in this book; how many connoisseurs have known the thrill of the chase, hunting that last missing copy which would assure him of a complete collection. How frustrating for the late 1960's or early 1970's teenager who declined the opportunity of paying a pound or perhaps less for one of the later books, only to find now that they are the hardest to obtain and where knowing who to ask yields more results than even the most diligent exploration of a town's secondhand bookshops. Whilst Anthony Buckeridge can derive some satisfaction from knowing that Jennings stories, in watered-down form, continue to appear on the children's bookshelves, he must derive infinitely more pleasure from the transactions between serious collector and serious dealer, with cheques for a hundred pounds or more being written for mint copies of batches of those elusive later titles.

What makes them worth collecting? A number of writers, critics and journalists have some answers.

Joseph Connolly, in his "Modern Children's First Editions," describes Buckeridge as **"creator of the funniest and best-written schoolboy books, bar none. Anthony Buckeridge is now enjoying a richly deserved revival following a dip in popularity during the 70's and early 80's - so much so that many of the Jennings books are being re-issued. Of course it is quite shameful(double ozard indeed) that they ever went out of print in the first place - but the re-issues are, I tremble to report, REVISED. This means, in effect, that all the glorious 50's prepschool language has been updated...I'm afraid I deplore this. Did they update Shakespeare? Jane Austen? What has become of period charm? And all references to Mr Carter and Mr Wilkins being pipe-smokers have been deleted. I-I-Corwumph! Collectors would be well-advised to look sharp if they want to gather this lot - Anthony Buckeridge is very collected."**

Humphrey Carpenter and Mari Prichard, writing in the Oxford Companion to English Literature, say: **"Buckeridge writes in the tradition of P.G. Wodehouse...he is a slick farceur with a command of verbal wit."**

The entry devoted to Jennings in Margery Fisher's "Who's Who In Children's Books" is worth reproducing in full, as it encapsulates beautifully the joy of the Jennings books: **"Jennings, an `eager, friendly boy...with untidy brown hair and a wide-awake look in his eyes' irrupted into the community of Linbury Court Preparatory School aged(he prompted Mr Carter precisely) `Ten years two months and three days last Tuesday, Sir.' His appearance, age and personality have not changed since the first story was broadcast about him in 1948 in the BBC Childrens Hour, although his favourite exclamation of `Gosh Fishhooks' has received various topical variations and his enthusiasms have moved with the times. Car noises have given place to space rocket countdowns and the clicking of a computer, and the expenditure of shillings and, later, new pence, has satisfied his desire for articles ranging from butterfly nets and foreign stamps to a snorkel. Like William, Jennings never deliberately causes trouble. The accidents and disasters for which he is regularly punished result from misplaced enthusiasm and an inability to appreciate the workings of cause and effect. Of all the schoolboys who have ever got lost on cross-country runs, engaged in elaborate financial transactions, experimented with home-made explosive devices, mistaken a visiting plumber or electrician for a school inspector, or a parent for a visiting plumber or electrician, none but Jennings could have turned a simple happening into such a hilarious sequence. Slapstick and farce must have an inner stability if they are not to become wearisome. The stories of Jennings are carefully and formally structured, with two or three story-lines prolonged, developed and intertwined until a final reckoning brings them all together and halts Jennings' impetuous course. He is supported by a skilfully varied cast of subordinate characters. His boon companion Darbishire provides a perfect foil for him; he is a polite child with a vicarage background, earnest and bespectacled, whose deliberate utterances sound as though they were in capital letters and who is helpless to escape from Jennings' forceful plans. The shrewd, imperturbable junior master Mr Carter is as important in Jennings' career as the testy Mr Wilkins, who is apt to make `a noise like an inner tube exploding under pressure' when roused and who never learns wisdom from his numerous encounters with Jennings. The varying attitudes and tactics of the people swept into the orbit of Jennings satisfactorily distract our attention and prevent** us from examining too closely the plausibility of this disarming and destructive schoolboy."

Isabel Quigly, in her history of the school story entitled "The Heirs of Tom Brown," provides a more academic but equally admiring view: **"It is significant that the only really popular school stories still being written, Anthony Buckeridge's Jennings books, are set in a prep school. Jennings is the middling schoolboy, direct descendant of Tom Brown, and Darbishire, a bespectacled, long winded clegyman's son, to provide comic contrast, is his friend and foil. The Jennings stories were first published soon after the Second World War and no one has since grown older; which shows not so much the anachronistic spirit of school stories as the agelessness of prep schools. No old-style public school could be used in a contemporary setting. The dimmest reader would know that teenage boys like that no longer existed. But Jennings, with his ` Please sir, yes sir' and the tireless routine of cricket matches and comic disaster, is still acceptable."**

The blurb on the dustjackets of the Collins editions is not surprisingly gushing in its compliments:
"School stories there have always been and in plenty, but here is a school story with a difference. The hilariously funny adventures of Jennings and his companions have exactly the sort of up-to-date humour which boys and girls appreciate."(JG, 1966 ed.)
"This new book is every bit as hilarious and amusing as his first, and re-establishes this juvenile writer's claim to be, as the reviewers have suggested, ` the Wodehouse of the school story.'"(JF, 1963 ed.)
"Jennings' popularity, both over the air and in print, is indisputable, and any boy or girl who meets him here for the first time will look forward to further encounters with this incomparable schoolboy character."(JA, 1954 ed.)
"Another ` Jennings' is really something to look forward to."(JD, 1962 ed.)
"Anthony Buckeridge's sparkling humour and racy style have provided riotous entertainment."(AT, 1958 ed.)
"Boys - and girls - love these humorous stories and recognise their authentic ring; they realise that they themselves, just like Jennings, often do the most fantastic things for reasons which the average adult is unable to appreciate, and so they can readily identify themselves with the boys of Linbury Court school."(FI, 1963 ed.)
"Writing in ` Growing Point,' Margery Fisher has this to say about the author of the Jennings books: ` He cleverly pushes the absurdities of real prep schoolboys so gingerly over the line of probability that the

"How should I know which card to choose?" said Darbishire

"Jennings!" Mr Wilkins shouted joyfully.
"Thank goodness you're safe, boy."

most literal-minded reader has no chance to measure real against fantastic. These are books to make an immediate hit with young readers and to please older ones(as they please many adults) by their inventive skill and unobtrusive good style.' A literary critic reviewing the Jennings books in a Swiss journal writes: ` Not since the Pickwick Papers, which we read in our childhood and have re-read many a time, do we remember laughing, and seeing children and grown-ups laughing, with so much joy and so many tears of mirth, as at a classroom reading of the adventures of Bennett.'"(SO and others)

A number of other tributes are shorter but still very much to the point:
"How refreshingly natural the voices of Jennings and his friends always sound!"(letter to Radio Times in 1962 concerning the Children's Hour broadcasts)
"Jennings is great!" (The Times AND The Sun)
"Magic...hilarious."(Daily Mirror)
"The hilarious Jennings books."(Daily Mail)
"For sheer entertainment a Jennings book gets top marks."(Children's Hour Book Review)
"In the field of school stories there is at present no rival to Anthony Buckeridge."(The Times)
"Jennings is rapidly and deservedly becoming the great contemporary schoolboy."(Manchester Guardian)
"The Jennings stories are full of humorous appreciation of the juvenile mind."(Tatler)

The publication of TH in 1994 produced another upsurge of interest in the Jennings books, and in particular this article by Stephen Pile in the Daily Telegraph;
"Fossilised fish-hooks! Jennings has come back from the dead. Over a quarter of a century Anthony Buckeridge sold five million copies of his 24 humorous novels about this amiable if disaster-prone pupil at Linbury Court prep school. And what gratitude did the world of publishing show for these decades of entertainment? Some crazed bazookas(as Jennings himself would put it) decided that these joyous books were old hat. Crystallised cheesecakes! What were these cloth-eared clodpolls doing? Trendiness triumphed over quality. It was a classic case of dispensing with ye babe and ye bath water. Those of us who had read these books when young assumed that Anthony Buckeridge had come to a sad end, growing old to find his life's work on the scrapheap. Not so. As with Jennings' plots themselves, things got pretty hairy, but there was a happy ending. (The Jennings Abounding

play) was the only sighting for a generation of that wonderful boy who acts according to a child's faultless logic that leaves the adult onlooker speechless. (Show Jennings a park railing and he will not only get his head stuck in it, but also have a perfectly reasonable explanation involving squirrels). Out of the blue in 1990, Macmillan decided to reprint the novels and to fire up Buckeridge to write new ones. There have been certain small updatings of currency and slang, but the essential world of child versus adult logic still remains charmingly unchanged. The question is: why the comeback? Bernard Ashley thinks it reflects the political climate. Jennings disappeared with comprehensivisation and reappeared with direct grant schools and the growing enthusiasm for private education. But Robert Leeson, author of the Grange Hill, detects a further explanation: `In my opinion, Jennings has come back because the books themselves as pieces of work were too good to be totally neglected. They are timeless. They have no snob attitudes. He is an accessible private schoolboy. The books concentrate on the absolute essence of school life; adults and children confined to the same building for weeks on end. It is them and us.'"

The Book & Magazine Collector magazine has printed two articles about the Jennings series. The first was by Helen Macleod in August 1986:
"Of all the great fictional schoolboys, the Linbury Court duo John Christopher Timothy Jennings and his acolyte, Darbishire(Charles Edwin Jeremy) are perhaps the funniest and most appealing. These `silly little boys' may have caused Mr Wilkins a few headaches in their time, but their youthful antics, chronicled in the...Jennings books, have amused and delighted millions of boys and girls(as well as their parents!) the world over since they appeared in 1950. The texts are enlivened with ebullient little line drawings, and the dustwrappers, illustrated by Mays and Biro among others, are particularly attractive."
The second was by David Schutte in May 1993:
"Walking into the children's section of any good bookshop in the 1950's, it was noticeable that the shelves were dominated by the works of a select handful of authors; Enid Blyton, Richmal Crompton, W.E. Johns - and Anthony Buckeridge. Their creations - respectively, the Famous Five, William, Biggles and Jennings - were the heroes of the postwar era, and in the Fifties, when television was still in its infancy, they all enjoyed a degree of popularity which is unmatched by that of any contemporary writer. The works of this elite group are now enjoying something of a revival, and although we lost the first three of these authors towards the end of the Sixties, Anthony Buckeridge is still going strong."

The writer Mat Coward contributed the following to the March/April 1992 edition of the magazine "Million:"

"I first read most of the Jennings stories, hiding from cross country runs and compulsory rugby, perched in trees or on top of haystacks. I tend to read them in bed now, but they still make me laugh loud enough to wake the neighbours. Certainly, as an adult, I enjoy aspects of Jennings that I previously missed - Mr Carter's sarcasm, for instance. I'm still laughing at the kind of humour which Buckeridge does better than any other writer this side of Wodehouse; comedies of errors and cross-purpose conversations. It's the brilliantly engineered misunderstandings which stay in the mind longest. Also reminiscent of Wodehouse - an influence which Buckeridge acknowledges - is a skilful use of both understatement and hyperbole. Buckeridge isn't afraid of using absurdism, but his humour is always grounded in exact observation and consistent characterisation; the jokes are believable, and that makes them all the funnier. This is true even when the laughs come from Goon-style logic-stretching. (The) sense of a term lasting almost a lifetime, in which any number of causes, enthusiasm and feuds can be pursued with utmost intensity and forgotten with startling rapidity, is typical of Buckeridge's keen understanding of the 11-year-old's mind; a month may pass in a flash for an adult, but time moves differently for children. Eleven is the only age Jennings could be, really; eleven is just old enough to be dangerously and excitingly independent, but from puberty onwards, according to my memory, sex and smoking largely take over from spaceships and tree-houses as a boy's main pre-occupations. By keeping his characters at that borderline age, Buckeridge is able to make his stories realistic, without exercising too much censorship. When I was eleven, `hoo-hahs,' `bishes' and `famous brainwaves' were not included in the normal schoolboy's vocabulary, nor did I ever hear a teacher preface a `frantic bate' with `I-I-corwumph!' but it's only in retrospect that I notice the anachronistic language. Jennings belongs, indisputably, amongst the first rank of funny fictional children."

It is now unlikely that there will be another Jennings story. The reader will have to be satisfied with the twenty-five volumes that Buckeridge has produced. No more, it seems, will we witness fresh dialogue of this kind:

"I say, Darbi," said Jennings through a mouthful of sponge cake, "What do you say to foxing out to Dunhambury this Saturday afternoon to get the new Anthony Buckeridge book?"

Darbishire gazed anxiously around him like a tribal explorer contemplating an area of uncharted African bush. "We haven't got per," he said doubtfully.

"I know that, you clodpoll! I just thought that we could get in ahead of those clueless bazookas like Ven and Atki who are getting a lift in the Archbeako's car after the Bracebridge match. I happen to know that his new book is fantabulous."

"Who's - the Archbeako's?"

"No, you coot - Anthony Buckeridge's."

Darbishire was quick to raise objections. "If this is another of your bat-witted schemes you can wizard well leave me out of it," he said. "How can we possibly fox out during the match?"

"We'll borrow some of the Bracebridge lot's dayclothes from the changing rooms. Then if some old geezer like Old Wilkie sees us stonking around town, he'll think we're Bracebridge boys."

"Crystallized cheesecakes!" Darbishire exclaimed. "I've met some beetle-brained schemes in my time, but this takes the gold medal for addle-pated bone-headedness against all comers! I mean, what if..."

Darbishire broke off as the door crashed open and Mr Wilkins hurtled across the threshold. For a moment he stood in silence, speechless with fury at the sight of the two boys who had wilfully disobeyed his orders.

"I-I-Corwumph!" he exploded, as the power of speech returned. "What in the name of thunder are you two silly little boys doing in here?"

"Er- just coming out, sir."

"Doh!" Mr Wilkins fumed. "I've just about had enough of your trumpery impudence, Jennings. If you're not out of here by the time I count to three, I - I - well, you'd better look out!"

BIBLIOGRAPHY

The writer repeats his indebtedness to all the authors/publishers of the books, newspapers and magazines listed below for permission to quote from them.

The Oxford Companion to Children's Literature - Humphrey Carpenter & Mari Prichard(Oxford, 1984)
Modern Children's First Editions - Joseph Connolly(Macdonald, 1988)
Clodpolls and Coots - Mat Coward("Million" magazine, March/April 1992)
Who's Who In Children's Books - Margery Fisher(Weidenfeld, 1975)
The "Jennings" and "Milligan" Books of Anthony Buckeridge - Helen MacLeod(Book & Magazine Collector, August 1986)
Another Happy Ending for Jennings - Stephen Pile(Daily Telegraph, 4.10.94)
The Heirs of Tom Brown - Isabel Quigly(Chatto & Windus, 1982)
Anthony Buckeridge at 80 - David Schutte(Book & Magazine Collector, May 1993)

ABOUT THE AUTHOR

David Bathurst is a solicitor and legal adviser to two benches of magistrates in West Sussex. His first book was The Selsey Tram, published by Phillimore in 1992, and this was followed by Six of The Best(see below), published by Romansmead Publications in 1994. He has also made contributions to the Justice of the Peace magazine, published by Barry Rose; his next book, a guide to enforcement of financial orders by magistrates, will also be published by Barry Rose. Whilst not writing he enjoys singing, hill-walking, cycling and teashops. He lives just outside Chichester with his wife Lizzie.

BY THE SAME AUTHOR

Six of the Best - by David Bathurst Price £ 4.95 post free.
Whether it is the Fat Owl of the Remove Billy Bunter bending over for another whopping from Mr Quelch, the impetuous Jennings with another supersonic wheeze, or the girls at St Chad's lining up for a rippingly jolly hockey match, British literary history has throughout this century been enriched by the much-maligned, much-imitated but also much-loved school story. David Bathurst's nostalgic tribute to six of this century's most famous exponents of the art not only examines the people behind the immortal catchphrases, the colourful characters and evocative settings, from Victorian public schools to modern suburban comprehensives; it traces, through the six chosen authors, the development of the school story over the past hundred years. Packed with illustrations, quotations, biographical detail, bibliographies and pure unashamed trivia, this book is a must for the nostalgia buff, the social and literary historian, and all who wish to become more familiar with this rich vein of children's literature. ORDER NOW from Romansmead Publications, 46 Mosse Gardens, Fishbourne, Chichester PO19 3PQ Tel: 01243 536156.